1987

FILMING LITERATURE

LITERATURE

The Art of Screen Adaptation

FILMING LITERATURE

The Art of Screen Adaptation

NEIL SINYARD

ST MARTIN'S PRESS
New York

Scholarly & Reference Division,
St. Martin's Press, Inc., 175 Fifth Avenue, New York, NY 10010
First published in the United States of America in 1986
Printed in Great Britain

Library of Congress Cataloging-in-Publication Data

Sinyard, Neil.
  Filming literature.
  Includes index.
    1. English literature — Film and video adaptations.
2. American literature — Film and video adaptations.
I. Title.
PN 1997.85.S5   1986   791.43   86-10118
ISBN 0-312-28939-1

Contents

Introduction

The legacy of the nineteenth-century novel is the twentieth-century film. In many novels of the Victorian and Edwardian era, with their burdensome cataloguing of details of the appearance of the external world, one senses an author who is either waiting for, or who will be made redundant by, the camera. One of the cinema's most immediate effects was to supplant the novel as the foremost art form of narrative realism.

The response of the modern writer to the coming of film was predictably variable. 'The cinema's swift change of scene, this blending of emotion and experience,' said Tolstoy, was much better than the 'heavy, long-drawn-out kind of writing to which we are accustomed. It is closer to life.'[1] Tolstoy saw it could activate a revolution in the methods of literary art. James Joyce, who founded the first cinema in Dublin, and Virginia Woolf, who contributed several thoughtful essays on the cinema, were similarly fascinated by the new medium. Part of their excitement was probably a feeling that the film could free them from what they saw as some of the more tedious responsibilities of the novelist (story-telling, the precise observation of everyday trivialities, entertainment) and allow them to develop the novel in much more interesting, esoteric areas — linguistic experimentation, mythological accretion, psychological complexity. (Significantly, neither of them has proved easy to adapt for the screen, Mary Ellen Bute's 1965 shot at *Finnegan's Wake*, and the Colin Gregg-Hugh Stoddard 1982 television adaptation of *To the Lighthouse* being much the best examples.) For writers like D.H. Lawrence and George Orwell, however, cinema was an enemy. It homogenised popular culture; it subdued art to industry and to the lowest common denominator of mass taste; it undermined the book and eroded literacy. The cinema has avenged itself on these two by generally ignoring Orwell and, with a few rare exceptions (like Christopher Miles's pleasing pastoral film of *The Virgin and the Gypsy* in 1970), by generally travestying Lawrence.

In its age of innocence, the film understandably wished to break away from the established forms of drama and the novel and establish itself as a distinctive entertainment and art form in its own right. Nevertheless, it had to acknowledge a heavy dependence for its material on adaptations of short stories, novels and plays. It also recognised a kinship with and influence from the narrative techniques of the novel — like Flaubert's anticipation of cinematic crosscutting in the scene of the agricultural fair in *Madame Bovary*, or Conrad's inclusion of a subliminal flashback in *Heart of Darkness* when Marlow prepares for a nocturnal meeting with Kurtz. Eisenstein drew parallels between the narrative methods of Charles Dickens and those of D.W. Griffith, and his own montage theories and practice had a precedent in a writer he greatly admired, James Joyce. The extraordinary opening chapter of Joyce's *A Portrait of the Artist as a Young Man*, with its free movement between time and space, is one of the finest examples of montage in fiction.

When the serious writer became involved in the movies, he found the going much tougher than promised by Herman Mankiewicz in his famous 1926 telegram to Ben Hecht: 'Will you accept three hundred per week to work for Paramount Pictures? All expenses paid. The three hundred is peanuts. Millions are to be grabbed out here and your only competition is idiots. Don't let this get around.'[2] F. Scott Fitzgerald, Nathanael West, William Faulkner, Aldous Huxley and Christopher Isherwood are only some of the major writing talents to have had considerable experience of Hollywood, and they could not muster a memorable original screenplay between them. They made quite a lot of money, and, in some cases, Hollywood provided the subject for some of their most important fiction, notably in Fitzgerald's *The Last Tycoon* and West's *The Day of the Locust.* But, in a lot of cases, the disdain of serious writers for the movie capital has sounded uncommonly like the sound of the crunching of sour grapes.

Conversely, the professional screenwriter in Hollywood has always been undervalued. Think of only some of the great original screenplays that have come from Hollywood and have, in many cases, become part of our common cultural and artistic heritage: *Citizen Kane* (Herman J. Mankiewicz and Orson Welles, 1941), *Sullivan's Travels* (Preston Sturges, 1942), *Monsieur Verdoux* (Charles Chaplin, 1947), *Force of Evil* (Abraham Polonsky, 1948), *Sunset Boulevard* (Charles Brackett and Billy Wilder, 1950), *All About Eve* (Joseph L. Mankiewicz, 1950), *Singin' in the Rain* (Betty Comden and Adolph Green, 1952), *North by Northwest* (Ernest Lehman, 1959), *Bonnie and Clyde* (David Newman and Robert Benton, 1967), *Chinatown* (Robert Towne, 1974), to name but a select few. How many of those names would mean anything at all to most literary academics, and even some film buffs? The professional screenwriter's situation in Hollywood has always been tinged with a sense of grievance, deriving from insufficient respect and recognition. During the 1930s and 1940s, the cavalier attitude of studios, actors and directors towards the text often drove writers into becoming directors in order to protect their own scripts, like Preston Sturges, Billy Wilder, John Huston and, later, Joseph L. Mankiewicz, Robert Rossen, Richard Brooks and Woody Allen. A further irritant came in the 1960s when the 'auteur' theory deified certain directors, at the expense of other collaborators, notably the writer. There is a story that Robert Riskin, exasperated at director Frank Capra's receiving all the credit for films like *It Happened One Night* (1934) and *Mr Deeds Goes to Town* (1936) which Riskin had written, once handed Capra a folio of blank paper and said: 'Here, let's see you put the famous Capra touch on that.' It is axiomatic that very few directors have become successful writers — Elia Kazan is a notable exception — whilst even Burt Reynolds and Sylvester Stallone can make technically competent directors. In the 1980s, it is good to see enterprising American publishers at last putting into print the screenplays of Sturges, Wilder, Samuel Raphaelson — Lubitsch's marvellous writer on *Trouble in Paradise* (1932) and *The Shop Around the Corner* (1939) — and others, at last acknowledging the Hollywood screen-play as a vital and viable contribution to twentieth-century American literature.

The writing achievements for film have been insufficiently acknowl-edged for a number of reasons (I have mentioned the sometimes unjustifi-able deification of directors), but one of them is undoubtedly the cinema's inferiority complex in relation to literature. This has been encouraged and perpetuated by the ignorance of academic institutions, the arrogance of media commentators, and by remarks from modern classic writers such as this one from Evelyn Waugh: 'Each book purchased for motion pictures has some individual quality, good or bad, that has made it remarkable. It is the work of a great array of highly paid and incompatible writers to distin-guish this quality, separate it, and obliterate it.'[3] In many ways, the purpose of this book is precisely to challenge that kind of prejudice, for many adaptations of remarkable novels have led to illumination, not obliteration. There are clearly many different motives for bringing a classic to the screen. One should not discount the commercial reason — the assumed existence of a ready-made audience for a film of a famous book. Yet films like Robert Z. Leonard's *Pride and Prejudice* (1940) and Robert Stevenson's *Jane Eyre* (1944), which were both co-scripted by Aldous Huxley, seem sincere and thoughtful attempts to make classic literature more accessible to a large audience. What is often interesting is the different strategies by which film-makers try to do this. For his elegant film of the imperishable *Little Women* (1933), director George Cukor expressed his policy of keeping in the faults as well as the virtues of a classic text, of not smoothing it out for fear of losing the atmosphere, essence and quality that had made it a classic in the first place. Conversely, an adaptor like Harold Pinter seems to focus immediately on a classic's weaknesses and then works backwards from them, correcting them and offering different perspectives on, for example, Burgess's suicide in *The Go-Between* or the Pre-Raphaelite paraphernalia of *The French Lieutenant's Woman*. Some works are modified in the adaptation process to make them relevant to the period in which they are made. Key changes are made to the narrative outcome of Bernard Malamud's *The Natural* in order to make Barry Levin-son's 1984 film conform to the optimistic mood of Reagan's America. In a different mood, the BBC's marvellous recent adaptation of Dickens's *Bleak*

House (1985) seems fired and inspired by a contemporary anger. Given the hideous cruelty and hypocrisy of the Victorian age that Dickens so devastatingly uncovers, it seems to say, could anyone but a historical simpleton and cultural imbecile seriously propose it as an example to follow and wish to take our political fortunes in that direction? It does seem to me that the great screen adaptations are the ones that go for the spirit rather than the letter of the text; or exploit a unique affinity between the personalities of the original writer and the present film-maker; or use the camera to interpret and not simply illustrate the tale.

During its development in this century, the film has discovered many curious parallels with literature. It has wrestled with the same tensions between art and entertainment, escapism and reality, that so preoccupied Victorian writers and critics. It has found film-makers who approximate to literary categorisations such as the epic (Eisenstein, Gance), the poetic (Vigo, Buñuel), the lyric (Renoir, Satyajit Ray); and who seem curiously analogous to corresponding personalities in literature (D.W. Griffith and Samuel Richardson, Humphrey Jennings and E.M. Forster, Max Ophuls and Arthur Schnitzler). This book has purposely tried to open up some of these areas and go beyond a consideration of straightforward correspondences between a specific film of a specific book.

The opening chapters deal with major attempts of the cinema to bring literary masterpieces to the screen in a popular form, concentrating on the films made from Shakespeare, James, Lawrence, Hardy and Orwell, and considering how far these films contribute to the critical literature on these authors and how far they succeed in becoming independent screen classics in their own right. Harold Pinter and James Agee are studied as writers who have made major contributions in other fields of literature but whose work for the screen seems a particularly revealing aspect of their artistic personalities. Other chapters draw analogies between the literature and film artist; discuss, with reference to four film adaptations, the notion that adapting a literary text for the screen is essentially an act of literary criticism; consider the cinema's attempt, through the genre of the bio-pic, to convey the social and intellectual life of the great writer; and survey the different ways in which the cinema has attempted to come to terms with adaptations from the stage.

The selection of material concentrates almost exclusively on the classic texts of British and American literature. European classics, popular literature and television adaptations are an equally valid subject for study, but the subject of adaptation is so vast that a line had to be drawn somewhere. The book is aimed at someone who loves film and literature equally, and who does not feel the necessity to demonstrate his or her cultural credentials by instantly expressing a preference for print over celluloid. As I hope the following pages demonstrate, the issue of adaptation is much more complex than that.

Notes

1. From Jay Leyda's *Kino*, as translated by David Bernstein. Quoted in Kenneth Macgowan's *Behind the Screen* (Delta, 1965), p. 375.

2. Quoted in *Anatomy of the Movies*, edited by David Pirie, (Windward Books, 1980), p. 141.

3. Macgowan, *Behind the Screen*, p. 383.

Chapter One

'In My Mind's Eye':
Shakespeare on the Screen

'I am less than ever convinced that there is an aesthetic justification for filming Shakespeare at all,' wrote Graham Greene in 1936. 'The effect of even the best scenes is to distract ...; we cannot look and listen simultaneously with equal vigilance.'[1] Admittedly, Greene was writing this immediately after seeing George Cukor's lavish but limp version of *Romeo and Juliet* — advertised in Greene's press book, apparently, as: 'Boy Meets Girl, 1436.' Also, prior to Greene's comment, Shakespeare on film had been littered with strange milestones. In the silent period, Hamlet was played by, amongst others, the distinguished Shakespearean actor Sir Johnston Forbes-Robertson, the Danish actress Asta Nielsen, and Buster Keaton (in a fantasy sequence from his 1922 short *Day Dreams*). A silent version of *Macbeth* was banned for excessive violence in, of all places, Chicago. Most notoriously, a 1929 version of *The Taming of the Shrew* credited the text as being 'by Shakespeare — with additional dialogue by Sam Taylor.' The year before his comment, Greene had seen the Max Reinhardt–William Dieterle version of *A Midsummer Night's Dream* (1935), which coarsens the humour and whose verse is badly spoken, but which has an occasional Mendelssohnian lightness of touch, notably in the performances of James Cagney as Bottom and a 14-year-old Mickey Rooney as Puck, and some effective visual moments (the descent of Oberon in his shining chariot).

Fifty years on from Greene's remark, one can see that the cinema's response to Shakespeare has been far more successful than its response to the Bible. But it might be as well to summarise some of the recurring difficulties. One of the problems is obvious: film is a commercial medium and Shakespeare, to borrow from *Hamlet*, pleases 'not the million' but is 'caviare to the general.' With the exception of Franco Zeffirelli's film of *Romeo and Juliet* (1968), which has everything going for it except a decent Romeo and Juliet, few Shakespearean films have been big commercial successes. This has a number of implications for Shakespeare on film: that the film might not be made at all; that if it does get made it will be done very cheaply, with a certain visual and artistic diminution of impact; and

1

that if it is made on a reasonable budget, it will need a big star that might serve as a financial guarantee but might not be ideal casting. I will give quick examples of all of these.

It is a source of great national shame that Olivier's ambition to make a film of *Macbeth* was never realised; and that the British cinema's contribution to the quatercentenary of Shakespeare's birth in 1964 was precisely nothing, while the Russians celebrated with Grigori Kozintsev's magnificent film of *Hamlet.* The George Schaefer 1960 production of *Macbeth*, with Maurice Evans as Macbeth and Judith Anderson as Lady Macbeth, is an example of the second category I mentioned: a cheap, quickie production, described as 'reverential' to Shakespeare which basically means that it is totally devoid of imagination, originality or spectacle. (One critic described Macbeth's castle as looking like two Weetabix stuck together.) Great artists, like Olivier and Orson Welles, can go some way towards surmounting these budgetary limitations, but it is still a pity they have to. Olivier's *Richard III* (1955) is a splendid film, but it is a shame that the crowd scenes (when Richard is exhorted to take the crown, for example) seem so sparsely populated, like friends gathering glumly for a thinly attended Equity meeting; or that the potential spectacle of the Battle of Bosworth is so obviously hampered by meagre resources. In Welles's *Othello* (1952), there is an exciting scene when Roderigo is murdered in a steam bath, a highly effective Wellesian invention necessitated by the unavailability of costumes for the cast. Money was not a problem for Zeffirelli's *The Taming of the Shrew* (1966), but did the commercial gimmick of casting Richard Burton and Elizabeth Taylor as the bickering lovers get in the way of the text? They speak the poetry intelligently, and Miss Taylor gives a tongue-in-cheek inflection to Katherina's final speech of submission to Petruchio that is both amusing and intriguing, but the stars cannot quite get away from the impression that it is a private joke at the Bard's expense. The starry cast of Stuart Burge's *Julius Caesar* (1970) did not save the film. Charlton Heston's third screen attempt at Mark Antony in his own 1975 production of *Antony and Cleopatra* (he had previously played the role in David Bradley's 1949 low-budget film of *Julius Caesar* and in the Stuart Burge version) did not come off, the responsibilities of direction seeming to diminish Heston's own performance. If George Cukor said that Zeffirelli's Juliet sounded too much like 'a chemist's daughter from Wimbledon,'[2] Frank Kermode was even unkinder about Hildegard Neil's Cleopatra: 'when she speaks of her majesty, as she often does, we take it as a kind of in-joke.'[3] According to Heston's journals, there was a proposal to reshoot the role of Cleopatra with a different actress, with the intention of integrating the new footage into that of the finished film.[4] Strangely, Cleopatra is the one major Shakespearean role that has yet to be given even an adequate performance on screen.

Quite apart from the intricacies of commerce, however, there is a more fundamental question to ask of filmed Shakespeare: namely, is there something in the nature of the film medium itself which makes it impossible to do justice to the dramatist? Do the visual images inevitably get in the way of Shakespearean poetic metaphor? Is there a kind of literalness, a photographic realism about the screen image which is fundamentally opposed to the symbolic, metaphoric, ritualistic theatrical elements in Shakespeare? Shakespearean language projects images on a mental screen: must it suffer if these images are put literally before you? It is often said that Shakespeare would have made a great screenwriter and that many devices he uses in his plays are very 'cinematic' — crosscutting between different planes of action, rapid shifts of location, counterpointing between scenes that work like good film editing. (Roger Manvell has demonstrated this in a concise way in his description of the rapid movement of action and location in *Macbeth*.)[5] The opportunity for visual expressiveness has been seized by the best directors, as in Olivier's reconstruction of the Battle of Agincourt in *Henry V* (1944). Modelled on Eisenstein's sequence of the battle on the ice in *Alexander Nevsky* (1938) (although, not surprisingly, Eisenstein hated Olivier's film), a sense of participation is heightened by a tracking shot along with the soldiers, an astounding shot of the flying arrows, judicious visual detail (for example, the movement of the flag) to suggest the fortunes of the battle, and fast cutting that gives a painterly sense of conflict whilst showing and spilling very little blood. Better still is Orson Welles's magnificent battle in the mud in *Chimes at Midnight* (1965), exuberance moving to exhaustion in a manner that captures the tone and theme of the film.

However, in an important respect, Shakespeare is not the equivalent of a screenwriter at all. He is our greatest verbal dramatist, relying on the associative metaphorical power of words to trigger the imagination. Visual imagination can sometimes make the words soar. Equally, however, too much embroidery can distract from the poetry, as in Olivier's rendering of 'To be or not to be' in his *Hamlet* (1948). It is valid and interesting to handle the speech not as a soliloquy but as an internal monologue, just occasionally punctuated by exclamations like 'Perchance to dream!' which he says aloud, as if the thought has suddenly pushed itself to the forefront of his consciousness. But there seems too much business going on: Walton's rather maudlin musical accompaniment, prefaced by melodramatic cascading strings to introduce the soliloquy; Hamlet's delivery of the soliloquy at the edge of a cliff, looking down at the ocean, as if the philosophical question has been reformulated as 'To jump or not to jump.' As Jean Renoir remarked: 'You feel dizzy when you look down from a great height? So what? What has that got to do with Shakespeare?'[6] More effective is Grigori Kozintsev's use of the soliloquy as internal monologue in his film of *Hamlet* (1964). For example, the 'O what a rogue and peasant slave' soliloquy comes immediately after the player's speech, and we hear it as an internal monologue, as Hamlet sits mute and withdrawn and the players look on with dismay at this pale, distraught figure. It is so effective because unspoken thought is a key aspect of the world of *Hamlet* as conceived by Kozintsev, which he expresses in this way:

The interior monologue will be particularly interesting if it is successful in giving the impression of an explosive force of thought which betokens danger for the government of Claudius. Spies have instructions to shadow this dangerous man, and not to let him out of their sight. And Hamlet unhurriedly and calmly strolls about the room. The camera goes closer; we hear the words of his thoughts, but the sleuth who clings to the door hears nothing. He has nothing to write down in his report: steps, quiet.

Hamlet ... thinks. There is nothing more dangerous.[7]

The old notion that so theatrical and artificial a device as the soliloquy could never work in the more 'realistic' world of the cinema ('of all conventions in the cinema this is the strongest: no character within a film may look at us and by that look announce the existence of a medium, a mechanical, optical, aesthetic structure that stands between us and the people and events it creates')[8] was scotched definitively by Laurence Olivier in the title role of *Richard III*. There Olivier brilliantly used the camera as friend, a confidant to whom he could direct his private thoughts. It had exactly the right feeling of complicity between actor and audience which, because the character is a villain, deepened the audience's moral responses and reactions. But, quite apart from soliloquies, there are equal problems of filming the interaction or Shakespeare's poetic dialogue. In *Julius Caesar* (1953), producer John Houseman and director Joseph L. Mankiewicz decided as far as possible to cut out reaction shots, for they felt these would disrupt the rhythms and cadences of Shakespearean speech. They also attempted to get round the problem of the archaic nature of Shakespearean speech and drama by emphasising the contemporary relevance of the play — the film a post-Second World War reading of the text as a play about dictatorships (with Louis Calhern's Caesar analogous to political gangsters like Hitler and Mussolini) and with the monochrome photography giving the impression of contemporary newsreel. Intelligent film interpreters of Shakespeare are always thinking of specific ways to make clear their feelings about individual moments or scenes through visual means, and their contrasting solutions to the same problem are very revealing. For example, in Peter Brook's film of *King Lear* (1971), the storm scene opens on a huge close-up of the King, superimposed over a shot of the heath and the sound of thunder and lightning: in this reading, the storm is essentially a psychological storm raging inside Lear's head. In complete contrast, in Kozintsev's film of *King Lear* (1970) the storm scene opens with an astonishing fast zoom towards the ever-blackening sky, followed by a tremendous aerial shot of the tiny figure of Lear, trying to make himself heard, and a completely different facet of the scene is highlighted: the contrast between the huge world of Nature and Lear's 'little world of man', and a revelation of the sudden vulnerability of a man who previously had thought he was everything.

Given a Shakespearean text to film, it seems you must do either one of two things. The first is to throw away the text altogether. Prior to filming *King Lear*, Peter Brook tried to escape from the text by commissioning the poet Ted Hughes to translate the play into his own poetic terms, but found eventually that the original had a force and emotional power that no paraphrase or translation could match. Akira Kurosawa's version of *Macbeth, Throne of Blood* (1957), ditches Shakespeare's poetry but replaces it with a supercharged atmosphere, a fascinating translation of Shakespeare into the Noh tradition of Japanese drama, and a richly textured visual surface to reflect the psychological extremities of the hero. It might not be Shakespeare in a literal sense, but it is certainly Shakespearean in atmosphere, — full of sound and fury, signifying everything.

The second alternative is, in Peter Hall's words, to 'work with the text, cut the text first, and make the camera support its close interpretation'.[9] Sometimes a subtle camera movement can render a particular line unnecessary. For example, in the Russian *Hamlet*, the camera tilts slightly and eerily upwards as Horatio first tells Hamlet of the ghost, as if to serve as a visual correlative to the line: 'There are more things in heaven and earth ...' A detail can be selected and subjected to entertaining visual elaboration, like that amusing shot of Baptista's bedraggled crowd waiting outside the church for Petruchio's belated arrival for his wedding in *Taming of the Shrew*, looking like a Proms audience waiting for the Albert Hall to open. Olivier's *Henry V* has one of the most foolish examples of fidelity to the text: namely, the retention of Falstaff's death scene, which is not only meaningless without the two parts of *Henry IV*, but is a reminder of a darker, meaner side to the King that the rest of the interpretation is at no pains whatever to endorse. Yet, in the same film, there is one of the best examples of a close matching of visual style to the text: that is, Olivier's delivery and direction of the 'Feast of Crispian' speech. It is not simply that Olivier speaks the words so thrillingly. Great care is also taken to render visually the rising excitement, the heroism, the persuasiveness, the skill of the man in whipping up emotion. The King begins the speech as he strokes a white horse, a correlative to the pure heroism of a character. As he continues, the camera tracks before him, almost as if his purposefulness is driving the camera back. The gathering of the men around him suggests his magnetism and powers of persuasion, and the growing unison of the men at the hypnotic pull of the words is reflected simply in the way the film frame seems to grow ever more crowded. The final touch is the moment the King moves on to the platform to conclude his speech, a movement which suggests his rising excitement, the sense of him as a man above the ordinary, but also a man who is lifting the spirits of his subjects with his soaring rhetoric. At the point of climax, the camera pulls away in a movement that conveys the sense of a contagious excitement spreading amongst the men, but also allows one to see the King more clearly in relation to his fellows. A less skilled director might have ended the speech on a close-up, thereby restricting its range, but Olivier instinctively senses that a screen climax (a close-up) and a Shakespearean climax (a fine gesture and a loud declamation) might not match, and that the camera should go back when the character raises his voice.

The subject of Shakespeare on film is too vast to be covered comprehensively in a single essay, and this survey chooses instead to concentrate on a comparison between two important versions of each of the following plays: *Hamlet, Othello, Julius Caesar, Macbeth* and *King Lear*. The comparison will be supplemented by brief comments on other filmed interpretations of these texts, and notes also on modern updatings which are sometimes fascinatingly oblique, analogous commentaries on the Shakespeare original. But, before then, some quick comments are probably in order about fine interpretations of other Shakespearean texts. For all the execrable verse-speaking and sentimentality, Zeffirelli's *Romeo and Juliet* has an Italianate verve that undoubtedly makes the play work for young audiences, and John McEnery's Mercutio is an unusual and vivid interpretation. At the other end of the scale, Orson Welles's *Chimes at Midnight* is a film imbued with wisdom and age, Welles's own performance as Falstaff having a lurking melancholy and nobility that underline his interpretation of the character as 'the greatest conception of a good man, the most completely good man, in all drama'.[10] Of more recent interpretations, undoubtedly the finest is Derek Jarman's film of *The Tempest* (1979), a work of true imagination as befits a play about artistic imagination. The film is shrouded in an atmosphere of dream, fantasy and darkness, moving gradually to a dawn in which young love awakens and colour floods the screen. Although Jarman cannot do much with the lumbering comedy of Stephano and Trinculo, Miranda and Ferdinand are unusually full of life, and the masque is wonderful, with Elizabeth Welch on hand to do an ostensibly incongruous but gloriously apposite rendering of 'Stormy Weather'. Jack Birkett rightly garnered a lot of attention for his striking and threatening Caliban, but equally fine are Heathcote Williams's Prospero and Karl Johnson's Ariel. Together, they reinforce the interpretation of the play as a vision of the powers of artistic creation — Prospero the poet, Ariel his inspiriting imagination which can produce the felicities if kept on a tight enough rein, Caliban the raging symbol of Dionysiac indiscipline. Prospero is always at his books and here dreams his own most sweetly executed plot, instilled with a sense of fresh beginnings but also with a cold apprehension of his own imminent death. It is an interpretation that takes liberties, but is true to Shakespeare in the sense that Jarman makes him seem the most exciting of playwrights.

Hamlet

Apparently, the response of one Rank executive on seeing the rushes of Olivier's *Hamlet* was: 'It's wonderful, you wouldn't know it was Shakespeare.'[11] Some purists have said the same thing about the film with rather less enthusiasm. 'He has stripped the play and his production to the essentials,' said James Agee. 'In the process, he has also stripped away a few of the essentials.'[12] One can certainly do without the second gravedigger but the key soliloquy 'O what a rogue and peasant slave . . .' is sorely missed, as are Rosencrantz and Guildenstern. The cutting of Fortinbras inevitably means the exclusion of the 'How all occasions do inform against me' soliloquy. The effect of these cuts is to eliminate the politics from *Hamlet* and concentrate entirely on the central character and on the family drama.

'This is a tragedy of a man who could not make up his mind,' we are informed at the outset. This preface is then reinforced by a recitation of Hamlet's 'So oft it chances in particular men/That, for some vicious mole of nature in them'[13] speech to underline the film's interpretation of Hamlet's tragic flaw as hesitancy and indecision. In Olivier's hands, Hamlet becomes almost a *film noir* hero, suffering a mental block, being swept along by Fate and traumatised by a devotion to a woman that has been twisted into vicious misogyny. Throughout, he treats Ophelia with undisguised contempt: there is not an atom of love there (one is reminded that Hamlet never refers to Ophelia in his soliloquys). Borrowing a stage-note suggestion in John Dover Wilson's classic text, *What Happens in Hamlet* (1934), Olivier shows that Hamlet has actually overheard Polonius's plot to find out the secret cause of his discontent by 'loosing' Ophelia to him. So when Ophelia appears, Hamlet immediately smells a rat, seeming to sniff suspiciously around in her presence. When he catches her out in a lie ('Where's your father?'/'At home, my lord'), he loses all control at this confirmation of feminine duplicity. The Laurence Olivier/Jean Simmons casting seems exactly right here: the younger actress terrified by the knighted actor, as is the common girl by the Prince of Denmark.

Olivier's reading is strongly Oedipal and heavily influenced by the Freudian interpretation of the play by Ernest Jones. 'The call of duty to kill his stepfather cannot be obeyed,' says Jones, 'because it links with the unconscious call of his nature to kill his mother's husband, whether this is the first or the second; the absolute repression of the former impulse involves inner prohibition of the latter also.'[14] In their opening scene, Gertrude treats her son almost as a disappointed lover and her farewell kiss is so affectionate that Claudius's 'Come, madam' is said in a tone of some annoyance. The closet scene is very passionate, and the ghost appears menacingly at a moment when Hamlet seems about to kiss rather than kill his mother. In the final scene, the Queen spots Claudius's treachery and deliberately drinks the forbidden cup. The words 'O Hamlet, I am poisoned' are spoken in a tone of quiet satisfaction, knowing he will understand and recognise the sacrifice she has made for him.

Roger Furse's set has often been criticised — the argument being that Olivier cuts key soliloquys and characters and then wastes time roaming around the huge, bare set — but Furse has explained that 'Olivier wanted a dream-like cavernous place as the setting for a drama which is centred in the shadowy regions of the hero's mind . . .'[15] Olivier's preference for black-

and-white was determined by his insistence on employing deep-focus photography which he felt would permit unusually long scenes and create shots of unusual beauty. In this decision, Olivier was undoubtedly influenced by his traumatic but formative experience under the exacting eye of William Wyler in *Wuthering Heights* (1939), which employed deep-focus to such compelling effect.

Olivier's *Hamlet* might be simplified Shakespeare, but it is unquestionably exciting. Oliver might not encompass the full tragic dimension of the role (he is not an actor who thrives on the intellectual, contemplative personality), but his feeling for the comedy and cruelty in the role is incomparable, reminding one of Pushkin's comment that 'Hamlet's jokes make your hair stand on end.' The pantomime that accompanies Ophelia's description of Hamlet's madness now looks a little stiff, as does the visualising of Ophelia's death in the manner of Millais's painting. But there are vivid moments of tension (the amplified heartbeats that introduce the ghost), and inimitable theatrical dynamics for the finale: a ferocious duelling sequence, and a staggering leap as Claudius's treachery is unmasked and Hamlet swoops down on his prey. As a piece of cinema, *Hamlet* is much more integrated and incisive than the stylistically uneven *Henry V* or the visually impoverished *Richard III*. Small wonder that Roman Polanski boasted he had seen this film twenty-five times.

Grigori Kozintsev's *Hamlet* offers a very different reading. An example of the difference is that the 'vicious mole of nature' speech, which is at the heart of Olivier's interpretation, is cut from Kozintsev's. (The line of Hamlet's that is the key to Kozintsev's interpretation is: 'Denmark's a prison.'[16]) Throughout, his cuts seem more sensible, less crucial, than Olivier's — for example, the cutting of the ''Tis not alone my inky cloak' speech, or of Hamlet's advice to the players. Predictably, Kozintsev keeps Fortinbras, whose belligerent decisiveness contrasts so strikingly with Hamlet's psychological paralysis, and whose external menace is the reason why Elsinore, in the Russian film, resembles a fortress more than a palace. Also unlike Olivier, but predictably, Kozintsev keeps Rosencrantz and Guildenstern, who are very well acted here and who are essential to a full understanding of Hamlet's threatened, isolated state where even former friends are potential traitors and informers. Shostakovich, whose score for this film even surpasses Walton's Olivier scores and is one of the greatest ever written for a motion picture, has given a very interesting, darkly Russian reading of this relationship: 'I'm particularly touched by Hamlet's conversation with Rosencrantz and Guildenstern when Hamlet says that he's not a pipe and he won't let people play him. A marvellous passage. It's easy for him, he's a prince, after all. If he weren't, they'd play him so hard he wouldn't know what hit him.'[17]

Unlike Olivier's cavernous Elsinore, which sometimes resembles a stately home out of season, Kozintsev's Elsinore is fully populated. Hamlet's first soliloquy is an interal monologue heard as he pushes his way through a crowd of bustling, jostling courtiers, emphasising his isolation.

'The architecture of Elsinore does not consist in walls,' said Kozintsev, 'but in the ears which the walls have. There are doors the better to eavesdrop behind, windows the better to spy from ... Every sound gives birth to echoes, repercussions, whispers, rustling.'[18] Elsinore is vividly represented as a claustrophobic castle, with its own secret police. If this is not the greatest *Hamlet*, it is the most vivid Elsinore, a place of stone, fire and iron, even down to a detail where Ophelia has to be locked into her garments of mourning for her father's death. The sharp, flinty atmosphere is reinforced by diamond-hard editing (as Kozintsev said: 'no film transitions: no blackouts, fade-ins, or double exposures. The life of government, individual and military flow together, merging');[19] and by Shostakovich's mighty score, harsh, percussive and metallic at the first materialisation of the ghost — a palpable figure of the night, with his cloak billowing in the wind — and whipping up the duelling scene into a whirling cauldron of excitement.

Innokenti Smoktunovsky's Hamlet misses some of the fire and the humour of the character, though his scene at the graveyard with Laertes is a memorable display of scorn, anger and grief; and there is a splendid moment of dry insolence when the men following Hamlet in their endeavour to discover the whereabouts of Polonius's body are compelled to stop dead in their tracks as the Prince pauses casually to pick a stone from his shoe. Smoktunovsky is riveting when on the move, whether sweeping a torch out of a guard's hand prior to his interview with Claudius (a nod perhaps to that moment in Olivier's film, when the enraged Claudius cries, 'Give me some light!' after the play scene, and Hamlet thrusts a torch in his hand); or contemptuously disposing of Laertes in the sword fight. Equally fine is Mikhail Nazwanov's performance as Claudius, bringing out the politician in his character, even having the self-composure to rise and applaud the players after their performance before leaving to plan Hamlet's downfall. The occasional touch of sentimentality (the gull flying away from Ophelia's corpse, presumably symbolising her soul) does not mar the power of the lament for the plight of the intellectual and the individual in a police state — in Kozintsev's words, 'the fate of humanity in the condition of society based on inhuman conditions'.[20] After reading *War and Peace*, William Morris once declared that Hamlet ought to have been a Russian rather than a Dane. He would have admired this film very much.

Of the other versions of *Hamlet*, the most interesting is Tony Richardson's 1969 version, unimaginatively shot in seemingly unremitting close-up, but with strong performances by Nicol Williamson as a snarling, neurotic Hamlet and Anthony Hopkins as Claudius, and a graphic and gruesomely effective staging of Gertrude's death. However, outside of Olivier and Kozintsev, the most imaginative screen version of *Hamlet* is probably Marlon Brando's remarkable western, *One-Eyed Jacks* (1960). Like Hamlet, Brando's Rio is a man set on revenge who finds himself inexplicably sidetracked; who kills all the wrong people; whose obsession brings death and destruction on innocent people around him; and who eventually kills his inveterate enemy almost by accident and only under extreme provocation, having really lost his will for vengeance. His antagonist is the significantly named 'Dad' Longworth (Karl Malden), a man who, like Claudius, is a surrogate father figure professing affection whilst plotting destruction because he knows the hero is the one person in the community who knows his guilty secret. Why does Rio not just go into town and kill his enemy? 'That's not my style,' he says, as adept as Hamlet at finding reasons for delay. To which the gunman replies, echoing many audiences' impatience with Hamlet's prevarication over four hours and five long acts: 'Then you better change your style, 'cos your style's a little slow.'

Othello

The difference between Orson Welles's 1952 film of *Othello* and the 1965 film record of Olivier's National Theatre performance can be stated very easily: in the latter, the star is the actor whereas in the Welles, the star is the camera. One certainly cannot go to Welles's film with the expectation of hearing a great play well spoken. For one thing, Welles has cut half the text; for another, much of the text retained (including the part of Roderigo) seems to have been dubbed in post-production by Welles himself. Many of the oddities in this production have to do with the chaotic and well-documented circumstances under which the film was made. It took nearly four years, with a frequent change of cast as actors and actresses proved either unavailable or unsuitable; improvisations of decor, costume and setting; Welles having to appear in films like *The Prince of Foxes* (1949), *The Third Man* (1949) and *The Black Rose* (1950) to help finance the film and suffering a nervous breakdown in the process; and Micheal MacLiammoir, who plays Iago, describing the film company after all these setbacks as a chic but highly neurotic lumber camp.

As Othello, Welles conveys little passion in his love for Desdemona: certainly none of Olivier's fire and magnetism here. His breathless delivery of many of the lines, said MacLiammoir, 'with his great bulk and power, gives an extraordinary feeling of loss, of withering, diminishing, crumbling, toppling over, of a vanishing equilibrium'.[21] This is even more eloquently suggested by the camera, with its odd angles creating a world of vertigo and delirium, and with its pervasive imagery of webs, nets and cages (for example, the introduction of Iago in his cage as he watches the funeral procession of Othello and Desdemona, the film, like *Citizen Kane*, beginning with the hero's death and then working backwards). In Welles's film, one remembers the imagery, not the poetry: the upside-down shot of Othello that opens the film, a visual premonition of the complete upending of his world; the dark shadow of Iago that follows Othello at one stage as he walks from the camera; the temptation scene on the ramparts, where the camera movement is even more expressive than the performance in suggesting Othello's agitation — hesitant, scurrying madly forward, pausing, then stopping dead, as if numbed, thunderstruck.

'I like Orson's design for the growing dependence of Othello on Iago's presence,' said MacLiammoir, 'the merging of two men into one murderous image, like a pattern of loving shadows welded.'[22] Throughout his career, Welles has been fascinated by the confrontation of innocence with evil, although he is often happier when playing the heavy character (like Macbeth, or Quinlan in the 1958 *Touch of Evil*, for example) rather than the innocent, and then revealing the fragility behind the authoritarian façade. Because of the circumstances of its making, it is a very fragmented film (Truffaut counts nearly 2,000 shots) which gives it more the flavour of a percussive suspense thriller than a sustained tragedy. It is the small touches one remembers more than the performances or any swelling tones, like the detail of Othello's strangling Desdemona with the handkerchief that has been the cause of all the anguish. Welles's good-luck charm, Joseph Cotten, has a walk-on as a senator; Joan Fontaine also appears as a page-boy. It looks stunning, with an especially vivid depiction of the riot in Cyprus, and throughout there is a flair and intelligence about the film that makes it more than just a technical *tour de force*. The literary academics will grumble at the verse-speaking and the liberties taken, but as Welles said in justification: 'In *Othello*, I felt that I had to choose between filming the play or continuing my own line of experimentation in adapting Shakespeare quite freely to the cinema form. Without presuming to compare myself to Verdi, I think he gives me my best justification.'[23] Coincidentally, the Shakespearean heroes whom Verdi has set to music — Macbeth, Othello, Falstaff — are the heroes whom Welles has portrayed on film.

Olivier's performance as Othello (in Stuart Burge's film transcription of John Dexter's National Theatre production) could almost be described as 'Verdian', on account of its extraordinary vocal range. Olivier has said that a problem of playing Othello is that, from Act III onwards, he is always moaning, and the actor somehow has to find a different vocal inflection for every complaint against Fortune. Olivier somehow does it, soft and child-like before Desdemona's dead body, 'Cold, cold, my girl! Even like thy chastity', rising to a terrifying, bestial howl of pain, 'O fool! Fool! Fool!' on learning how he has been deceived by the handkerchief trick. The vocal music of this production is one of its most notable features, Frank Finlay's Iago assisting in scenes whose incisive rhythms and surging climaxes have an overwhelming sense of a rising tide of ungovernable emotion.

Dexter and Olivier have said that the initial inspiration for the interpretation was not Verdi but F.R. Leavis — the suggestion in his essay in *The Common Pursuit* (1952) of monstrous egotism in Othello. By seizing on that, Olivier gives himself a framework for the scale of his performance and makes the tragedy genuinely Othello's, and not just that of a man unfortunate enough to be within range of an evil figure like Iago. In the early scene before the Senate, Olivier deliciously conveys the hero's sly condescension before the Duke, his pride at his own prowess as a warrior, his scarcely concealed sexual satisfaction at having enticed a lovely creature like Desdemona. He is not a stupid gull but a tremendous figure whose sheer presence can quell a riot. His fatal flaw is not his gullibility but an excessive delight in his own intelligence. Ironically, in the temptation scene, he feels he is in control, exuding satisfaction at his ability to spot Iago's unseemly and suspicious reserve. When the seed of jealousy is planted, Othello goes berserk, tormented not so much by Desdemona's infidelity but by the knowledge that he, of all people, should have been deceived ('False to *me*?'). Olivier's performance from this point is one of unnerving intensity, as the character flagellates himself with his own emotional excesses, as if his egotism demands that he must suffer more terribly, more memorably, than anyone else who has ever suffered. The poetry fuses with the character. The man deliberately plays with verbal conceits to punish himself the more — the variations on the word 'lie', for example; the ironic 'Cassio shall have my place,' which Olivier turns into a sexual joke against himself. Yet Olivier's Othello is not Leavis's Othello. Behind the self-dramatisation is genuine grandeur, the touching vulnerability of an outsider in a hostile community, the true isolation of a tragic hero whose only confidant is the man working hardest for his destruction, and the greatness of heart that leads him to suicide as the only honourable course of atonement for a man whose life has been determined by action.

Filmically, the only decision for the director is to judge the camera range in relation to the scale of the performance. Like Iago himself in this production, the camera gives Olivier's Othello room to range around the stage like a wounded lion, which merely needs the occasional flick of Iago's whip to move in the intended direction. Frank Finlay's Iago is filmed more often in close-up, as befits a performance and character of whispers and conspiracy. At one stage, for Iago's speech 'He takes her by the palm', the camera frames Iago foreground left of the frame, whilst in the background and to the right, Cassio and Desdemona unsuspectingly mime their actions to his words. Much later in the film, this composition is to be reversed — Othello foreground right listening to an incriminating conversation between Iago and Cassio, background left — and the visual similarity subliminally links the two moments, a reminder of the incipient stages of Iago's treachery when we are witnessing its full effect later with Othello's jealousy in full cry. Finlay's Iago emerges as a bitter, impotent, low-minded man, proud of his own smartness, resentful of anyone who prospers (notice that scowl as he sees Othello taking Desdemona blissfully by the hand). Derek Jacobi makes capital out of Cassio's drunk scene; Robert Lang's Roderigo is a definitive rendering of this difficult role.

Of the other adaptations of *Othello*, Sergei Yutkevitch's 1955 version, with Sergei Bondarchuk in the title role, is rather stolid. Basil Dearden's modern-dress version, *All Night Long* (1961), is distinguished by Patrick McGoohan's subtle and insinuating Iago. In George Cukor's *A Double Life* (1947) Ronald Colman plays a famous actor who finds that the role of Othello is taking over his personality: it won him an Oscar, but he seems a little too gentlemanly for Othello's terrifying rage. Delmer Daves's western, *Jubal* (1957), is the most intriguing variation, with an evil ranch hand (Rod Steiger) beginning to poison the mind of his boss (Ernest Borgnine) against a suave new foreman (Glenn Ford) who seems rather too gentlemanly towards the boss's wife. As one might expect, Rod Steiger plays Iago with authentic resentment and relish. He has envy to burn.

Julius Caesar

The 1953 John Houseman–Joseph L. Mankiewicz production of *Julius Caesar* remains the finest Shakespeare film ever done by a major Hollywood studio. It might seem a surprising vehicle for MGM, but *Quo Vadis* (1951) and *The Robe* (1953) had made Roman themes very popular and it also meant that they could reuse the costumes of *Quo Vadis* and save money. The film did very well, justifying *Variety*'s irreverently uncultured prediction: 'Socko Shakespeare, seven stars, boffo B.O.'

Houseman had been closely involved with the famous Orson Welles stage production for the Mercury Theatre in 1937, which had particularly emphasised the play's contemporary relevance through its timeless psychologising about dictators and demagoguery. Something of that 1930s political atmosphere is felt in the opening scene, where disgruntled commoners are arrested by Caesar's political police, and in the scene of Caesar's acceptance of absolute power at the ceremonial games, which evokes the atmosphere of Hitler's appearance at the 1936 Olympic games (the crowd's cries sound like Nazi slogans). For Mankiewicz, however (who has described himself to me as a completely unpolitical man — 'I've never voted *for* any politician in my life, I only vote against them'), the politics are secondary to a cluster of themes that have recurred elsewhere in his particularly rich film-making career. In *Julius Caesar*, the spirit of Caesar is to haunt all the characters and become even more powerful after his death, a motif which occurs in other Mankiewicz films like *The Ghost and Mrs Muir* (1947), *House of Strangers* (1950) and *Sleuth* (1972) where ghosts have a life of their own and the dead never seem to stay dead. The themes of *Julius Caesar* seem especially congenial to Mankiewicz whose films often deal with the impact of the past on the present and the clash between generations as one succeeds the other. As *All About Eve* (1950) and *The Barefoot Contessa* (1954) also demonstrate, Mankiewicz is an intrigued observer of back-stabbing conspiracies: indeed, he has murdered Julius Caesar twice in his film career (the second time was in his 1963 film, *Cleopatra*). He is also interested in theatrical people, figures who only come alive before an audience and, among other things, *Julius Caesar* is an interesting play about theatrical charisma: Brutus and Cassius do not possess it, but Antony does, and it will be their downfall. (One of the highlights of the film is Antony's entrance at the Forum, displaying Caesar's mutilated body to the crowd as a blood-curdlingly effective theatrical prop, a dramatic coup that completely upstages Brutus.) Finally, Mankiewicz is a director who loves good talk in film, and is thus eminently suited to the filming of Shakespeare's poetry.

There are lots of fine visual and histrionic moments: the scene at Brutus' home with the conspirators, very tense and brooding; the build-up to the murder at the Capitol, finely scored by Miklos Rozsa; the entry of Antony after the murder of Caesar, a slow approach down a long corridor and with Brutus and Cassius jockeying nervously for position; Antony's contemptuous inspection of his hand, as if for signs of contamination, after having it shaken in friendship by the murderers. Antony's thrilling speech to the crowd must have had a lot of resonances for Mankiewicz: a reminder of his own masterful speech at the traumatic Screen Directors' Guild meeting in 1951, which had saved his presidency and vanquished the forces of Cecil B. De Mille arrayed against him; and a terrifying example of the ease with which a mob can be emotionally manipulated, a relevant spectacle in America during the McCarthyist period.

The most controversial aspect of the film remains the casting. Perhaps surprisingly, two of the best performances are from Hollywood stalwarts: Louis Calhern's portrayal of Caesar as a paternalistic mobster; and Edmund O'Brien's characterisation of Casca as a cynical mimic (both James Mason and Spencer Tracy said they felt O'Brien gave the best performance in the film). Brando is a forceful Antony, perhaps a little given to ranting, and John Gielgud's Cassius was his best screen performance up to that date, partly through the skill with which the camera accommodates Gielgud's essentially theatrical delivery of the lines. James Mason's Brutus remains problematic, certainly more telling than Gielgud in close-up (the argument scene between Brutus and Cassius is one of the best things in the film), offering an intelligent reading of the lines, but so subdued that the charisma and moral authority of the character fail to come through. In a way, this might have been part of the point. Apparently, Mankiewicz saw Brutus as a sort of Adlai Stevenson figure — cultured, much more intelligent than any of his opponents, but quite unable to sell himself to the mob or to stamp his authority on the hurly-burly of everyday politics. The consequence was that he would be forever outmanoeuvred by the rhetorical rabble-rousers and the coarse opportunists. In this respect, the casting works well. Cassius has the intelligence, Brutus has the best arguments, but it is Antony who has the charisma — and in Ancient Rome, as in Hollywood (in Mankiewicz's film of *Cleopatra*, one could hardly make the distinction), star quality wins.

In his journals, Charlton Heston says that the 1969 version of *Julius Caesar* basically made three mistakes — its choice of cameraman (Ken Higgins), director (Stuart Burge) and Brutus (Jason Robards).[24] This is a fair assessment and, as one can imagine, these mistakes are fairly devastating. The weakness of Brutus in this film is especially disastrous since it is on this character that the film places the weight of its interpretation. Its approach to *Julius Caesar* is to see it as a play about the morality of political assassination (a sensitive but relevant theme at the tail-end of the devastating 1960s decade in America). The assassination scene in the film is very violent indeed. Originally, Orson Welles was considered for the role of Brutus ('Oh, but he's much too fat for it now,' was John Gielgud's characteristically tactful response to this idea), but the part went to Jason Robards Jr, who did not turn up for rehearsals but professed a preference for saving the freshness of his performance for the camera. During the filming, tales emanating from the production insisted on the remarkable performance Robards was giving; but, in the event, it turned out to be languid and bemused. John Gielgud is a witty, aristocratic Caesar, Heston a sensual Antony, Richard Johnson a creditably bitter Cassius, and Robert Vaughn an effectively oily Casca. The battle scenes are better done than in the Mankiewicz film, but otherwise it is inferior in almost every other respect, stolid and unimaginatively filmed.

Macbeth

Two of the most excitingly cinematic examples of filmed Shakespeare are both versions of *Macbeth* — Akira Kurosawa's *Throne of Blood* (1957) and Roman Polanski's *Macbeth* (1971). Both films leave a lot to be desired in terms of the verbal poetry and the speaking of the blank verse. The sub-titles of Kurosawa's film reduce famous Shakespearean utterances to banalities like 'What weather! I've never seen anything like it!' whilst Polanski trivialises the 'Is this a dagger' soliloquy through crude special effects. In both cases, the films compensate by vivid visual imagery which brings the atmosphere of the play to frightening, pulsating life.

Kurosawa's opening is breathtaking: two Japanese warriors, Washizu (Macbeth) and Miki (Banquo), encounter a single witch, who has a chalky-white complexion, a loom that seems to symbolise both the thread of life and the wheel of Fate, and is surrounded by skulls that cast her as a sinister harbinger of death. After this fateful meeting, the troubled warriors cannot find their way out of the forest, the film frame seeming a cage which they cannot escape, an invisible barrier which they cannot get beyond. It is a play and film about advancement and about a man whose ambition drives him to murderous impatience: yet the film's visual patterning seems constantly to put obstacles in this Macbeth's way.

The key scene between Macbeth and Lady Macbeth, where the latter impels her husband towards murder after he has told her of the witch's prophecy, is done in a very stylised way. It is mostly composed in full shot, which apparently confused Kurosawa's camera crew who were used to moving closer for moments of emotion. At the beginning of their dis-cussion, she is seated and he paces, but when he has resolved to do the deed, he is seated as she says about Duncan's guards 'I will offer them some wine' — Macbeth's position emphasising his submission to her prompting. Her dominance has been prefigured before then in a moment when he is seen pacing as we hear *her* voice, almost as if she is the voice of his inner self. The formalised exchanges between husband and wife (in the film they never touch or even seem to face each other, being connected only by the blood of the King) are punctuated by shifts of tempo: the fast tracking shot when Macbeth hears of the approach of his Lordship; the astonishing shot of his Lordship's approach with his men — distanced but advancing, slow but inexorable, twisting like a snake into the dark hole of the hero's head as the opportunity for the dread deed presents itself. The film's visual correlatives for the hero's mind are cleverly handled throughout. In Kurosawa's filmic imagination, the mist-laden forest corresponds to Macbeth's moral confusion, just as the moving of Birnam Wood to Dunsinane visually represents his increasing mental derangement. Toshiro Mifune's leading performance is a splendid rendering of a definite Kurosawa protagonist who shows unshakeable obstinacy in the teeth of adversity. Equally fine is Isuzu Yamada as a chillingly spidery Lady Macbeth (Asaji), whose nervous breakdown in Kurosawa's interpretation is precipitated not by guilt or remorse but by a miscarriage which dashes her hopes of a son for future succession (an ingenious addition to the play).

Kurosawa came at *Macbeth* from the rituals and traditions of Noh drama, and has produced a memorably exotic interpretation. Polanski also refracts the play in an idiosyncratic way, but to very different ends. When his film appeared in 1971, it was attacked for its over-emphasis on the carnage at the expense of tragic nobility. But is is clear that Polanski was not interested in attempting to recreate the play's specifically tragic vision. Like Polanski's two previous witchcraft films, *Rosemary's Baby* (1968) and *Dance of the Vampires* (1969), *Macbeth* is about the overwhelming power of evil. What Polanski brings to the material specifically is his own dark personal history (most notably, his horrific childhood experience in Nazi-occupied Poland, and the murder of his wife, Sharon Tate, by the Satanic Manson family). He also brings his tastes and skill as a cineaste, by which *Macbeth* is transformed into a fascinating fusion of horror film and *film noir*.

The *noir* elements are in the reading of the characters and the atmosphere: the seduction of a weak but ambitious hero by a strong heroine who impels him to murder, set against a shadowy world that is dark with something more than night. The horror elements are contained in the film's specific stress on the power of the supernatural. In Polanski's version, *Macbeth* becomes the tragedy of a man who believes what he was told by three witches.

Polanski has said that he was determined to cut across theatrical clichés, and this reinterpretation of the work in terms of specific film forms allows for a liberating irreverence towards stuffy readings of the play. Macbeth (Jon Finch) and Lady Macbeth (Francesca Annis) are unusually youthful and impetuous figures who see the witches' prophecy as potential triumph more than tragedy, but whose attempt to fulfil their destiny reveals a black-hearted corruption to their natures that they never suspected. 'Fair is foul' is a line that begins to apply to this ostensibly attractive couple as they absorb the witches' malignant demonism.

Other changes are equally striking. Unlike the play, where the King is killed offstage, Polanski's film shows Duncan's murder. Nevertheless, this is not a gratuitously gory scene but tensely and intelligently done: entering the chamber, knife in hand, Macbeth still seems hesitant and afraid and it is the fact that Duncan suddenly awakens and sees him that compels him to strike — for what else could he be doing there but plotting murder? Lady Macbeth's sleepwalking scene in the nude aroused predictable critical ribaldry, but Polanski's reasoning seems eminently sound — she would hardly have been asleep fully clothed and her nakedness makes her seem more vulnerable. Ross (John Stride) has been transformed into a major Machiavellian monster who appears unexpectedly as Shakespeare's enigmatic third murderer to assist in Banquo's assassination, but who later appears with Macduff's forces to oppose Macbeth. The porter scene is very funny. According to Polanski's film, he takes such a long time to get to the gate because he is drunk and has to urinate on the way.

Such relief is rare in the film, though. Mainly *Macbeth* is seen as a Jacobean bloodbath whose ruthlessness has clear references to some of the horrors of the modern world committed in the name of overweening ambition. It is a film that could well have been endorsed by a fellow-Polish Shakespearean like the critic Jan Kott (author of the significantly entitled *Shakespeare our Contemporary*). The horrific scene where Lady Macduff and her small son are murdered was based, says Polanski, 'on a childhood experience ... I suddenly recalled how an SS officer had searched our room in the ghetto, swishing his riding crop to and fro, toying with my teddy bear, nonchalantly emptying out the hatbox full of forbidden bread. The behaviour of Macbeth's henchmen was inspired by that recollection.'[25]

The other major film version is Orson Welles's 1948 B-picture quickie, shot in twenty-one days on a minuscule budget, with some fine visual moments (Macbeth's mind 'full of scorpions' illustrated by an unmistakably Wellesian shot of the hero's face reflected through a distorting mirror) but otherwise scrappily structured and flimsily acted. A bizarre updating of the play occurred in Ken Hughes's gangster movie, *Joe Macbeth* (1955), with Paul Douglas as the hero responding to the appearance of the ghost of Bankie (Sid James) with the inelegant Shakespearean pastiche: 'Which o' you guys have done this?' The most imaginative plot stroke is to have Macbeth accidentally kill his wife (Ruth Roman), but, as indicated before, *Macbeth* is *film noir* material, not gangster, and the material is therefore intolerably strained. The Shakespeare play that most closely follows the classical gangster conventions or rise/fall structure and rueful audience rooting for its audaciously appalling hero is *Richard III*. The gangster movie that recognises this best is probably Richard Wilson's *Al Capone* (1958), which has a scene straight out of *Richard III*: Capone (Steiger) succeeding in courting the widow of a man he has killed, she both disgusted and fascinated by his love for her, he both awed and disorientated by her attraction to him.

King Lear

Roman Polanski's view of *Macbeth* was undoubtedly influenced by its relevance both to his own experience and to modern history. However, the Shakespeare tragedy which has seemed to strike a particular chord with twentieth-century sensibilities is *King Lear*. This is interesting for, according to A.C. Bradley at the beginning of the century, *King Lear* was certainly 'the least popular' of the tragedies, 'the least often presented on the stage, and the least successful there'.[26] Bradley wrote that in 1904: if it were true then, it is clearly no longer true. Although the play seems to have attracted some hostility amongst nineteenth-century artists, notably Tolstoy (whose last years then had an uncanny parallel with Lear's), it has certainly fascinated modern artists and critics. Ted Hughes has attempted a poetic version of its themes; Edward Bond's play *Lear* brings out some of its most challenging implications for modern audiences; Samuel Beckett's *Waiting for Godot* is often compared to the work, notably by Jan Kott; even Lennon and McCartney quote Oswald's dying speech from the play in their absurdist song 'I am the Walrus'. Why this interest? In what does its modernity consist?

Firstly, there is a modernity of style. Here *King Lear* is audacious in two particular areas. It has a theatrical self-consciousness and self-awareness, drawing attention to its artificiality, its heightened rhetoric, its allegorical atmosphere. It never wants you to forget that you are in a theatre watching a play. It would be too strong to label this pre-Brechtian alienation, but it is a play less concerned with psychological plausibility than with projecting an audience headlong into startling, stylised, ritualistic scenes. In the first scene, one senses Lear as a petulant tyrannical patriarch dividing the kingdom according to his whim: but one equally senses Lear as an actor-manager who, after the main business on the agenda, demands a chorus of acclaim from his supporting actors and is dismayed when one of his underlings refuses to play the game. In a similar way, the trial scene in the hovel has Lear as actor and Edgar as director having a debate on the 'motivation' of the other characters. Small wonder the Ronald Harwood found Lear so congenial a sub-text for his play *The Dresser*: the relationship between Sir and the dresser is analogous to that of Lear and his fool, but it also emphasises that the relationship between Lear and the Fool can be seen in terms of that of actor–manager and dresser.

King Lear is not only a play of alienation; it is one of the earliest candidates for inclusion in the theatre of the absurd. It is a play that presents a world of irrationality and nothingness, a play built on absurdist paradoxes in characterisation — a wise fool, a perceptive blind man, a rational madman. When Lear and Gloucester converse on Dover beach we have the spectacle of two philosophical tramps who seem very akin to the plays of Beckett and Pinter. *King Lear* is a tragedy with an intensity and bitterness that almost topples it into farce, notably in the extraordinary scene between Edgar and Gloucester when the latter is persuaded that he is jumping to his death from a prodigious height and is actually falling over on a flat stage. Like a lot of Pinter, it is a play that is funny until it gets to that crucial point at which it is *no longer* funny — then turns, and dares an audience to laugh. Of novelists, only Dostoevsky and Hardy have had an equivalently piercing perception of the humour in horror, the close proximity of tragedy and farce; in the cinema, the rape sequence of Kubrick's *A Clockwork Orange* (1971), choreographed to the strains of 'Singin' in the Rain', has a similar sense of outrageousness, a kind of sadistic slapstick that unnerves and challenges an audience.

If *Lear* is modern in its style, it is equally so in its theme. It presents a terrifying spectacle of the innate savagery in humanity which is reinforced by the recurrent animal imagery that seems to uncover the degenerate essence of man when the restraints of civilisation have been removed. In this, *Lear* shares its perception with some of the key texts of modernism — Joseph Conrad's *Heart of Darkness*, J.G. Frazer's *The Golden Bough*, Freud's *Civilisation and its Discontents*, William Golding's *Lord of the Flies*. In addition to its perceptions about human primitivism, *Lear* is Shakespeare's most radical play, with Lear himself becoming the most extreme social critic in the whole of Shakespeare's work. It sees a world of intolerable injustice and cruelty and, with overwhelming compassion, follows the gradual process by which Lear begins to identify with the sufferings of the poor and sees the necessity of forging a bridge between the governors and the governed. However, although this vision of Lear's is felt as truth by the audience, it is expressed as madness, as hysteria. The only way of perceiving society's madness is by becoming mad yourself, like Edgar in his disguise as Poor Tom; at the same time, hypersensitivity to the injustice and cruelty of the world might *truly* drive you mad, as happens to Lear. *King Lear* offers a radical revaluation of what sanity and truth are, and also the subversive proposition that madmen rule and those who voluntarily obey them are blind not to see the insanity of society.

Finally, perhaps the most modern aspect of the play is its moral elusiveness. *King Lear* has often been interpreted as a deeply Christian play, demonstrating redemption through suffering and the triumph of Good over the forces of Evil. Yet the most morally sensitive of all critics, Dr Johnson, was neither convinced nor comforted by this, finding the death of Cordelia particularly intolerable. 'Why should a dog, a horse, a rat, have life/And thou no breath at all?'[27] cries out Lear to his dead daughter in the final scene. The question remains unanswered. When, on the point of death, he seems to see the feather stirring that would signify Cordelia's breathing, it is either Lear's redemption or yet another example of his seeing only what he wants to see, his most profound self-delusion. Through its ambiguity and anguish, *King Lear* speaks to the moral chaos and confusion of our time.

The most celebrated production of *King Lear* in modern times is probably Peter Brook's production for the Royal Shakespeare Company in 1962, starring Paul Scofield as the King. It was a happy idea to preserve this interpretation on film and, unlike Olivier's *Othello*, to reconceive and adapt this reading of the play in terms of the cinema. The film was shot in wintry conditions in North Jutland, which has two immediate effects: to reinforce the play's contrast of hot emotions in a cold climate; and to give the visual texture of the film a kind of Dark-Age, Nordic bleakness that recalls the Bergman of *The Virgin Spring* (1958). It is a film of incessant movement in crude and lumbering wooden wagons: the play's theme of painful journey made vividly actual. Whatever reservations one might have about the overall interpretation of the text as it develops, the steady bony grip of the narrative (after a rather fragmented start) makes this unquestionably Brook's finest film to date.

One complaint at the time about the Brook–Scofield *Lear* was the downbeat nature of the treatment — deplored, in Laurence Olivier's phrase, as an exercise in 'cutting the hero down to size and slicing away his majesty'.[28] For some time, this is a low-key rendering of the play, in which the characters genuinely converse rather than declaim (surely a more natural mode of speaking for members of a household who know each other well). This has its own rewards, notably in Scofield's withering delivery of Lear's curse to Goneril in Act I Scene iv — no loss of control here but a deadly cumulation of resentment, punctuated by Scofield with a terrifying caesura halfway through the speech and a short look away as if seeking additional inspiration for the horrors of vengeance he hopes will befall his daughter. Part of Brook's purpose in keeping Lear's early tirades on a leash is probably to avoid a sense of anti-climax in the later part of the film, when Lear disappears for a large part of the action. The points of physical climax are done with graphic effectiveness: the ghastly blinding of Gloucester; the violent suicide of Goneril (played with fearsome brilliance by Irene Worth) who dashes out her brains against a rock. But the real heart of the film is the meeting of mad Lear and blind Gloucester on the beach, ruined old men with a new fount of wisdom to impart, alternately shot in heart-breaking close-up and almost comically detached long shot that combines to make the scene richer and more moving than in any other production I have seen.

The second main criticism against the Brook–Scofield *Lear* was the deliberate decision to cut the redemptive moments of the play: the servants' rising up against Cornwall's barbarity to Gloucester; Gloucester's happy death; Edmund's conversion. This version is irredeemably grim. Nevertheless, it seems to me convincing in its own terms and to reinforce Brook's deterministic reading of the text. Gone is Edmund's death-bed line, 'Some good I mean to do/Despite of mine own nature,'[29] not only because the director sees it merely as an implausible plot device, but because it is a disruption of the play's inner logic. In Brook's reading, *King Lear* charts the tragic collision that occurs when the characters follow through the consequences of their own basic natures: Lear's stubbornness and pride, Kent's outspokenness and loyalty, Cordelia's reticence and obduracy, Edmund's resentful opportunism, Edgar's naive nobility,

Gloucester's superstitious gullibility. The concept is probably behind Brook's much criticised decision to reallocate certain speeches to different characters. For example, Edgar's lines to the dying Edmund, 'The gods are just ... the dark and vicious place where thee he got/Cost him his eyes ...'[30] are ingeniously and much more plausibly given to Cornwall, sadistic even at a moment of encroaching death, and played with all the malice and malevolence that the inimitable Patrick Magee could command.

Human nature is placed in terrifying conjunction with other aspects of Nature that are to be thrown awry — the storm that symbolises universal discord; the bonds of nature, between fathers and children, which become terribly twisted; the theme of 'back to nature', in which Edgar disguises himself as a naked madman and Lear actually becomes a naked madman; and the theme of 'back to nature' in another sense, in which the emotions of the characters become increasingly primitive, savage, bestial, monstrous. In this reading, Albany's tirade against Goneril in Act IV Scene ii ('Humanity must perforce prey upon itself/Like monsters of the deep'),[31] assumes particular significance. Overall, Brook's reading of the play has an intelligence and intensity that establishes *Lear* indelibly as a milestone of modern theatre: the Theatre of the Absurd, the Theatre of Cruelty, Brechtian alienation and the profundity of Beckettian silence are all somehow encompassed in this monumental interpretation.

In his book *The Empty Space*, Peter Brook talks of the particular impact the Royal Shakespeare Company's production of *King Lear* had when touring between Budapest and Moscow. 'These audiences,' he says, 'brought with them three things: a love for the play itself, real hunger for a contact with foreigners and, above all, an experience of life in Europe in the last years that enabled them to come directly to the play's painful themes.'[32] It was therefore probably inevitable that, after the success of his *Hamlet*, Grigori Kozintsev would seek to make an equally powerful film of *King Lear* (1970). The world he immediately evokes, even before a word is said, is one of ruin and refugees, of, in his phrase, 'footsteps filled with blood':[33] we follow the tired trek of the people towards Lear's court in the vain hope that his renunciation of power will mean some alleviation of their suffering.

The opening scenes are especially well done, with the courtiers manoeuvring for position, Lear appearing in a slightly distracted manner after joking with his fool, and Kent standing with ostentatious solidity in the centre of the frame as an indication of his honesty and directness. As in *Hamlet*, Kozintsev presents a number of the speeches as internal monologues, including Lear's curses on his daughters. One misses Lear's rage but the King's internalisation of his anger is an effective way of suggesting a self-laceration that could lead to madness. Lear's 'poor naked wretches ...' speech is similarly handled and gains immediacy and poignancy through Lear's being actually in the presence of beggars in the hovel sheltering from the storm. In the play, this moment can seem abstract, theoretical and self-pitying: but here, Lear is genuinely moved by first-hand contact with their suffering, a feeling that seems almost involuntarily to generate the speech.

For Kozintsev, the play is a political tragedy as much as a personal one, about the gap between the rulers and the ruled, between wealth and value, and between a ruler's conception of his world and the reality of ordinary life outside. This has a number of implications which make the weighting of the interpretation quite different from Brook's. Gloucester is relatively unimportant (his scene with Lear on the beach, which is the highlight of Brook's interpretation, is done very cursorily here). On the other hand, the progress and character of the political Machiavel, Edmund, are followed with great care, and Edmund's dying change of heart, which Brook omits, is given significant visual emphasis by Kozintsev — an inverted close-up to suggest a kind of last-minute political conversion. Lear's final speech to Cordelia is bewitchingly done by the actor Yuri Jarvet, but the point Kozintsev makes from it has more to do with politics than with passion: someone who can move the feelings of people like that is politically danger-ous. The more touching the scene between Lear and Cordelia, the more powerful is Edmund's motive for ordering their political murder.

'Shakespeare saw a black cloud encroaching on history,' said Kozintsev, 'a black death threatening to annihilate history, to return it to primeval horror. And he expressed it with all the demonic power of tragedy. But he also wrote of how Cordelia found within herself the strength to say "no", and of Edgar's brave behaviour and, first and foremost, of the fearlessness of Lear's thoughts.'[34] His interpretation of the play is more humanistic and romantic than Brook's, though finally less moving, and also less impressive than Kozintsev's *Hamlet* (the plot a little confused in the telling, the performances less striking and integrated, Shostakovich's music less thril-ling). It is a distinguished reading, nevertheless, with a gleam of hope to set beside the unremitting, brilliant barbarity of Brook's version. Nothing illustrates this better than in the directors' respective attitudes to the Fool, to whom Brook gives little attention but whose life is spared by Kozintsev. When asked at a National Film Theatre lecture in 1972 why he had departed from the text and allowed the Fool to live, he replied gently: 'Because I love him very much and I didn't want him to die.'

As I write, new versions of *King Lear* by Jean-Luc Godard and Akira Kurosawa are in production. It is a great pity that Anthony Mann did not live to direct his western version of *King Lear*, for no director could drama-tise the theme of sibling rivalry and hatred with keener intensity. It is a convention now to see shades of *King Lear* in the western *Broken Lance* (1954), in which a tyrannical ranching patriarch has his heart broken by his three sons. Spencer Tracy, one of the American actors who could have made a great screen Lear (one thinks also of Lee J. Cobb and Rod Steiger), is imposingly impressive in the leading role. Outside of Brook and Kozint-sev, however, perhaps the most interesting cinematic *King Lear* is Steve Rumbelow's cut-price 1976 version for the British Film Institute Produc-tion Board. It makes a virtue of limited resources: a cacophonous soundtrack that effectively evokes a world of chaos; a bare natural setting that locates the play's action on the fringes of civilisation; stark black-and-white photography that polarises the characters between extremes of good and evil. It is a critical essay on the play, written with the camera. Like all critical essays, it selects and highlights certain aspects of the play to the exclusion of others. Thus it omits Cordelia, gives little space to Edmund, but a lot of space to Lear and Gloucester. The central visual motif seems to be suggested by Lear's 'I am bound/Upon a wheel of fire.'[35] The pervasive fire imagery implies many things: the flashes of lightning that, in the storm, have obliterated the old order; the over-heated intensity of Lear's mind; the wheel of fire as the crown of England; a vision of life itself as a baptism of fire; and a suggestion that, as G. Wilson Knight argues in his essay on the play in his book *The Wheel of Fire* (1930), the play itself is an experience of Purgatory, a world of darkness that is momentarily illuminated by flares of passion and madness but is almost burnt out.

There is unquestionably a separate chapter, even a book, to be written about films that use Shakespeare as an inspiration, if not a direct source, for their material. Paul Mazursky modernises *The Tempest* (1982), just as *Forbidden Planet* (1956) transfers its events to the world of science-fiction. The structural patterns of *The Winter's Tale* — remorse, rebirth and renewal (with an interval of sixteen years) — lurk behind the romanticism of Brian De Palma's *Obsession* (1975); *Titus Andronicus* is reinterpreted in the language of Hammer horror in the ingenious Vincent Price comedy thriller *Theatre of Blood* (1973); Price plays Richard III in Roger Corman's lacklustre *The Tower of London* (1962); and there is a delightful Shakespearean allusion in Bill Forsyth's *Gregory's Girl* (1981), when an English class on *A Midsummer Night's Dream* is used subtly to anticipate Gregory's change of partners and his subsequent enchantment in the woods on midsummer's night later in the film. *Psycho* is the *Macbeth* of the modern horror film, complete with strange 'castle', a host murdering his guest with a knife and then using a little water to clear up the deed, and obsessed with the imagery of blood, darkness, and with filial devotion and psychological disintegration.

The great tradition of Shakespearean cinema is represented by the interpretations of Olivier, Welles, Kurosawa, Kozintsev, Brook, Mankiewicz, Polanski and Jarman. Their reverence for the text is evidenced not by cautious copying, but by the quality of imaginative invention they bring to the task of making the classic text fresh and exciting for a modern audience. Those who are not strictly faithful to the literal text are often profoundly faithful to the play's spirit, and perhaps provide a working answer to the question of what Shakespeare would have used in place of the written word if he had made films instead of writing plays. The great examples of filmed Shakespeare are a fusion of great literature, cinema and theatre, and they are reverential to Shakespeare in the only way an interpreter can be truly reverential: they do him justice.

Notes

1. Graham Greene, *The Pleasure Dome* (Secker & Warburg, 1972), p. 111.
2. Gavin Lambert, *On Cukor* (W.H. Allen, 1973), p. 102.
3. Frank Kermode, 'Shakespeare in the Movies' in *Film Theory and Criticism*, edited by Gerald Mast and Marshall Cohen (Oxford University Press, 1st edn 1974), p. 324.
4. Charlton Heston, *The Actor's Life* (Penguin, 1980), p. 453.
5. Roger Manvell, *Shakespeare and the Film* (A.S. Barnes & Co., 1979), p. 10.
6. Quoted in Raymond Durgnat's *Films and Feelings* (Faber, 1967), p. 49.
7. Grigori Kozintsev, *Shakespeare: Time and Conscience* (Dobson, 1967), p. 250.
8. Robert Philip Kolker, *A Cinema of Loneliness* (Oxford University Press, 1980), p. 151.
9. Quoted in Manvell's *Shakespeare and the Film*, p. 125.
10. Joseph McBride, *Orson Welles* (Secker & Warburg, 1972), p. 154.
11. Patricia Warren, *The British Film Collection* (Elm Tree Books, 1984), p. 141.
12. *Agee on Film* (Peter Owen, 1963), p. 389.
13. *Hamlet*, Act I, Scene iii, ll.23-4.
14. Ernest Jones, *Hamlet and Oedipus* (W.W. Norton, 1949), p. 90.
15. Manvell, *Shakespeare and the Film*, p. 45.
16. *Hamlet*, Act II, Scene ii, l.242.
17. Dimitri Shostakovich, *Testimony* (Faber, 1981), p. 84.
18. Kozintsev, *Shakespeare: Time and Conscience*, p. 225.
19. Ibid., p. 231.
20. Manvell, *Shakespeare and the Film*, p. 80.
21. Micheal MacLiammoir, *Put Money in thy Purse* (Methuen, 1952), p. 28.
22. Ibid.
23. André Bazin, *Orson Welles* (Elm Tree Books, 1978), p. 111.
24. Heston, *The Actor's Life*, p. 325.
25. *Roman by Polanski* (Heinemann, 1984), p. 291.
26. A.C. Bradley, *Shakespearean Tragedy* (1904) (Macmillan, 1965), p. 199.
27. *King Lear*, Act V, Scene iii, ll.306-7.
28. Quoted in Kenneth Tynan's *Othello* (Rupert Hart-Davis, 1967).
29. *King Lear*, Act V, Scene iii, ll.243-4
30. Ibid., ll.172-3.
31. Ibid., Act IV, Scene ii, ll.48-9.
32. Peter Brook, *The Empty Space* (Pelican, 1972), p. 45.
33. Quoted in Sergei Yutkevitch's article, 'The Conscience of the King: Kozintsev's *King Lear*', in *Sight and Sound* (Autumn 1971), p. 195.
34. Grigori Kozintsev, *King Lear: The Space of Tragedy* (Heinemann, 1975).
35. *King Lear*, Act IV, Scene vii, ll.46-7.

Chapter Two

Historian of Fine Consciences: Henry James and the Cinema

'The historian of fine consciences':[1] this was Joseph Conrad's phrase for Henry James (1843-1916) and the description is apt. James is the supreme analyst of sophisticated sensibilities. The excitement of his work is not in physical incidents nor in racy plots, but in the process by which a sensitive mind slowly uncovers, analyses and elucidates all the nuances of a complex situation. Intelligence, decorum, discrimination: these are the hallmarks of a James novel.

For some, it is all a little contrived and cerebral. In *Aspects of the Novel* (1927), E.M. Forster considered the patterned structure of *The Ambassadors* and its cost to variety and liveliness of characterisation and concluded: 'Beautifully done, but not worth doing.' In *Boon* (1915), H.G. Wells likened James's style to that of a hippopotamus juggling with a pea: there was somehow a disproportion between the intricate technique and the insubstantial content. To some readers, James has seemed a miniaturist on a grand scale, ponderously and portentously belabouring a limited range of effects. Take this moment from the beginning of Chapter 15 in his novel of 1897, *The Spoils of Poynton*, where an incipiently passionate scene between the heroine, Fleda, and the hero, Owen, is interrupted by the arrival of the mother of Owen's fiancée, Mrs Brigstock.

> Mrs Brigstock, in the doorway, stood looking from one of the occupants of the room to the other; then they saw her eyes attach themselves to a small object that had lain hitherto unnoticed on the carpet. This was the biscuit of which, on giving Owen his tea, Fleda had taken a perfunctory nibble: she had immediately laid it on the table, and that subsequently, in some precipitate moment, she should have brushed it off was doubtless a sign of the agitation that possessed her. For Mrs Brigstock there was apparently more in it than met the eye.[2]

For Jamesians this is the kind of detail that delights; for his detractors, even if one grants the humour, it is too ponderously trivial. James might be the only major classical novelist who can make a sexual object out of a broken biscuit, but he is also the only major novelist who would particularly wish to do that.

Nevertheless, although James cannot be viewed as a social critic in the manner of a Dickens, he can be seen as a moral critic in the manner of a Jane Austen. The basic themes in James are not conflicts on a global scale, but intense psychological skirmishes in which self-respect battles with selfish desire, worldliness attempts to subdue innocence, and scrupulous conduct defends itself against egoistic ruthlessness. In his preface to *What Maisie Knew*, James says:

> No themes are so human as those that reflect for us . . . the close connection of bliss and bale, of the things that help with the things that hurt, so dangling before us for ever that bright hard metal . . . one face of which is somebody's right and ease and the other somebody's pain and wrong.[3]

That kind of duality is the essence of Jamesian drama, and perhaps a hint of the sinister ferocity and cruelty which James seems to have felt about life. It is the resolution of this moral tension that tests and reveals character, and it is part of James's tragic vision that the characters who are morally vindicated (Catherine in *Washington Square*, Fleda in *The Spoils of Poynton*, Strether in *The Ambassadors*) so often lose what they really want.

What is there in Henry James that would attract the film-maker? There is, of course, his classic status. Most Jamesian adaptations have not been frankly commercial exercises but have been what one might call the 'art' end of the popular cinema. There is an appropriateness to this since, for all his esoteric literary armoury, James always yearned for popular esteem: one might call him the Merchant–Ivory of the novel form. Also one should remember that James was an art critic, a visually sensitive man whose writings place great emphasis on impressions and pictorialisation: the *visual* bent of his analysis and imagination should not be underestimated. The difficulty and yet the challenge of filming James stems from his combination of psychological analysis and pictorial dramatisation. It would probably be impossible to render visually Isabel's wonderful internal monologue in Chapter 42 of *The Portrait of a Lady* (1881), when her darkest fears about her marriage to Gilbert Osmond are laid bare. Yet the moment in Chapter 40 when she interrupts her husband in conversation with Madame Merle and something about their posture tells the truth about their relationship is exquisitely pictorial ('But the thing made an image, lasting only a moment, like a sudden flicker of light. Their relative positions, their absorbed mutual gaze, struck her as something detected').[4] The tortuous style of *The Ambassadors* would be hard to approximate visually, but again the crucial event in the novel is an act of seeing: the moment in Book 11, Chapter 4, when Strether glimpses two people in a boat on the river and suddenly realises that two people he has idealised are having a squalid affair. The effectiveness of the moment is entirely due to James's almost cinematic use of point of view, angle of vision, and his rendering of Strether's skill in reading off the correct meaning from the image he inadvertently sees. One could even see Strether's situation and behaviour through the novel as analogous to that of the film spectator: he is a man who watches but does not act, who feels but cannot touch.

Given this basic stimulus which James offers, the cinema's reponse to his work has been a generally honourable one. It has attempted to do him justice rather than make him fashionable. Of the major adaptations, only Peter Bogdanovich's film of *Daisy Miller* (1974) is a complete disaster, and that is mainly because of the miscasting of Cybill Shepherd in the leading role. She is so shallow and unalluring that it has the effect of reinforcing F.R. Leavis's characteristically anti-American response to the novella: 'Daisy Miller's freedom in the face of European social conventions is of a kind that would make her insufferable in any civilised society.'[5] Otherwise James has been fairly treated.

Inevitably, the cinema has been attracted to James's early work, with its strong narrative outlines, lively dialogue and detailed characterisation, rather than to the more highly wrought and symbolic later novels. Two films — William Wyler's *The Heiress* (1949), based on *Washington Square*, and Jack Clayton's *The Innocents* (1961), based on *The Turn of the Screw* — have drawn heavily on theatrical adaptations of the novels rather than directly on the novels themselves. (One of the ironies of James's career was that, although his own experience as a playwright was disastrous, culminating in his being booed off the stage after the opening night of *Guy Domville*, his novels have been adapted very successfully for the stage.) There have been adjustments in dramatic scale to compensate for the absence of spectacle and big climaxes in James. *The Heiress* and James Ivory's film of *The Europeans* (1979) have skilful dance sequences that enlarge and elaborate on scenes in the original. François Truffaut's *The Green Room* (1978), based on *The Altar of the Dead*, changes the period and the setting; Martin Gabel's *The Lost Moment* (1947), based on *The Aspern Papers*, changes the tone and style. Yet within the different stylistic and audience demands of the cinema, all seem to have rendered the essence of James's world with a fair degree of intelligence and sensitivity. It is on these films, plus Merchant–Ivory's recent adaptation of *The Bostonians* (1984), that the following commentary will concentrate, in chronological order of films.

The cinema's 'first really bold stab at Henry James' (to borrow a phrase of the screenwriter DeWitt Bodeen)[6] was *The Lost Moment* (1948), an imaginative adaptation of the 1888 novella, *The Aspern Papers*. An antiquary (Robert Cummings) on the trail of a dead poet's letters insinuates his way into the house of the poet's former mistress, Juliana (Agnes Moorehead), now more than a hundred years old. He does this by consciously finding favour with Juliana's ward, Tina (Susan Hayward). In the novella, there are three particularly interesting facets of James's handling of the drama. There is his delight in the creation and inhabitation of what he called, in his preface to the novel, 'a palpable, imaginable, *visitable* past'.[7] There is also his exploration of the split between art and life, in which he is no more sympathetic here to an 'art for art's sake' attitude than he was to be later in *The Spoils of Poynton*. (Frequent criticism of his work along these lines is thus both ironic and insensitive.) The final facet of particular interest is James's highly original use of first-person narrative. Although *The Lost Moment* tries at various points to accommodate all these facets, ultimately it has the good sense to go its own way.

One of the fascinations of *The Aspern Papers* as a literary text is the way the story is told. On one level, it is simply a means of narrating the events from one particular point of view. But the tone evokes the past with such vividness and obsession that one simultaneously catches a vision of the character of the narrator. One mentally compares the artistry of *The Aspern Papers* with Thomas Mann's *Death in Venice* — also about an artistic temperament in search of beauty in the most historically resonant city in the world. One also thinks of Pushkin's *The Queen of Spades*: about a ruthless hero who is seeking to steal a precious secret from an old woman. Intriguingly, the first-person narration is not simply a self portrait but an unwitting self-condemnation. James expands in novel form the dramatic monologue technique of his favourite poet, Robert Browning, and provides the nearest approximation in fiction to Browning's poetic masterpiece, 'My Last Duchess': common to both is the theme of art and life in which the art object is treasured above human consideration, and a first-person narration that becomes an unconscious self-disclosure and critique. In *The Aspern Papers*, James's own voice is not to be identified with that of the narrator, but is felt as the invisible ironic tone underneath the words that allows them to echo so hollowly.

James's sophisticated device of the unreliable narrator (some critics controversially feel that *The Turn of the Screw* can be read in the same way) would be difficult to approximate in film. Hitchcock ran into a lot of critical fire when he had the impudence to use a lying flashback in *Stage Fright* (1950). Billy Wilder often uses narration in his films in such a way that one is given a greater insight into the character of the narrator than the subject of the narration — *Sunset Boulevard* (1950), *Sabrina* (1954) and *Witness for the Prosecution* (1957) are all good examples of this. On the whole, though, popular films encourage involvement and identification and discourage distantiation. *The Lost Moment* chooses to discard any attempt at Jamesian detachment and irony. But what it substitutes is quite interesting: not bland realism but eccentric Gothicism.

The character of Tina, who is a shy recluse in the novel, is transformed in the film into a romantic schizophrenic who sometimes confuses her own identity with that of Juliana. James talked about an 'imaginable, *visitable* past': *The Lost Moment* takes this literally. Tina becomes Juliana in the past, with a ring that transports her into a palpable other world. In the film's words, Tina is a woman 'who walked dead among the living and living among the dead'. Intriguingly, this is identical to the François Truffaut character of *The Green Room*. Tina's destructive obsession with the past and the world of the dead, however — in the film, it is even more poisonous than the hero's — is a reminder of James's impassioned invocation in his stories and notebook 'to live all you can; it's a mistake not to ... Live, live!'[8]

By shifting the dramatic energy of the story from the hero to the heroine, *The Lost Moment* becomes a romantic ghost story with a lot of correspondences to numerous successful Gothic excursions in 1940s Hollywood cinema. As a black-clad, somnambulist Tina walks in straight lines during her trances, one can be forgiven for being reminded of Mrs Danvers in *Rebecca* (1940), similarly obsessed by ghosts and the past: the mysterious house with its magic rooms has a strong aura of Manderley. There is also a suggestion of the influence of David Lean's film of *Great Expectations* (1946), which had been very successful in America. Here too we have a strange old lady with romantic memories living in a room petrified by the past and who is ultimately to be consumed by fire. What James would have thought about being rendered in the manner of Dickens and du Maurier is anybody's guess, but it makes for an intriguingly eccentric and atmospheric film.

The style of the film is distinctly Wellesian, for two reasons perhaps: the success of the film version of *Jane Eyre* (1945), another slice of Gothic romance in which Orson Welles had appeared as Rochester; and because the director of *The Lost Moment*, Martin Gabel, had been a member of Welles's Mercury Theatre.[9] Like Welles's *Citizen Kane*, the film is dominatd by a stylised use of depth and shadow (the idea that 'to love a shadow is not love' is one of the key motifs of the film); by a Gothic house like Xanadu; and by a journey into the past, dominated by women. Like *The Magnificent Ambersons*, it stars Agnes Moorehead and takes place in a huge mansion that is a treasury of the past. The hero's weakness (his failure to stop the beating of the maid, for example) is echoed by the lameness of his friend, a characteristically Wellesian *doppelgänger* who represents the black side of the hero's enterprise — business and malice as opposed to romance and idealism.

There are many atmospheric moments — a well-created Venice, all shadow, mystery, stillness; a spooky scene when the hero attempts to steal the poet's letters and a bird comes swooping at him out of the darkness, like an avenging spirit; the house as a presence which keeps the old lady alive ('As long as I stay here I'll never die') but which stifles the hero and Tina (as he enters the house, he comments: 'The door to the present shut behind me'). The main problems of the film arise from the somewhat uneasy casting: Robert Cummings is not overly expressive as the hero (Pauline Kael's vicious phrase for him is 'unattractively untalented'), and Susan Hayward's firebrand temperament seems a little melodramatic. Yet Agnes Moorehead as Juliana is magnificent, and Hal Mohr's photography is richly textured. For all its odd notes, it is more imaginatively audacious, both visually and dramatically, than either of the two more recent *Aspern* variations. Merchant–Ivory's *Hullabaloo over Georgie and Bonnie's Pictures*

(1978) has an Englishwoman and an American connoisseur on the trail of a maharaja's collection of miniatures in India. It is a genial piece but also, as writer Ruth Prawer Jhabvala honestly admits, rambling and unfocused. Eduardo de Gregorio's *Aspern* (1983) transposes the tale from nineteenth-century Venice to twentieth-century Lisbon with some loss of atmosphere, and casts the block-like Jean Sorel as the hero with some loss of tension. However, the final scenes — perhaps James's most sardonic exposition of the price to be paid for artistic obsession — gather a satisfying force.

Unfortunately, *The Lost Moment* was not a great success with either press or public, but the next major James adaptation, William Wyler's film *The Heiress* (1949), fared much better, winning four Academy Awards and respectable box-office takings. Based on Ruth and Augustus Goetz's theatrical adaptation of *Washington Square* (a play that at least fully exploits James's mastery of dialogue), the film preserves the novel's basic narrative line for about two-thirds of its length. A plain, unsparkling heiress, Catherine Sloper (an Oscar-winning performance by Olivia de Havilland), is courted by a dashing suitor, Morris Townsend (Montgomery Clift), to the amusement and then the chagrin of a fearsome father, Dr Sloper (Ralph Richardson), who suspects that the young man is only interested in his daughter's money. Where film and novel most noticeably part company is in the handling of the ending. The novel dwindles into a kind of diminuendo of disillusionment. Structured as a more dramatic series of false hopes, failed elopements, and vengeful rejections, the film ends on a note of tight-lipped triumph.

It is customary to attack the film for glamorising the novel, but this would be unfair. The changes represent a thoughtful response to the differences of form. The film cannot hope to duplicate the ironical tone of voice of the novel's narrator, but it compensates for this absence by sharpening the dramatic conflict. Moreover, the shifts of emphasis in characterisation are not all in the direction of over-simplification. Catherine is less stoical in the film, and, particularly in her scenes with Aunt Penniman (Miriam Hopkins), there is a suggestion of wit and life, light and shade, that hint of deeper feelings under a docile manner. She moves from feminine reticence at the beginning to feminist self-assertion by the end, though the actress's detailed attention to Catherine's hardening of voice and behaviour reveals the painful cost of that development. (Unlike the novel, Catherine refuses to attend at her father's death-bed: the moment has something of the chill of that episode in Wyler's 1941 film, *The Little Foxes*, when the wife refuses to come to the aid of her despised, dying husband.) Dr Sloper has more varieties of mood in film than novel. James ensures that Sloper's range from irony to anger is kept on a tight leash, but in the film, Sloper momentarily loses control in a series of carefully constructed stages — his deteriorating health, his discovery that Townsend has been using his home in his absence, his exasperation at Catherine's obstinacy — and he utters wounding words of contempt to Catherine that, tragically for both of them, can never be unsaid. In the novel, Townsend's true intentions are evident by the end of Chapter 6, and the drama then becomes a slow, suspenseful consideration of the crushing fate that awaits Catherine from Townsend's treachery and Sloper's arrogance. But in the film, thanks to Montgomery Clift's sensitive performance and Wyler's cunning in hiding Townsend's face from full view at key points in the drama, there is more ambiguity and the uncertainties are sustained much longer.

Taking up a hint from the novel about Morris's tenor voice, the film includes a scene where he serenades Catherine on the piano with a rendition of 'Plaisir d'Amour'. It is seemingly a romantic moment. Catherine certainly registers it as such and fails to notice that the piano is out of tune (we are quickly reminded by Dr Sloper that, by contrast, her mother had 'a perfect ear for music'). But as Morris recites the words, against his slightly discordant accompaniment, a darker premonition resonates: 'The joys of love/Last but a short time/The pains of love/Last all your life/All your life.' More than in the novel, romantic loss is to become one of the film's main themes. It is not simply that, in Wyler's and de Havilland's hands, Catherine will be transformed into one of the great jilted heroines of American cinema. The theme also implicates Dr Sloper and his beloved wife, who has died shortly after giving birth to Catherine. A picture of Sloper's wife is prominently displayed in the scene when Sloper interviews Townsend's sister and introduces her to Catherine. The implication is that his wife has played the same role in Sloper's life as Townsend (the subject of the conversation) is destined to play in Catherine's: that is, the briefly idealised romantic object that will disappear almost as soon as it has been claimed. Indeed, Townsend himself might be implicated in this theme. In the novel, when he returns twenty years later, James makes clear that he is still the same shallow opportunist he always was. In the film, when he returns four or five years later, a certain ambiguity and attraction still cling to Morris. He is still handsome and, very surprisingly, still has not married. There is a hint that a residue of feeling still remains for Catherine, and that it is she who has changed, not him.

In the film, all the major characters grow more and more like the embittered Sloper. 'We like the same things,' says Townsend about Sloper, meaning the objects of the house rather than a liking for Catherine: the implication is that his opinion of her at that time is not very different from her father's. Catherine grows harder, despising her father as he has despised her, and reversing roles in her final scene with Townsend: he now seems foolish, gauche, romantic whilst she is controlled, detached, ironical. 'How could you be so cruel?' says Aunt Penniman, when she realises Catherine has no intention of running off with Townsend this second time as she had led him to believe. 'Yes, I can be very cruel,' replies Catherine, 'I have been taught by *masters*.' The word 'masters' is significant: not simply 'experts' but people who have bullied and dominated her, trying to turn her life into one of caution and subservience. When she has worn her mother's red dress to an engagement party (a disastrous red dress is worn by the heroine in a famous scene from another Wyler film, the 1938 *Jezebel*), her father has commented with withering finality: 'But Catherine, your mother was fair; she *dominated* the colour.' Sloper is obsessed with dominance. In a claustrophobic masculine house, in which the sliding doors seem to turn the rooms into so many cells, the heroine is variously buffeted by the rival challenges of an impersonal rationalism (her father), excessive romanticism (her aunt) and mercenary opportunism (her suitor). She finally takes a stand of independence and individuality against masculine dominance and control. As in *The Desperate Hours* (1955), *Friendly Persuasion* (1956), *The Big Country* (1958) and *Ben-Hur* (1959), Wyler shows his fascination for the passive and pacific figure who is slowly transformed into an anguished agent of revenge. *The Heiress* is one of Wyler's most powerful examinations of 'the worm that turns'.

At the end of the novel, Catherine has rid herself of an elderly, balding Townsend and returned to her needlework — 'for life, as it were'. The film opts for a different treatment. Here Townsend is still a desirable prospect. But Catherine wants no more part of his deceit, and his return seems to galvanise her into closing for ever that disastrous page of her life. She completes her final embroidery, sewing the letter 'Z' and then snipping the last thread at the precise moment that the doorbell rings. The maid is instructed to bolt the door, the house at this juncture becoming, in effect, Catherine herself, barred from outside feeling and from a masculine hammering at her defences. From the outside, Townsend sees the light going out above the door: the fading of her feeling for him, and of his hopes. As he continues to hammer at the door, she climbs the stairs. It is the third significant staircase shot in the film, each one marking a crucial stage in her situation and character. The first has occurred when she joyously ascends the stairs after Townsend's declaration of love. The second has been an ascent of abject misery, when she realises the man has backed out of his promise of elopement and confirmed himself as the fortune-hunter her father suspected. Failing to leave the house, Catherine's only alternative is to dominate it, which at the end she does in the final staircase ascent.

One suspects that what attracted James and Wyler to the basic situation was very similar: the theme of domestic tyranny. James also explores the theme, with painful intensity, in his great novel, *The Portrait of a Lady*, and it is a preoccupation of numerous Wyler films, which are obsessively concerned with marriage and the family and the clash of generations. *The Heiress* shares with a later film of Wyler, *The Big Country*, the situation of a daughter needing to rid herself of the influence of an awesome father figure; and the situation of a younger generation ultimately rejecting the example of embittered or corrupt parent figures runs all the way through Wyler films from *Come and Get It* (1936) and *The Little Foxes* to his last film, *The Liberation of L.B. Jones* (1970). Ultimately, the basic difference between novel and film lies in their choice of central character. For James, it is Dr Sloper. For Wyler, ever interested in heroines kicking against the constraints of a patriarchal order (he would have made a great film of

Hedda Gabler), the central character is Catherine. The final difference between novel and film, then, is not only one of medium but also one of personality, and perhaps sexual politics. Wyler's Catherine — not James's — could become a feminist on a par with Olive Chancellor in *The Bostonians*.

If irony is the essence of James's *Washington Square*, ambiguity is the key to his haunting ghost story *The Turn of the Screw*, published in 1898. Of all James's stories, this one has never lacked for critical interpretation, though basically the views can be grouped, with variations, under one of two headings. On the one side, it is an allegory of Good and Evil, the virtuous governess fighting to save the two children in her charge from becoming possessed by the demonic spirits of the former governess, Miss Jessel, and the evil valet, Quint. On the other, it is a pre-Freudian study of sexual neurosis, in which an unbalanced Victorian spinster with a colourful imagination starts seeing things, believes that these visions are connected with the children and starts behaving in such a manic way that ultimately she terrifies them to the point of nervous breakdown and death. Jack Clayton's stylish, imaginative and genuinely frightening film version, *The Innocents* (1961), while retaining some of the Jamesian ambiguity, leans definitely in the directon of the second of the two interpretations.

One would have thought that this might pose certain visual problems. How could you show that the ghosts are figments of the governess's imagination? That ghosts would have to be shown if the governess's state of mind were to be understood at all and, once seen, would surely convince a spectator of the validity of her visions. In fact, these appearances are visually insubstantial in a very satisfying way (the first sight of Quint on a tower being particularly eerie). But Clayton's major visual solution is brilliantly simple. He reverses cause and effect by always showing the governess's reaction to what she sees before we see the thing itself. In this way, a close-up of the governess's horror before the visions appear gives the impression that it is her own sense of horror that is actually producing the visions.

James tended to dismiss *The Turn of the Screw* as a mere pot-boiler, but one can read it in more serious terms, notably as a trenchant criticism of Victorian values. The most interesting thing about the tale is the way in which evil is actually defined. One of the things which most offends the governess about Quint's affair with Miss Jessel is its disturbance of her sense of social decorum — the servant not knowing his place. But mainly it is the sexual nature of the relationship and the fact that the children might have seen something that generates from the governess a protective attitude towards them that borders on possessiveness. Certainly in Michael Winner's typically gross film *The Nightcomers* (1971), which deals with what went on before the governess arrived, the relationship between Quint and Miss Jessel is a very kinky affair and worth protecting anyone from, but this was not Clayton's view for *The Innocents*. 'I don't think that Quint and Miss Jessel have done anything but have a perfectly normal sexual relationship,' he said.[10]

So who is terrorising the children — is it the ghosts or is it the governess? Clayton's film seems less about the horrors of evil than about the horrors of innocence. The children are protected from 'knowledge' (by Miles's headmaster, who expels him from school for 'saying things'; by the housekeeper; and particularly by the governess) and are persecuted and suffocated by the perverted puritanism of typical Victorian authority figures. It is this which accounts for the children's strange behaviour, not any evil spirits. In this reading the work becomes a potent indictment of Victorian sexual inhibition and hypocrisy: the elders are horrified by sexuality yet also fascinated by it, and transmit their poisonous prurience to the bewildered children.

This is underlined by the characterisation of the governess, whose very presence throws Nature into disarray and who seems to bedevil the chance of anything natural surviving. She touches some flowers and they instantly collapse; she first sees Flora as an upside-down reflection; she hears the sound of a piano when the keys are still; winds howl, thunder crackles, and all animal life in the film has a hard time, particularly a hapless tortoise called Rupert.

Clayton amplifies this hot-house of repression with a skilful soundtrack, in which Georges Auric's music adds mystery, and with some bravura cinematic passages. There is a particularly fine scene when the governess is wandering the house hearing voices and sounds of laughter but is unable to find anything. She tugs at the doors only to find them locked (an implicit image of her sexual repression since earlier in the film the image of 'open doors' has had overtones of sexual licence: it is an interesting parallel to Catherine's locked door at the end of *The Heiress*). Clayton caps her frustration and hysteria with an overhead shot of her turning back and forth in the corridor, unable to find an unlocked door, twisting, turning — like a screw. Elsewhere the imagery is beautifully attuned to the film's sense of enigma and suggestion rather than overt horror, as in that wonderful moment when the governess's evidence that the ghost of Miss Jessel is real is simply a wet tear on a school desk that evaporates almost as soon as it materialises.

Michael Redgrave's appearance as the uncle, a crucial figure outside the main narrative, is a rather interesting anticipation of his appearance in Joseph Losey's *The Go-Between*. It is a reminder of the similarity between both the Clayton and the Losey films, and the James and Hartley novels: similar opening journeys to a large house, games of hide and seek, a sinister relationship between the mistress of the house and a servant, and the insidious equation of sexuality and evil, which has such a traumatic impact on the minds of the children. One sometimes wonders how directors manage to coax such performances from children in this kind of situation, but one can only record that Jack Clayton has always been a marvellous director of children (see also the young performances in his 1964 film *The Pumpkin Eater* and his film of 1967, *Our Mother's House*) and that the performances of Martin Stephens and Pamela Franklin in *The Innocents* are remarkable.

The revelation is Deborah Kerr's governess. It is one of those performances that is felt so far from the inside that she seems physically to change as the film develops, particularly emphasised by a flashback structure which cuts from her face after the traumatic events to her appearance before them, and we wonder what has changed her from one to the other. In Miss Kerr's astounding performance, the governess becomes more and more like Miss Jessel, sitting at her place at the desk, wearing black. In her final scene with Miles, the governess acts out her vision of the Quint–Jessel relationship — he bullying, she supplicating; and, at Miles's death, she howls like a wild beast in the way Jessel is said to have howled at Quint's death. The casting of Deborah Kerr is especially resonant, since her screen persona has always polarised her between purity and sexual frustration (from the nuns of *Black Narcissus* and *Heaven Knows Mr Allison,* to the nymphomaniac of *From Here to Eternity* and the tempted teacher of *Tea and Sympathy*). Perhaps one could take the casting as a delicious black joke on her famous governess role in *The King and I* (1955). In *The Innocents,* whenever Miss Kerr's governess feels afraid, she does not whistle a happy tune: she takes it out on the children.

Although James has long been accepted as a classic author in England and America, his acceptance in France as an artist of major status has apparently been considerably delayed. The attitude has been: why do we need Henry James when we have Marcel Proust? One of the events which has assisted a greater recognition of James in France is François Truffaut's film *The Green Room,* based mainly on James's short story of 1895, *The Altar of the Dead* (though with some themes that also recall another James Story, *The Beast in the Jungle*). In some ways, it is a surprising choice of work to adapt. The story is one of James's most morbid and critically neglected, and its sombre theme is rather unexpected from a director of Truffaut's affirmative personality. Seen in retrospective over Truffaut's whole career and particularly from the perspective of his untimely death in 1984, it looks an increasingly revealing, impressive work.

The film deals with the hero's obsession with the memory of his dead wife (in the original story, it is the hero's fiancée), which becomes an immersion in the rituals of death itself and a desire to preserve the memory of his dead friends by dedicating a chapel to their honour. Like many of James's heroes, the man is a spectator of life, wounded by life's cruelty and sickened by the impermanence and instability of human relationships. After a remarkable opening sequence in the film, when he supports his friend's 'undignified' grief at the death of his wife against the pious platitudes of the clergy, he is deeply distressed to find later that his friend has remarried. His loyalty is admirable up to a point ('In this pitiless cruel world, I insist on the right not to forget,' he says), but his idealism makes for an uncomfortable inflexibility. His intensity makes him overlook until too late the attentions of a girl (Nathalie Baye) who is devoted to him. His moral fastidiousness ultimately drains him of all life. The part is played in an appropriately stiff and intense manner by Truffaut himself.

The tone of the film might seem uncharacteristically morbid for Truffaut, but there are certain preoccupations which can be traced to his other work. He has always been fascinated by obsessive love which drives people into peculiar excesses of behaviour — from *Jules et Jim* (1961) to *The Story of Adele H* (1975) and *The Woman Next Door* (1980). The worshipping attitude to woman, prominent in his Antoine Doinel films, is here taken to an extreme of discomfort and claustrophobia. The style too takes on a particularly personal colour, with a plot that has echoes of Hitchcock's 1958 masterpiece, *Vertigo* (the absorption with death and the preservation of a dead girl's memory), and a terse manner that recalls Bresson: both considerable influences on Truffaut. The personal note breaks out overwhelmingly in the film's central sequence, when Julien allows the girl into the chapel to participate with him in the consecration of his dead friends. The pictures displayed are those of men who have helped form Truffaut's own artistic sensibility — James, Proust, Oscar Wilde, Cocteau, the actor Oskar Werner and the composer Maurice Jaubert. It is both a tribute to the way in which the cinema has allowed Truffaut to preserve his own artistic friends and treasures; and, in its sense of claustrophobia, a very Jamesian suggestion of how his own cinematic and literary obsessions might have stifled his capacity for life. The scene is to generate a later and typical Truffaut nightmare scene, in which past and future are aligned and soundtrack noises of war jostle with images of flame at the altar.

One addition to the James original is the inclusion of the relationship between Julien and his housekeeper's young boy, who has a severe speech impediment. As Richard Roud has pointed out in *Sight and Sound* (summer 1978) the scenes between them recall Truffaut's *L'Enfant Sauvage* (1970). The child seems to represent a positive force in the film but a force whose gestures are restricted and difficult, a foreboding of the problematical future awaiting the generation emerging from the scars of the First World War.

This brings us to the second major change from the original: Truffaut's updating of the material to the period after the First World War. Here it would be worth quoting Henry James's own despairing outburst at the outbreak of the war. 'The plunge of civilisation into this abyss of blood and darkness,' he said, in a letter to Howard Sturges, 'is a thing that so gives away the whole age during which we have supposed the world to be, with whatever abatement, gradually bettering, that to have to take it all now for what the treacherous years were all the while really making for and meaning is too tragic for any words.'[11] For James, the war was a terrible denial of what the nineteenth century had stood for and a terrible premonition of what the twentieth century was in for. Truffaut's use of this period gives the film a more modernist sensibility than the James original. Although the film's death-in-life atmosphere was more often compared to Edgar Allan

Poe than Henry James, Truffaut's examination of a hero who has seen death at first hand through his experience in the war, who has felt the horror of the modern age, actually links *The Green Room* with the death-ridden culture of the twentieth century — from T.S. Eliot to Samuel Beckett, from Virginia Woolf to Sylvia Plath. It might even be most appropriate to approach *The Green Room* not as filmed James, but as a cinematic sequel to Alain-Fournier's great 1913 novel, *Le Grand Meaulnes*, a work of romance and death whose air of lost pastoral and nightmarish forebodings seems almost to prophesy the coming holocaust. The hero Meaulnes is also to lose his wife and is to have a dream of a green room, a dream which seems close to nightmare and loss. 'Chilled to the marrow, he recalled a dream, or rather a vision ... he was in a long green apartment with curtains the colour of foliage ...'[12] It is not surprising that a director of Truffaut's literary sensibility would be drawn to a linguistic stylist like James, but he has transmuted the Jamesian themes into an individual, dark romanticism that seems quintessential Truffaut.

Truffaut is an unexpected director of Henry James, whereas the sensibilities of James and the director James Ivory seem made for each other. Ivory is an American who has spent much of his life abroad, like James, and this no doubt accounts for his similar fascination with the conflicts that arise between people of different cultures, in films such as *Shakespeare Wallah* (1965), *Autobiography of a Princess* (1975) and *Heat and Dust* (1983). Like James also, Ivory is fascinated by cultures and societies which seem at the twilight of their development, grimly existing in the present but with their hearts in the past and resisting for as long as possible a pull towards the future. Aided by the most sympathetic of collaborators (producer Ismail Merchant and writer Ruth Prawer Jhabvala), Ivory is therefore ideally cast for handling the culture conflicts of *The Europeans* (1979) and the transitional social and sexual tensions of *The Bostonians* (1984).

Set in Boston a decade or so before the American Civil War (the novel was written a decade or so after, in 1878), *The Europeans* deals with the impact on a wealthy American family, the Wentworths, of a visit from their sophisticated European cousins, Eugenia and Felix. Although the events of the narrative might seem little more than a series of courtesy calls, one is constantly made aware of the importance of the issues at stake: the confrontation tests the values by which people live. 'We are to be exposed to peculiar influences,' says old Mr Wentworth, and his horror at European affectation and frivolity is beautifully conveyed in the film by Wesley Addy, particularly his stuffy but understandable disapproval of the fascination Felix has for his impressionable daughters. On the other side, the Europeans are genuinely attracted by the American innocence, making Eugenia, in particular, more aware of the limitations in herself and of something precious in her life she has lost. Lee Remick had previously revealed herself as an actress of Jamesian sensibilities through her performance as Maria Gostrey in a fine BBC television production of *The*

Ambassadors, with Paul Scofield as Strether. She might not have the intimidating imperiousness of Eugenia (Ivory has said that his image of the character was of a younger Bette Davis), but does have poise and style and a crucial suggestion of vulnerability.

There is a fine moment early on in the film when the cousins have all met, and Mr Wentworth says gravely, 'You have come very far.' The remark stops Eugenia momentarily in her flight of strenuous graciousness and unaccountably almost reduces her to tears. Is she acting for sympathy, or has the remark struck deeper than intended? Momentarily, in Lee Remick's face, there is a sudden confusion: gratitude that she might at last have landed in a haven of rest, but also a chilling awareness of the unintended irony of Wentworth's remark — of what a disappointing journey her life has actually been.

The tension in the film is felt most acutely in the relationship which develops between Eugenia and Robert Acton. Acton, finely played by Robin Ellis, is an admirable figure who is nevertheless unduly passive (Tony Tanner has pointed out that his name is 'Action without the "i"')[13] and is always in danger of putting humanity on a pedestal. The film finds skilful embellishments to enhance this impression of Acton: his soft-focus imagination, and — a detail not in the novel — the exquisite gift he purchases for Eugenia of a jade ornament, which exactly conveys his remotely idealised image of her. It is a gift which is eventually to go to Acton's sister when he discovers that Eugenia has a flaw. An incident of subdued farce (the discovery of young Wentworth hiding in Eugenia's room) is enough to knock Acton's ideals awry and upset the relationship sufficiently to ensure that its fragile balance can never quite be restored.

Eugenia has potential; however, her bitter experience of life has encrusted her with a self-protective but unattractive veneer of cynicism which, in this case, is to deny her what she wants. (This is unlike her less complex brother — his hobby of sketching is a correlative to the happy superficiality of his outlook on life — who winds up with everything.) There is a finely sustained and acutely uncomfortable party scene — another skilful invention of Ivory's and Jhabvala's — where Eugenia's gushing affectation, to some degree prompted by the cruelty of Acton's sister, presents a distorted picture of her to the others which can never be entirely eradicated. Nevertheless, even under the most massive blows of misfortune, she has a resilience which enables her to retain a sense of self-esteem — always one of the most attractive aspects of both Ivory's and James's view of character. Both film and novel end with an exquisite modulation between incident (the profusion of prospective marriages) and tone (the prolongation of poignant melancholy). In the film, Larry Pizer's photography is predominantly autumnal, as if taking its hues not from the young lovers but from Eugenia's romantic disillusionment and from Mr Wentworth's resigned recognition of a fading world. These two characters add a shade and a depth to what could have seemed a summery and superficial work.

No one could find James's novel *The Bostonians* (1886) superficial: it is one of his major achievements. It tells of a struggle for the heart and mind of a young lady, Verena Tarrant, who, encouraged by her eccentric and religious father, is a dazzling public speaker on the rights of women. She is ardently supported by Olive Chancellor, whose feminist ideals are partially defined by her strong dislike of men ('There are women who are unmarried by accidents, and others who are unmarried by option,' comments James, 'but Olive Chancellor was unmarried by every implication of her being').[14] Verena is passionately courted by a conservative gentleman from the American South, Basil Ransom, who sees the role of women as a form of decorative slavery, and is as enamoured of Verena as he fears and despises Olive and her influence over her. Ransom's feeling is that Verena is in thrall to Olive and is merely a mouthpiece for ideas in which she does not believe. Olive's feeling is that Ransom is the incarnation of the enemy they are fighting and that his seduction of Verena is simultaneously a ploy to discredit an emancipation movement he loathes. Verena is torn between the two of them — between principle and passion, loyalty and love, and between ultimate commitment to a person whose values are as reactionary on the one side as they are radical on the other.

The Bostonians has always struck me as one of James's most American novels, and perhaps the most influential of all his works on other American writers. (Appropriately enough, the film begins with an organ performance of 'America', played with all the stops out.) The spellbinding power of James's female orator now seems an influence on the character of Sister Sharon Falconer in Sinclair Lewis's novel *Elmer Gantry,* a comparison emphasised by the quirky religious background shared by both works and by the dubious conjunction noted by both James and Lewis of sermonising and showbiz. 'There's money for someone in that girl; you see if she don't have quite a run!' says the newspaperman, Mr Pardon, of Verena:[15] her father ensures that he extracts his share from Olive for Verena's services. Also, in its archetypal tensions between male and female, *The Bostonians* has a strong sexual charge that takes it in the direction of *A Streetcar Named Desire.* In the novel, Olive tells Verena that 'there are gentlemen in plenty who would be glad to stop your mouth by kissing you!'[16] — a particularly powerful image of the brute male seduction that attempts to overwhelm the woman's identity. In a hysterical denunciation of Ransom towards the end of the novel, Olive claims that 'it was because he knew that her voice had magic in it, and from the moment he caught its first note he had determined to destroy it'.[17] In her view, Ransom's fascination for the virginal heroine is inseparable from his determination to tear her down from her pedestal: he is the epitome of masculine oppression, the kind of male who will not let a woman breathe. James is a long way from Tennessee Williams but he has a similar sympathy for the sensitive, frail and vulnerable and a similar horror for those with a ruthless drive, determination and power — sympathies which would inevitably draw him towards the softness of the female against the aggressive assertiveness of the male. A final comparison that suggests itself is Lillian Hellman's play *The Children's Hour*, which deals with a close personal and professional relationship between two women that is disrupted partly by the insistent presence of the male: the lesbian sub-theme and the critique of a stuffy Bostonian society have much in common with the James work. In *The Bostonians*, James comments that 'Olive had a fear of everything but her greatest fear was of being afraid.'[18] In her self-portrait in the tale 'Julia' in *Pentimento* (a story to be filmed in 1977 by Fred Zinnemann, with Vanessa Redgrave as Julia), Ms Hellman has an almost identical phrase: 'you are afraid of being afraid, and so will do what sometimes you cannot do'.[19] Lewis, Williams and Hellman are an odd cluster of Jamesian legatees, but *The Bostonians* is the James novel that has most to say about the puritanism, pomposities and prejudices of American society and it is not surprising that fine writers have been so stimulated and affected by James's example.

What, then, would specifically attract Ivory to the material? Like most of his works, it is a literary subject with a strong theme, a lot of attractive historical detail (including here an Independence Day fireworks display, a Cape Cod beach party, a period stroll in Central Park) and a suspenseful dénouement. It takes up the theme of patronage with which Merchant–Ivory have frequently been concerned, most notably in their fine 1981 adaptation of Jean Rhys's anguished, autobiographical novel, *Quartet*. Above all, the material has two splendid parts for women, and the Merchant–Ivory–Jhabvala films have been especially notable for their discovery of young actresses and for their sensitive portrayals of women in patriarchal societies. In the novel of *The Bostonians*, one feels that the 'emancipation of women' theme is more the occasion for character conflict than the subject of debate itself: it is important background colouration but the theme is basically that of *Washington Square* — the struggle over a soul by two egos of equal strength pulling in opposite directions. In the film, the emancipation theme is given much more prominence, for three main reasons: its modern topicality; Vanessa Redgrave's extraordinary performance as Olive; and the film's calculated, emphatic refusal to accept James's defeatist conclusion.

Ivory has a particular gift for filming James: he knows how to film dialogue so that each pause is given its due weight. When Olive effuses over Verena's 'divine gift', the particular weighting and inflection of the single word 'Oh' by Olive's sister Adeline (Nancy New) imply volumes about how often she has seen such effusions in the past. Alert direction and editing counterpoint the dialogue in such a way that sometimes the stress of a scene is felt somewhere different from its ostensible subject. Olive talks to Mr Pardon whilst Verena talks to two students, but the point of the scene is in neither of the dialogues but in Olive's gathering agitation at Verena's flirtatiousness, her obvious ease and pleasure in the society of men. Ransom has to cope with Adeline at the Wednesday Club whilst simultaneously trying to hear what Verena has to say in her public speech, and dialogue and image weave a spellbinding counterpoint: between Ransom's innate Southern courtesy and his barely suppressed irritation at Adeline's interruptions; between Verena's impassioned speech and the kind of polite society implied by the setting, a kind of community that is patronising towards commitment and frivolous about injustice.

The film was criticised in some quarters for emphasising the romance at the expense of the novel's social comedy, but it seems to me quite alert to this dimension in the work. Martial drum rolls over the soundtrack amusingly accompany the self-important entries of Ransom, and the brisk precision of Linda Hunt's performance as Doctor Prance brings out the dry irony of a character whose views in the novel are closest to James's own ('there is room for improvement in both sexes. Neither of them is up to the standard').[20] The film is equally attentive to the novel's suspense. Olive searches for Verena against a lurid night sky, fantasising about her drowning, or worse, finding her with Ransom: this vivid episode from the novel is splendidly visualised in the film, as is the prolonged tug-of-war over Verena prior to her big theatrical performance, where Ransom finally paralyses her into sexual submission. As Verena, Madeleine Potter's performance does not have the range to suggest the character's stage charisma, but she does convey well the fragile and unguarded charm of the private character. As Ransom, Christopher Reeve has the right kind of pompous authority: clearly Henry James brings out his subtleties as a performer, away from his superstar status. (Strangely, the same thing happened to Richard Chamberlain who, on the heels of Dr Kildare, surprised everyone with the sensitivity of his performance as Ralph Touchett in a memorable BBC production of *The Portrait of a Lady*.)

The great performance of the film, however — to the extent of transforming the novel's theme — is that of Vanessa Redgrave as Olive. It is built up from small details, very often the gesture of clapping her hands to her ears at unwelcome sounds. She does it to the clatter of Adeline's noisy son (the gesture implying how she has shut out the sound of children from her world); also to the discordant dinner gong, during a tense conversation with Verena over the latter's feelings for Ransom, in which Olive is compelled to listen to things she would rather not hear. A nervous cough that punctuates the polite civilities of tea, when she is given another warning about Verena by Mrs Burrage (the excellent Nancy Marquand), is another tiny mannerism that suggests a character as tense as a coiled spring: it absolutely fulfils the Jamesian maxim of aiming for the maximum intensity with the minimum of means. There is no attempt to sentimentalise Olive — her buying off Verena's father is seen in all its moral dubiousness — but nor is she turned into a monster. Her sincerity for the cause is clearly genuine; her feelings for Verena are honestly confused (admiration or love?); her fear of Ransom for his ideas, as well as his sexuality, is certainly well founded.

In his famous essay on James in *The Triple Thinkers*, Edmund Wilson thought that there was no ambiguity about Olive in *The Bostonians*:

'though tragic perhaps, she is definitely unhealthy and horrid, and she is vanquished by Basil Ransom'.[21] In fact, James's conclusion is considerably more ambivalent and melancholy than Wilson allows. Ransom has rescued Verena from Olive but James's final sentences read: '... he presently discovered that, beneath her hood, she was in tears. It is to be feared that with the union, so far from brilliant, into which she was about to enter, these were not the last she was destined to shed.'[22] Clearly rejecting Wilson's interpretation of the characters, the film also refuses to follow James's equivocal conclusion. Olive has certainly lost, but Miss Redgrave's performance seems to demand that she has the last word and so she does, addressing a speech to the sparse audience remaining after the débâcle of Verena's desertion. Verena's loss does not discredit the movement, it merely shows that the message was being relayed through the wrong vessel: but the struggle will go on.

Some critics felt that this finale represented a disruptive and unconvincing break from the original, disfiguring James in order to provide a sop to the modern feminists. However, as well as having some justification for it in the original text (Verena has exclaimed to Olive that 'you are quite a speaker yourself!'),[23] the ending has a similar implication to Wyler's ending for *The Heiress*: a modern insistence on giving the heroine a voice; a refusal to accept James's resigned conclusion that the heroine must put up with docile defeat. In Ivory's *Bostonians*, the conviction of Olive's final speech comes mainly from Miss Redgrave's beautifully evolving performance, but also, it must be said, from her powerful persona. James Ivory has made a link between Vanessa Redgrave's performance in *The Bostonians* and the personal battle she was simultaneously waging against another example of Bostonian prejudice:[24] namely, the decision of the Boston Symphony Orchestra to fire her without notice as narrator for Stravinsky's *Oedipus Rex* because of her controversial political opinions, a decision which Miss Redgrave bravely contested in court. Something of the actress as well as the character comes through in that final speech in *The Bostonians* and, with it, Henry James is hauled, kicking and screaming, into the twentieth century:

I say we will be as harsh as truth. As uncompromising as justice. On this subject, we will not think, or speak, or write with moderation. We will not excuse — we will not equivocate — we will not retreat a single inch. And we will be heard!

In conclusion, it can be said that the history of James on screen has seen directors of the calibre of Wyler, Clayton, Truffaut and Ivory sincerely and intelligently seeking to respect the broad outline of his themes whilst also striving to make James relevant for both a modern age and a modern medium. What cannot be duplicated is his style, his tone of voice, and what one might call his aesthetic idealism. James is of crucial importance to the history of the novel not only because of the dramatic situations he devises, but because of his visionary ideas about the form itself, and his conscious endeavour to raise its intellectual level and refine (to as near perfection as he could) its literary discourse. For him the novel transcended the boundaries of history, philosophy, science, and was a form of limitless potential — its power of suggestion immense, its responsibilities awesome. That kind of idealism, with its appeal to the connoisseur and its stress on artistic sensitivity, is most potently expressed in his prefaces and his momentous critical essay 'The Art of Fiction' (1884). It is the kind of purist fervour which would be difficult to apply in a ruthlessly commercial world like the film industry. Adaptations of James tend to make him more accessible, more dramatic, but some find a more Jamesian flavour in works that are analogous to James rather than strict adaptations — like Jacques Rivette's free-form variations on Jamesian themes in *Celine and Julie Go Boating* (1974), or Billy Wilder's supremely sophisticated epic comedy *Avanti!* (1972), which offers a very Jamesian confrontation between the values of America and Europe and of innocence and experience. If one thinks of Jamesian directors, one probably thinks of people like Eric Rohmer (with his moral and stylistic fastidiousness, though without James's current of tension) or Satyajit Ray (with his humanism, sense of character and sensitivity to form). If one thinks of a Jamesian film style, which would combine absolute precision of form with an infinity of nuance and a sense of the pressure of passion, Joseph Losey's extraordinary direction of *The Go-Between* might come to mind. Over the last decade, a lot of exciting sounding projects have been mooted — a Franju version of *What Maisie Knew*, Ivory tackling *The Portrait of a Lady*. But the spirit of James is elusive, distilled as it is in a sensibility and style essentially attuned to an era before the film age. Still, this is a matter more of record than regret. A cinema that has produced its own rosebud need not lament the absence of a golden bowl.

Notes

1. Quoted in *A Selection from Scrutiny: Volume Two* (Cambridge University Press, 1968), p. 108.
2. Henry James, *The Spoils of Poynton* (Penguin edition, 1963), p. 121.
3. Henry James, *The Art of the Novel* (Scribner edition, 1963), p. 143.
4. Henry James, *The Portrait of a Lady* (Penguin edition, 1963), p. 408.
5. F.R. Leavis, *The Great Tradition* (Peregrine edition, 1962), p. 159.
6. DeWitt Bodeen, 'Henry James into Film', *Films in Review* (March 1977).
7. James, *The Art of the Novel*, p. 164.
8. See James's preface to *The Ambassadors*, in *Art of the Novel*, p. 308
9. John Houseman's *Run-Through* (Allen Lane, 1972) contains an interesting account of the Mercury Theatre and Gabel's connection with it. Regrettably, *The Lost Moment* was to be Gabel's only film as a director. He went on to make a solid career as a reliable supporting actor in films, notably as the malicious Strutt in Hitchcock's *Marnie* (1964) and the crazy psychiatrist in Billy Wilder's film of *The Front Page* (1974).
10. Interview with Clayton in *Films and Filming* (April 1974).

11. *The Letters of Henry James*, vol. 2 (Scribners, 1920), selected and edited by Percy Lubbock, p. 384.

12. *Le Grand Meaulnes* (Penguin edition, 1966), p. 47.

13. James, preface to *The Europeans* (Penguin edition, 1984), p. 23.

14. James *The Bostonians* (Penguin edition 1984), p. 17.

15. Ibid., p. 56.

16. Ibid., p. 119.

17. Ibid., p. 327.

18. Ibid., p. 14.

19. Lillian Hellman, *Pentimento* (Quartet, 1976), p. 106.

20. James, *The Bostonians*, p. 37.

21. Edmund Wilson, 'The Ambiguity of Henry James', in *The Triple Thinkers* (Pelican, 1962), p. 115.

22. James, *The Bostonians*, p. 390.

23. Ibid., p. 120.

24. *Sight and Sound* (spring 1985).

Chapter Three

Another Fine Mess: D.H. Lawrence and Thomas Hardy on Film

Lawrence and Hardy are not exactly the comic double-act of modern English fiction, but most of the film versions of their work are something of a joke. I wish to discuss some of the difficulties of adapting these two writers successfully in visual terms, but, before that, something should be said about the symbiotic relationship between them in terms of creative personality and artistic concerns.

The finest critical essay on Thomas Hardy is by D.H. Lawrence, which he wrote, he said, out of anger at the First World War (can one see Little Father Time in *Jude the Obscure* as a prophecy of this horrific future, and of what Hardy calls the 'coming universal wish not to live'?). With all its eccentricity, Lawrence in his book-length essay comes closer than anyone to defining and imaginatively entering the special quality of Hardy's world:

> This is a constant revelation in Hardy's novels: that there exists a great background, vital and vivid, which matters more than the people who move upon it ... Upon the vast incomprehensible pattern of some primal morality greater than even the human mind can grasp, is drawn the little, pathetic pattern of man's moral life and struggle, pathetic, almost ridiculous ... setting a smaller system of morality, the one grasped and formulated by the human consciousness within the vast, uncomprehended and incomprehensible morality of nature or of life itself, surpassing human consciousness.[1]

For Lawrence, this quality is what makes Tess and Jude genuinely tragic figures, for they sense and feel the moral and physical constriction of normal society but must inevitably be destroyed in their attempt to push beyond it. For Lawrence, Tess is much finer than the world around her, and it is her inability to transcend the ideology of her immediate society that causes her downfall, as it does Anna Karenina's. Tess is not at war with God, or Nature, or Fate, only with Society. She is cowed by society's judgement on her, even while feeling in her own soul that she is right, and this eventually erodes her will.

Lawrence writes brilliantly about Hardy because they share many of the same themes and even some of the same personality traits, notably a massive inferiority complex. Lawrence continues wholesale the literary tradition that Hardy bequeathed. Both men are social outcasts of a kind, ill at ease in the literary establishment, Hardy painfully self-conscious about his self-education, Lawrence alienated from his own working class and unable to function within a middle-class ambience which he regards as fundamentally sterile and dead. They are out of step also in that both write books that are condemned for their sexual frankness, and both are suspicious of contemporary progress. Hardy's phrase for it in *Tess of the d'Urbervilles* (1891) is 'the ache of modernism';[2] Lawrence's phrase, in his seminal short story 'England, My England', is 'the spear of modern invention'.[3]

Hardy bequeathes to Lawrence a romantic feeling for the country and nature, a passionate distrust of nineteenth-century progress ('the age of the mealy-mouthed lie'[4] is Lawrence's characterisation of Victorianism) and a hatred of industrial, technological society which mechanises man. Hardy's Jude is an anticipation of the Lawrentian working-class hero, notably Paul Morel in *Sons and Lovers* who, like Jude, like Tess, is a person pulled between flesh and spirit in his relationships. Hardy's pioneering spirit which, as he writes in *Jude the Obscure*, put Jude and Sue fifty years ahead of their time, is echoed by Lawrence in *Lady Chatterley's Lover* (1927), which takes thirty-three years to find its way legitimately to our library shelves. Like Hardy, Lawrence rails against sexual taboos, pleads for sexual freedom, attacks sexual hypocrisy. Like Hardy, he is also a poet, and this leads to a strain between the realist and the symbolist mode in his writing but also to passages of overwhelming beauty and power. They both write elemental dramas of earth and landscape and, in so doing, strain the very form of the novel to breaking-point.

A novel like *The Rainbow* is almost inconceivable without the prior trail-blazing of *Jude the Obscure*. When Hardy talks about his heroine, Sue Bridehead, in his 1912 preface to *Jude* ('the woman of the "feminist" movement — the slight pale "bachelor" girl — the intellectual, emancipated bundle of nerves that modern conditions were producing, mainly in cities as yet; who does not recognise the necessity of most of her sex to follow marriage as a profession'); he is describing with remarkable accuracy Lawrence's characterisation of Ursula in *The Rainbow*. *The Rainbow* starts in the Victorian period and, as it develops, gives an extraordinary picture of a changing society, an encroaching industrialism, and an evolution in attitudes about the situation of women in society. At the end, Ursula has rejected marriage and is attempting to make her way in a man's world: she is Sue Bridehead one step on. Hardy's fearful view of social change is a broad theme which Lawrence follows through. There is the same terrible tension between man's potential and how life turns out for him, in fact. There is the same terror at the failure of the individual to find fulfilment, and the submission of the individual life to impersonal and

destructive social and industrial forces. Yet there is a ringing vitality in
Lawrence that becomes the resurgent flipside of Hardy's equally valuable
dire warnings. 'The universal wish not to live' is transformed by Lawrence
into something more affirmative in tone. Remember what he said was the
message of *The Rainbow*, of the new generation to the old, of the modern
world to the Victorian: 'the older world is done for, toppling on top of us,
... There must be a new world.'[5]

As I mentioned at the beginning, one other quality they share is that
they are exceedingly difficult to film. In the case of Lawrence, this is not
immediately surprising. Harry T. Moore's biography *The Priest of Love*
mentions that the silent version of *Ben-Hur* made Lawrence almost
physically nauseous, and his poems are full of hostile utterance against
film, which he saw as symptomatic of the mass industrialisation of society
which he so opposed in his novels. 'For God's sake, let us be men,' he
writes, 'Not monkeys minding machines ... /The radio or film, or
gramophone/Monkeys with a bland grin on our faces.'[6] One should not be
surprised if Lawrence's work in some way was not simply uncinematic but
anti-cinematic.

Hardy is a somewhat different case. In *Working with Structuralism*
(1981), David Lodge has argued that Hardy is the most cinematic of novelists; whilst Charles Barr has drawn a parallel between Hardy's *mise-en-
scène* for Tess's confession scene in *Tess of the d'Urbervilles* and a correct
use of Cinemascope.[7] Hardy's characters are often figures in a landscape
and their states of mind are represented physically more than psychologic-
ally. Hardy's novelistic devices are not really the intense analysis of
thought, but a variation of long shot and close-up detail to exact the
maximum drama. For example, in that moment in *Tess of the d'Urbervilles*
when Tess is goaded by Alec into striking him across the mouth with a
glove, Hardy chooses not to concentrate on what Tess is thinking prior to
this incident, but to concentrate on the shape and size of the glove ('heavy
and thick as a warrior's'): a close-up detail to add presence and surprise. As
an example of Hardy's visual sense, one need only quote Troy's sword
display for Bathsheba in *Far from the Madding Crowd*, a passage which
Gerard Manley Hopkins thought was one of the finest pieces of prose he
had ever read:

Beams of light caught from the low sun's rays, above, around, in front
of her, well-nigh shut out earth and heaven — all emitted in the marvellous evolutions of Troy's reflecting blade, which seemed everywhere at
once, and yet nowhere specially. These circling gleams were accompanied by a keen rush that was almost a whistling — also springing from all
sides of her at once. In short, she was enclosed in a firmament of light,
and of sharp hisses, resembling a sky-full of meteors close at hand.[8]

After that — and particularly the emphasis on the dazzling light of the sun,
and the uncanny, sinister, hissing sound of the sword through the air —

there is no need for any elaborate analysis of Bathsheba's attraction to Troy or the danger he represents.

Although this scene is very well done in John Schlesinger's 1967 film (and certainly exceptionally photographed by Nicolas Roeg), it highlights two particular problems with adapting Hardy. One is that Hardy is so intimidatingly visual as to make the camera seem almost redundant: the director can only duplicate, not enhance. The second is the peculiar combination of realism and symbolism. Hardy instinctively moves from one to the other. A pedestrian director like Schlesinger, grounded in British documentary, cannot rise to this extra poetic dimension. He can duplicate the sword display because it is there for him in the novel. But nothing in the rest of the film suggests a similar sort of sensibility, so it becomes almost an extractable set-piece. Everything else in the film is so laboured — the heavy-handed humour and condescension towards the workers, the lumbering cranes and pans to suggest atmosphere, the obvious subjective tracking shot when Troy approaches Boldwood's house — that one cannot help but recall Andrew Sarris's comment on Schlesinger: 'Everything he does is so wrong that the accumulation of errors resembles a personal style.'[9]

The pastoralism of the film is merely decorative and quite without Hardy's irony and savagery. A storm is reproduced when it is necessary to the narrative, but Hardy's fogs and swamps for important symbolic and emotional colouration (for Fanny Robin's funeral and Bathsheba's awakening to Troy's true nature, respectively) are entirely absent. Conversely, on another occasion, the sound of the sea drowns out a crucial conversation between Bathsheba and Troy at Weymouth for no discernible reason, other than an inability on screenwriter Frederic Raphael's part to imagine what they might be saying to each other. One especially ludicrous scene crosscuts between Oak asleep and his stampeding sheep — as if his attempt to fall asleep by counting sheep has gone madly out of control. For miscalculated montage, this scene would take some beating. The casting is uneven. The shepherd, Gabriel Oak, looks exactly what he is — Alan Bates with a beard. As Bathsheba and with her accent fluctuating from scene to scene, Julie Christie has a modern aura that clashes with the desired image of a nineteenth-century country maiden. Only Peter Finch as Boldwood has the requisite agony and forcefulness. Hardy's novel is an imposingly imagined tale about the bond and struggle between man and Nature. Schlesinger's film is simply a visually clumsy melodrama set against an attractive landscape.

A much more intelligent film-maker, Roman Polanski, does not make the same mistake with *Tess* (1980). He recognises that the film-maker can either go for the realist in Hardy or the symbolist, but that he cannot have both if he is to make a cohesive film. One might have expected Polanski to have had a field-day with Hardy's more melodramatic surreal imaginings in *Tess of the d'Urbervilles* (the death of the horse; the sleepwalking of Angel; the heart-shaped bloodstain on the ceiling after Tess's murder of Alec).

But these are precisely the moments that Polanski chooses to cut or modify. Why? Because, for him, the strength of the novel, surprisingly, is in its social truth and its narrative logic:

> Hardy's *Tess of the d'Urbervilles* is the story of innocence betrayed in a world where human behaviour is governed by class barriers and social prejudice. It is also a study in causality. All the evils in Tess's life are the fortuitous products of the small but momentous coincidences that shape our destiny. Had there been no chance encounter between her drunken father and a parson who tells him he has aristocratic blood in his veins, there would have been no tragedy. Tess would have lived out her uneventful days as a Dorset peasant woman. She would never have met Alec d'Urberville, never have been raped by him, never have ended on the gallows.[10]

Polanski might have underplayed some of Hardy's metaphoric melodrama and visual omens, particularly the imagery of fire connected with Alec and sun with Angel, and the recurring colour motif of red on white that mesmerisingly binds the novel together. But the narrative has rarely seemed more unerringly logical and convincing. No one seeing the film could possibly suspect that Hardy has often been accused of narrative contrivance and the over-use of coincidence. Polanski clearly identifies with Hardy's heroine — someone victimised through one mistake in the past and hounded for it to the death for going against a social law. Nothing — certainly not the symbolism nor the subconscious in the novel — must distract or detract from what Polanski perceived as the terrifyingly plausible linearity in Tess's fate.

Polanski's overall tone is different, however. Hardy quoted Gloucester's lines in *King Lear* as a key to the mood of the novel: 'As flies to wanton boys are we to the gods/They kill us for their sport.' Polanski's epigraph to Tess could also be from *King Lear*, one feels, but this time Edgar's lines to Gloucester: 'Men must endure/Their going hence even as their coming hither;/Ripeness is all'. 'Have they come for me?' asks Tess at the end. 'I am ready.' Polanski ends with this, stressing the nobility of Tess's acceptance of her fate rather than the horror of the fate itself. The film's poignant quiet romanticism at the end has the sense of Tess, and perhaps Polanski himself, coming out of a nightmare to a renewed 'ripeness' and maturity. It is a dignified interpretation, but for all the excellence of the direction and Nastassia Kinski's performance, there is nothing very Hardyesque about it. It is a subdued and sober film, Hardy without the glaring faults, but without the sublimity as well.

Another problem the cinema would have with Hardy is the handling of his pessimism. Is there not something inherently contradictory in Hardy's view of life and that of an industry whose philosophy, as Ryan O'Neal's film teacher in *Irreconcilable Differences* (1984) puts it, is: 'never leave an audience feeling empty'? A film of *Jude the Obscure* which would do justice to the novel is almost inconceivable. The two major Hardy adaptations I have mentioned are both emotionally tentative and, for cinema that one could call Hardyesque, one must look elsewhere. Terrence Malick's *Days of Heaven* (1978), with its rural vistas, its stunning sense of Nature, and its intense and quirky plot, forges a true Hardyesque alignment between the fateful passions of its characters and the awesome workings of the natural world. Mike Newell's *Dance with a Stranger* (1985), his film about the last woman to be hanged in Britian, Ruth Ellis, has an unexpected but authentic Hardyesque quality. Ruth is a Tess of the 1950s, a victimised heroine, who, like Tess, loses a baby; waits in vain outside a churchyard for a sight of the man she loves and his family; wears a red scarf over her blonde hair (compare Tess's red ribbon and her white dress); kills her lover and is hanged for going against the law (criminal, social and sexual) of her bigoted and prurient community. Also few films communicate a more gruelling, more Hardyesque sense of complete pessimism than *Dance with a Stranger*.

The problems D.H. Lawrence poses for the cinema are different from those presented by Hardy, but equally difficult. They relate to Lawrence's particular characteristics as an artist and as a moralist. Unlike Hardy, Lawrence is not a great visual writer. His most original feature as a novelist is his experimentation with language and imagery to express the unconscious. Lawrence's visual set-pieces tend to be isolated moments of intensity, like Ursula's encounter with the horses towards the end of *The Rainbow*, which, without the accompanying psychological analysis, would probably simply look like someone being frightened, quite reasonably, at the possibility of being stampeded. Lawrence's symbolic flourishes often look either obvious or absurd when visualised. The crude Nature/industry, male/female contrast of that moment in *Women in Love*, where Gerald brutally forces his terrified mare to stand its ground as a train thunders past, seems even more ponderous when Ken Russell films it: it looks like an O-level guide to symbolism. Gudrun's dance before the cattle in Russell's film not only looks ridiculous but reverses the meaning of the scene in the novel: Gudrun appears stupid rather than rapt, Gerald reasonable rather than stolid. Aside from Lawrence's symbolism not travelling well to the cinema, another problem he poses is that he has no great narrative flair. He does not tell stories: he dissects relationships, with great psychological penetration. The novel can convey the essence of such things much better than a film, which conveys substance. As the above examples show, the substance of Lawrence's world does not translate very easily into visual terms, into the essence of his characters' feelings.

The major difficulty with filming Lawrence is more fundamental, however. It has something to do with certain basic characteristics of the national cinema and of the national character. Prestige British cinema has invariably tended to conform to the three Rs: realism, rationality and restraint. Lawrence stands at the opposite end of that tradition, which is more appropriate to novelists of a more limited calibre, like Wells,

Galsworthy, Bennett, Maugham, where everything is subsumed under the tenets of realism and 'good taste'. The qualities Lawrence has — passion, poetry, prophecy — are exactly the qualities which some observers so miss amidst the stolid sobriety of most British cinema. There are British film-makers who aspire to Lawrentian poetry and passion. Unfortunately, they are not Jack Cardiff, Christopher Miles or Claude Whatham, who have tried to film Lawrence. Funnily enough, Ken Russell is one of those directors who one feels might have the necessary daring and devil to scale the Lawrentian heights. But his highly acclaimed film of *Women in Love* (1970) has always seemed to me one of Russell's most tepid and visually boring movies, of what I have always found to be one of Lawrence's most unpleasantly tendentious and misogynistic novels. *The Rainbow* would suit Russell better. Amongst other things, *Women in Love* is grotesquely miscast. Eleanor Bron, for no good reason, seems closer to Isadora Duncan than to Hermione. Oliver Reed as Gerald is a complete disaster. It is not simply that Reed is quite the opposite of Lawrence's Nordic conception of Gerald in the novel — he is supposed to be Birkin's opposite, not his twin. It is that Reed, given a lot of Lawrence's dialogue, offers no indication that he has any idea of what it means. His ponderous mud-splattered entry into Gudrun's bedroom ('I came — because I must'), and his final death-wander into the snow (Russell's homage to the first shot of the little boy in *Citizen Kane*) are further examples of the visualisation of Lawrence that provoke mirth more than metaphoric revelation.

From time to time, the industry has tried to cash in on Lawrence as an erotic writer — though, for the most part, this eroticism has been defined only in the prurient or voyeuristic terms which Lawrence despised and sought fundamentally to change. The result has either been to soften or coarsen the material, which has been equally unsatisfactory. The French version of *Lady Chatterley's Lover* (1955) probably generates more passion than a British film would have of similar date, but the crucial context of the novel (its attack on the industrialisation of England and hence the necessity and urgency of personal relationships) is completely lost. The American version of *The Fox* (1969) distorts both the context and the sexuality. It is set in Canada; romanticises the hero (he is a boy in the novella); makes the lesbianism more crudely explicit; treats the triangular relationship as a lustier version of *The Children's Hour*; and replaces Lawrence's troubled ending with an upbeat one. The shifting and complex symbolism of the novella is flattened into a one-dimensional device: fox equals male intruder. But a fox, when photographed, is not a symbol of the male: it is simply a fox. Something of the same bland literalism infects Claude Whatham's film of *The Captain's Doll* (1981), which takes half an hour to get a proper sense of camera range in relation to characters and setting and has Jeremy Irons juggling embarrassingly with a Scottish accent whilst breaking up his sentences into even smaller units than John Wayne. As the characters tread ever more tediously on to higher physical and philosophical planes, they become steadily less convincing, and Lawrence's shrill revenge against womankind becomes even more offensive than in *Women in Love*. Robert Bierman's 1982 short film of the short story 'The Rocking Horse Winner' avoids the moralising of the 1949 Anthony Pellisier version, which tacks on a cosy ending to dilute the irony and harshness of Lawrence's critique of materialism. But it cannot find much in the way of visual imagination to take it beyond the realm of a quaint supernatural tale. More imaginative is Colin Gregg's film *The Trespasser* (1980), which attempts to fuse narrative, Nature and performance into a distinctive and unusual visual rhythm to accentuate the mood of the characters. Images of the moon, water, windows, are linked mesmerisingly to dreams, internal monologues, lingering fades to transform the reality of the world into a liquid subjective reverie. Pauline Moran as the heroine is first rate, and Alan Bates makes Siegmund an anguished Lawrentian self-portrait of the artist stifled by his home life.

Outside of Russell's *Women in Love*, the most famous Lawrence film is Jack Cardiff's sturdy but cautious *Sons and Lovers* (1960), which is more a paraphrase of the novel than an adaptation. The film focuses immediately on the character of Paul (it reduces William, omits Annie, and kills off Arthur), which is understandable, except that it makes the title more or less meaningless. It is oblique rather than forthright in its depiction of physical relationships, which makes Paul's hang-ups harder to understand; and the Leivers family is somewhat caricatured, particularly Rosalie Crutchley's gruesomely frigid mother figure. There are some good visual moments: the father's grease mark on Paul's picture; the mine disaster conveyed initially by a ripple on the water (an addition to the novel, but a permissible one, and a vivid analogue to the theme of the impact of industry on Nature and human nature); and the motif of the snowdrop which Paul picks and discards and which relates to both his relationship with Clara (the snow queen whom he melts before the fire) and Miriam (the epitome of frigid fidelity, to whom he bids farewell in the snow). As a romantic drama, the film serves well enough, but the weak visual imagination and Mario Nascimbene's lush music dampen the Lawrentian complexities.

When writer/producer Larry Kramer invited F.R. Leavis to a screening of *Women in Love*, he predictably received the following, almost incoherently irate, letter in reply:

> It's an obscene undertaking to 'write it again' for the screen ... No one who has any inkling of the kind of *thing* the novel is, or how the significance of a great work of literature is conveyed, or what kind of thing significance is, could lend himself to such an outrage. Great writers even where they're dead ought to be protected.[11]

This is a bit extreme perhaps, although, curiously enough, the directors who seem closest to Lawrence in spirit are directors who (as yet) have never come near him. With his acute understanding of English class, sexuality and puritanism, Joseph Losey could have made a superb

Lawrence film, true to the dense symbolism and psychology of the writer. Larry Cohen's *Q — The Winged Serpent* (1982) is the nearest film we have had to *The Plumed Serpent*, and Cohen's analysis of the tensions of bisexuality and homosexuality within our patriarchal social structures in his film *Demon — God Told Me To* (1977) seems a logical continuation of Lawrence's own wrestling with the complexities and contradictions of sexual roles in stories such as 'The Blind Man' and novels like *Women in Love* and *Lady Chatterley's Lover*.

Above all, there is Nicolas Roeg. *Don't Look Now* (1973) might be based on Daphne du Maurier but, in feeling, it is much closer to Lawrence's short story 'England, My England'. Both works have heroes estranged from their environment who foresee, without being able to avert, tragedies involving their children. The bold experimentation with narrative time in both (Lawrence makes magnificent use of a concealed flashback) gives enormous force to their similarly ominous openings and hallucinatory, death-haunted finales. The Freudian symbolism and tormented heroine of Roeg's *Bad Timing* (1980) who is liberated but punished for that liberation, seem a very Lawrentian combination of elements, as do the destructive, self-tormenting, raging relationships in *Eureka* (1983). Something about the free physicality in Roeg, the poetic associations of his editing, the intense dissection of relationships, his distaste for narrative linearity and everyday reality, seems very like Lawrence. He films with his own nerve-ends exposed, in the way Lawrence wrote. His films make the everyday look strange, as his heroes step out of their moral background into an alien world. His films exalt the instinctual over the rational and expose the limitations of earth-bound experience — of civilisation, if you will. Lawrence was a visionary who attempted to restore a sensual, instinctive way of life to a materialist age. This is exactly the programme and theme of Nicolas Roeg. For a long time, Lawrence was a prophet without sufficient honour in his own country. Similarly, Roeg has had to struggle for honour, and distribution, in his conservative, class-bound, tasteful, rational home country and national film industry. 'English, in the teeth of everything,' said Lawrence, 'even in the teeth of England.' Roeg could say the same. If Lawrence is one of the glories of English literature, the most fruitful tradition of British cinema (passionate poetry rather than tasteful realism) could be said to be Lawrentian. Roeg is the most scintillating modern representative.

Notes

1. D.H. Lawrence, 'Study of Thomas Hardy' (1914). From *Selected Literary Criticism of D.H. Lawrence* (Heinemann Educational Books, 1967), pp. 176-7.

2. Thomas Hardy, *Tess of the d'Urbervilles*, Chapter 19.

3. D.H. Lawrence, 'England, My England' (1922), in *England, My England* (Penguin, 1960), p. 11.

4. D.H. Lawrence, 'Pornography and Obscenity' (1929). See *Selected Literary Criticism*, p. 46.

5. Letter to Lady Cynthia Asquith, 7 February 1916.

6. D.H. Lawrence, 'Let Us Be Men', *Selected Poems* (Penguin, 1968), p. 146.

7. Charles Barr, 'Cinemascope: Before and After', in *Film Theory and Criticism*, edited by Gerald Mast and Marshall Cohen, (Oxford University Press, 1st edn 1974), pp. 135-6.

8. Thomas Hardy, *Far from the Madding Crowd*, Chapter 28.

9. Andrew Sarris, *Confessions of a Cultist* (Simon & Schuster, 1971), p. 112.

10. *Roman by Polanski* (Heinemann, 1984), pp. 371-2.

11. Quoted in *Films and Filming* (September 1970), p. 30.

Chapter Four

Age of Doublethink:
George Orwell and the Cinema

George Orwell was never very interested in the cinema and, until the year of 1984, the cinema has never been very interested in George Orwell. This is revealing on both counts. Although Orwell's critical accounts of aspects of popular culture such as comics, picture postcards and crime fiction were to facilitate the acceptance of contemporary cultural studies as a serious academic subject in Britain (writers like Raymond Williams and Richard Hoggart were to be indebted to Orwell's pioneering example), he remained suspicious of the mass media in general and cinema in particular: it was the modern opium for the masses. On the other side, if the cinema ignored Orwell's entire novelistic output of the 1930s, such as *Burmese Days* (1934), *The Clergyman's Daughter* (1935) *Keep the Aspidistra Flying* (1936) and *Coming Up for Air* (1939), this served to illuminate certain deficiencies of Orwell's fictional practice which would make him unsuitable for adaptation, notably his inadequate narrative sense and his absence of visual imagination. Nevertheless, there are aspects of Orwell's work that are of relevance to the cinema: the analogies one can draw between Orwell's writing and certain aspects of film practice, notably 1930s documentary; his brief career as a film critic; and the interesting film adaptations of *Animal Farm* and *1984*.

Although no film buff, Orwell seems to have been a casual filmgoer with tastes not too dissimilar from the popular preference. He liked Disney, Mickey Mouse, Charlie Chaplin, Douglas Fairbanks, and thought that Garbo's shot at Anna Karenina was 'not too bad'. He disliked the avant-garde. He hated Buñuel's *L'Age d'Or* (1930) largely, one feels, because of his detestation of Daliesque surrealism. Strangely, though, there is an image in Orwell's *1984* — Winston's discovery of a disembodied hand in the middle of the street — that might have come straight out of the Buñuel-Dali surrealist short film *Un Chien Andalou* (1928). He also disliked the Expressionism of *The Cabinet of Dr Caligari* (1919), a film he found 'merely silly, the fantastic element being exploited for its own sake and not to convey any definite meaning'.[1] For the most part, he disliked Hollywood escapism, if it had neither the fantasy nor the imagination of a Disney or a Chaplin.

In his more general writings, he elaborated on some of his attitudes to the cinema. In his essay 'The English People', he describes the English film as dismally reactionary but at least commendably classless, though this is more commercial necessity than a belief in social consensus ('Films ... have to appeal to a public of millions and therefore have to avoid stirring up class antagonisms').[2] In his 'As I Please' column in *Tribune* (28 July 1944), he comments on how the poor are kept in their place by film through the cinema's calculated recurring fantasy of the 'good poor man defeating the bad rich man' (he might be thinking there of the popular comedies of Eddie Cantor or the more overtly social comedies of Frank Capra, like *Mr Deeds Goes to Town* and *You Can't Take it with You*). Although this is not dissimilar from a criticism he was to make about Dickens and the limitations of his radicalism, it is more harshly expressed in relation to the cinema, for Orwell, like D.H. Lawrence before him and F.R. Leavis after, distrusted the industrial structure of film and the consequent mechanisation of art. 'Disney films,' he says darkly, 'are produced by what is essentially a factory process, the work being done partly mechanically and partly by teams of artists who have to subordinate their individual style.'[3] This is more than a statement of fact which anyone with the most rudimentary film knowledge would not need to be told: he makes Disney Studios sound like a labour camp. In that description, the cinema becomes an aspect of Orwell's distrust of totalitarianism, his fear of art being appropriated by the state. (He might there be recalling both Lenin's 'Of all the arts, the cinema is for us the most important', and the use made of Leni Riefenstahl's cinematic genius by the Nazis.) In his novel *Keep the Aspidistra Flying*, the cinema is seen in the most contemptuous terms, flickering drivel whose main purpose is to serve as a drug for friendless people. Like Lawrence, unlike Joyce and Virginia Woolf, Orwell disliked the cinema because he felt it was displacing the art he loved, taking away the realist, narrative function of the novel and reducing the significance of books.

Film lovers must find many of Orwell's remarks about the cinema distasteful and glib. He seems profoundly reactionary in his attitude to violence and experiment on the screen and, considering his social views, surprisingly snobbish. Dismissing popular cinema as 'treacly rubbish' is no substitute for a serious consideration of how films work and why they give so much pleasure to so many people. His narrow critical ethic of 'realism' and 'social relevance' does not allow sufficiently for visual style, and the specific way film communicates. It brings out the negative side of Orwell's posture as the honest, commonsensical man: an occasional philistinism and impoverishment of imagination, and unintellectual conservatism about new art forms and alternative modes of expression to realism. Just as his criterion for good prose as being 'like a window pane'[4] is aesthetically and stylistically limited, his implied preference for the camera as 'window on the world' also would impoverish the cinema's expressive range.

Admirers of Orwell, however, would find these criticisms interesting in the way they illuminate some of the strengths and concerns of his work. His willingness to discuss forms of popular culture rather than dismiss them out of hand — for example, his speculation about the relation between film-viewing and the dream state — is to be commended. Some of his quoted comments are an interesting anticipation of an ideological rather than aesthetic strategy for reading films, and, as might be expected, Orwell does have a sense of the underlying politics of film-making. He perceives the possibly disturbing link between state, capital or industry and the mass media, and the possibility of its leading to the kind of thought control depicted in *1984* ('The instrument, the telescreen, could be dimmed but there was no way of shutting it off completely').[5] Ahead of his time, Orwell was concerned about the possible destruction of a genuinely popular, national culture by an amorphously global mass culture, dominated by America. He would have understood what the directors of the New German Cinema of the 1970s (Herzog, Fassbinder, Wenders) meant when they talked of American cultural imperialism and how the Americans had colonised their subconscious.

During the 1930s, it is rather surprising that Orwell did not show more of an interest in the British documentary movement, whose ideals in many ways seemed quite close to Orwell's own. In fact, an interesting parallel can be drawn between Alberto Cavalcanti's famous short, *Coal Face*, made in 1935, and Orwell's *Road to Wigan Pier*, written the following year. A careful comparison between the two helps unravel some of the obscurities of method and theme that have accreted around both works, particularly the Orwell. *Coal Face* was a product of the GPO film unit masterminded by John Grierson, who had coined the term 'documentary' (and in the fullest sense of the term, Orwell's *Road to Wigan Pier* and *Homage to Catalonia* are documentaries). For Grierson, documentary meant 'the creative treatment of actuality' — there is no better description than that of everything Orwell wrote in the 1930s. For Grierson, like Orwell, film basically meant realism: he shared Orwell's disdain for Hollywood and the avant-garde. Film for Grierson, like writing for Orwell, in the 1930s, was basically a means of opening people's eyes to the lives and deprivations of the working class. *Coal Face* admirably fulfils this aim.[6]

Like *Road to Wigan Pier*, *Coal Face* is, on one level, an example of the documentary as information. The subject is life in the coal mine and we are told what the men do, where they are, and the conditions in which they work. But behind the flow of information is a tone of anger and criticism. Conditions of work are uncomfortable and dangerous (there is reference to the 'cramped position' in which men work, and the one-in-five chance of injury); and there is a sense of the subjugation of the men by the pit (lives 'bound up ... owned by ... dependent on the pit'). However, two stylistic traits modify the directness of that critique. The first is the use of Auden's verse and Benjamin Britten's music to aestheticise the angry observation (one might compare Orwell's comments on 'Why I write': 'I start from a feeling of anger ... but I couldn't write it if it were not also an aesthetic experience').[7] The other modifier is the point of view which, from the tone of the narration, is identifiably middle class not working class, and consequently the viewpoint of an outsider who sympathises but who does not belong. What *Coal Face* is doing is also exactly what Orwell does in *Road to Wigan Pier*. If Orwell's book is seen in terms not of an English literary tradition but in the tradition of 1930s documentary film, a lot of the problems that literary critics have found with it simply drop away.

For example, the book has often been attacked for breaking into two separate parts, which do not belong to each other: a first-hand observation of life in the pits; then a partial autobiography, in which Orwell outlines some of his difficulties about class and socialism. But far from being irrelevant to the first part, Orwell's personal revelations are essential to it. Through them, Orwell is offering an extremely sophisticated version of documentary, suggesting that the form is as selective and subjective as more overtly fictional forms (interestingly, the director of *Coal Face*, Cavalcanti, felt the same: 'Documentary is a silly term ... Films are the same, fictional or otherwise').[8] The subject of *Wigan Pier* is not poverty, or class, but Orwell himself. The book is fundamentally about not what is being described but who is doing the describing. Similarly, the subject of *Coal Face* is not the miners, but people who see miners in that particular way. An analogy with documentary film brings certain aspects of Orwell into sharper focus. *Wigan Pier* becomes a completely unified book. It is basically a journey into the depths on two levels — the physical (the mines) and the psychological (the personality of Orwell). It is clear evidence that Orwell was not really a novelist. His real field was the drama-documentary, of which he would have been a masterly exponent, had he lived. *Homage to Catalonia* (1937) is an even more vivid example of drama-documentary: a work unified by the physical and psychological concept of 'crossing frontiers' and a work where one can practically see Orwell as he talks, as it were, to the camera and the events unfold — come to life — behind him.

If Orwell has a value in clarifying by analogy certain fundamentals about documentary film, is there any other area of film study in which Orwell can be profitably applied? The one that most suggests itself is tracing how far Orwell's views on the English character are confirmed by characteristics of the national cinema. In his magnificent book *Ealing Studios* (1977), Charles Barr mentions the basic aim of Ealing, articulated by Michael Balcon, as the desire to 'project Britain and the British character'.[9] In analysing what that meant, Barr mentions that, almost in spite of himself, he kept feeling the necessity to refer to George Orwell, particularly the essays 'The Lion and the Unicorn' and 'The English People'. If one recalls Orwell's description of the English character — from its sense of family to its love of flowers, from its privateness and restraint to its belief in the restorative powers of a cup of tea, from its overt respect for the law to its covert admiration for the rebellious little man who cuts through red tape — one has a whole cluster of images that can be related quite specifically to famous Ealing films like *Passport to Pimlico* (1949), *The*

Blue Lamp (1950) and *The Lavender Hill Mob* (1951). Is there a more pertinent description of the image of elderly, paralysed, hallucinatory, hide-
bound England seen in *The Ladykillers* (1955) than Orwell's in 'The Lion
and the Unicorn': 'a family in which the young are generally thwarted, and
most of the power is in the hands of irresponsible uncles and bed-ridden
aunts'?[10] Without commenting directly on any film or on the cinema at all,
Orwell defined the underlying feeling and essence of one of the most
famous manifestations of British cinema — Ealing film — as well as
anyone.

Orwell's most direct contact with the cinema industry came when he
had a brief career as a film critic between 1940 and 1941, writing twenty-
six film columns for the magazine *Time and Tide*. It was not a post he took
up very graciously. 'Everyone in this world has someone he can look down
on,' he said, 'and I must say, from experience of both trades, that the book
reviewer is better off than the film critic, who cannot even do his work at
home, but has to attend trade shows at eleven in the morning and, with one
or two exceptions, is expected to sell his honour for a glass of inferior
sherry.'[11] All of his reviews are influenced by the war and he accuses the
cinema of being unaffected by it and carrying on with the same mindless
rubbish. This underrates the role of the cinema in wartime as an important
safety-valve of escapism, and also ignores the complexity of the Hollywood
situation, which had to reconcile its product with the isolationist political
policy of America at that time. During these years, Hollywood was wary of
trying to dictate its country's foreign policy and in fact, given that situation, Hollywood's record at that time is not ignoble: films as diverse as
Ninotchka (1939), *The Sea Hawk* (1940), *The Mortal Storm* (1940), *Hold
Back the Dawn* (1940) and *Foreign Correspondent* (1940) share an implicit
or explicit, coded or committed, indictment of Nazism and recommenda-
tion of involvement. Orwell refused to see that and kept up his barrage of
criticism against the frivolousness of Hollywood. He was even upset by the
violence of Raoul Walsh's *High Sierra* (1940), which now looks a remarkably lyrical Renoiresque film, and his condescension to American movies
makes him certainly less open-minded and perceptive a film critic than
Graham Greene. Orwell never evinced any interest in the art of the
cinema; seems to have had little concept of cinematic technique or of what
the director does; and could hardly even reconcile himself to colour (admittedly, not of a high standard in those days). When he did like a film, the
reasons are generally personal and easy to locate. Mitchell Leisen's *Arise,
My Love* (1940) is admired for its anti-isolationist stand (undoubtedly influenced by the contribution of co-writer Billy Wilder, a European who had fled
from Berlin at the accession of Hitler); and he praises Mervyn LeRoy's
Escape (1940), alluding in his review to the fading of 'justice' and 'objective
truth' and to a horrible child who spies — all anticipations of the apparatus
of his novel, *1984*. But the one film that Orwell praised above all others in
his brief critical stint was Charles Chaplin's *The Great Dictator* (1940).

Orwell had long been an admirer of Chaplin. For Orwell, Chaplin embodied the common man and his belief in decency. He felt Chaplin was wiser than the intellectuals, just as animals are wiser than men — suggesting the germ there of an idea to be developed in *Animal Farm*. Saying that Chaplin believes that giants are vermin, Orwell linked him with what he called 'one of the basic folk tales of the English-speaking peoples: Jack the Giant Killer — the little man against the big man'[12] (again perhaps anticipating Orwell's conception of the struggle of ordinary Winston Smith against Big Brother in *1984*). Orwell is not surprised that Chaplin's films were banned in Nazi Germany or that Chaplin was attacked by English Fascist writers, notably Wyndham Lewis in his *News Chronicle* column at the time, who condemned Chaplin for popularising 'infantile attitudes'. By contrast Orwell embraces Chaplin's socialism and his attack on the allure of power politics in *The Great Dictator*. It is everything that Orwell desires of a film: decent, political, committed, dealing with serious ideas.

In fact, it could be argued that *The Great Dictator* exerted a greater influence on Orwell than he, or anyone, realised: that it showed him a method, and offered him a range of imagery, for dealing with the themes which were to dominate his work. The satirical approach and style of *The Great Dictator* anticipates the satirical vein that Orwell was to exploit for the first time in his creative work in *Animal Farm* (1945). Chaplin's ferocious attack on totalitarianism and the cult of the Great Leader in the film looks forward to Big Brother and to *1984*. These are fairly loose and generalised connections between *The Great Dictator* and Orwell's two great, final works. Nevertheless, what is striking is the sheer amount of minor detail that Chaplin's film and Orwell's final works have in common. In a fascinating way, the film contains numerous hints of things to come in the Orwell of the future: from Big Bertha that opens *The Great Dictator* to Big Brother that closes *1984*; from Tomania and Bacteria in *The Great Dictator* to Oceania and Eurasia in *1984*; from Hinkel = Hitler, Napolini = Mussolini, Garbage = Goebbels in *The Great Dictator* to Major = Lenin, Snowball = Trotsky, Napoleon = Stalin in *Animal Farm*. Confusion of identity closes *The Great Dictator* and a similar confusion closes *Animal Farm*. Chaplin's Happy Hour (ordered by the state) in *The Great Dictator* is transformed in *1984* to Orwell's Hate Week; and Chaplin's filmic state of double-cross becomes Orwell's state of double think in *1984*. There is a clear cross-over of concerns, interests and influences from Chaplin to Orwell; and what confirms it above all is Chaplin's final speech in *The Great Dictator*, which Orwell deeply admired. It is a speech that is a turning-point in Chaplin's career when the tramp disappears for all time and Chaplin addresses us for the first time in his own voice; a speech which urges people, the common man, to unite in the name of democracy, to 'fight for a new world — a decent world that will give men a chance to work — that will give youth a future and old age a security'.[13] This speech is the cinema's closest analogy to Orwell's world philosophy of this time, as expressed in works like *Homage to Catalonia* and 'Looking Back on the Spanish War'. 'Shall people be allowed to live the decent, fully human life which is now technically achievable, or shan't they?' asks Orwell in his Spanish War essay. 'Shall the common man be pushed back into the mud, or shall he not? I myself believe, perhaps on insufficient grounds, that the common man will win his fight sooner or later, but I want it to be sooner and not later.'[14] There is the same tone of desperate hope that characterises the concluding speech of *The Great Dictator*. My feeling is that Orwell was deeply moved by the film and ransacked its style, tone and ideas more than any other work of art when he came to shape his two most profound works, *Animal Farm* and *1984*. During the 1930s Orwell had spent much of his time trying to find an appropriate aesthetic form for the expression of his social and political ideas. Above anything else, Chaplin showed the value of satire, and the lesson was not wasted.

To film audiences, Orwell's name will be most familiar for the screen adaptations of *Animal Farm* and *1984*. *Animal Farm* was inspired by Orwell's horror at the sight of a little boy driving a huge carthorse along a narrow path and whipping it whenever it tried to turn. It made him ponder what might happen if animals ever became aware of their strength; and it made him reflect that men's attitude to and exploitation of animals was not very different from the manner in which the rich treated the proletariat. Although written between 1943 and 1944, it was not published until 1945. Like Chaplin's *The Great Dictator* again, the novel was embarrassing because of its timing. In Chaplin's case, the embarrassment was an anti-Nazi film at a time when American foreign policy was isolationist and neutral. In Orwell's case, the embarrassment was a satire on the Russian Revolution when Britain was trying to forge a postwar alliance with the Soviet Union. On behalf of Faber & Faber, T.S. Eliot rejected it for publication on the grounds that 'we have no conviction ... that this is the right point of view from which to criticise the political situation at the present time'.[15] It was turned down in America by the Dial Press on he grounds that 'it was impossible to sell animal stories in the USA'.[16] It was eventually published by Secker & Warburg, became an instant modern classic, and Orwell's first popular success.

John Halas and Joy Batchelor's film version of *Animal Farm*, made in 1954 and released a year later, represented two firsts: the first full-length cartoon ever made in Britain; and the first British animated film on a serious theme. It took on the Disney mantle, in other words, and when the film appeared, it was immediately compared with Disney: the bright colours, the cute animals, the sense of it almost as a political *Lady and the Tramp*. Nevertheless, this is not an inappropriate comparison. Orwell admired Disney greatly, so the allusion would have delighted him (it might even have subconsciously influenced the original conception). Disney cartoons like *Three Little Pigs* (1933) and *Snow White and the Seven Dwarfs* (1938) often have elements of fear, sadism and cruelty (Pare Lorentz thought that Disney was the most violent director of the 1930s)[17] so in that sense also, the parallel is not inappropriate. The force of the story comes from its combination of fairy-story and ferocity, the setting of pastoral innocence against which bestial brutality takes place. With an amusing but sinister slogan ('Pig Brother is Watching You'), the cartoon offers a good, tidy adaptation of the story. It brings out the Dickensian poignancy of the death of Boxer which, in its way, is the most emotionally harrowing death scene in English fiction since Little Nell. It pleasingly omits the sexist characterisation of Molly, the mare whose principles are bought off (the human disposition to bribery sexistly symbolised by female skittishness and vanity). Its most controversial aspect is its dilution of the ending — transforming Orwell's 1940s pessimism into his 1930s desperate optimism. At the end of the novel, the animals are left looking through the window in horror as the pigs negotiate with the humans ('The creatures outside looked from pig to man, and from man to pig, and from pig to man again; but already it was impossible to say which was which').[18] Characteristically, in Orwell's work, the revolution has not only failed, but things are worse than when they began: here the pigs have become indistinguishable from the horror that brought them to revolution in the first place. The film ends with the animals storming the house and shattering Napoleon's portrait, the implication being that another revolution is on the way. Given Orwell's cynicism about the effectiveness of revolution, the renewal of the revolutionary cycle is not overly affirmative. Nevertheless, it does damagingly sidestep the bleakness of the original.

Animal Farm was followed a year later by a film version of *1984*, directed by Michael Anderson. Although the favourable reception of the cartoon undoubtedly facilited the prospect of another Orwell adaptation, there were other factors which made a film of *1984* a commercial proposition at this time. When published in 1949, a year before Orwell's death, the novel had been an immediate success with both public and critics. In a long review in *The Times Literary Supplement* (10 June 1949), the critic had stressed the similarity of Orwell's *1984* society to the rationed, drab, troubled England of the late 1940s (the British film which best conveys the tatty paranoia of postwar Britain at this time is probably the Boultings' 1950 production, *Seven Days to Noon*); and saw the main themes as a study of power and corruption and 'the corrosion of the will'. In *Tribune* (17 June 1949), Bruce Bain saw the novel not simply as a picture of a postwar world, but of a post-atomic-bomb world. The novel had its crudities, he felt: the insertion of Goldstein's history as an undigested, undramatised chunk of material; the use of Julia as a 'dumb siren'; the melodrama of Winston's fear of rats (though one might remember Orwell's comment in *Homage to Catalonia* that 'if there is one thing I hate more than another it is a rat running over me in the darkness').[19] Mostly, it is a powerful warning about what *Tribune* defined as Orwell's fear of 'the apathy of the common people and the general acceptance of the standard of power politics'. Following the success of the novel was a notorious BBC television production of *1984*, starring Peter Cushing as Winston and André Morell as O'Brien, which created such controversy that its live production was repeated only weeks after its first transmission, attracting British television's biggest-ever viewing audience up to that time. To complaints that the work was 'disgusting' and 'immoral', Michael Barry (head of TV's drama section) retorted: 'It is grim, frightening and shocking — shocking in the sense of its portrayal of man's inhumanity to man.'[20] In general, Orwell's reputation was soaring during the 1950s amongst the public and the intelligentsia. Ironically, Orwell was being championed with equal fervour by literary movements that otherwise had quite opposite ideals. For example, to the poetry group known as the 'Movement', which included such notably conservative figures as Philip Larkin, Robert Conquest and Kingsley Amis, Orwell was a hero both for his opposition to the Soviet political system and his suspicion of experimentation and obscurity in art, sharing their preference for a plain, comprehensible, transparent literary style.[21] Yet Orwell was equally a hero at this time to radical movements in theatre and literature, who liked his ideas and his insistence on attempting to fuse literature with politics and to make art relevant to society. In fact, one could regard the heroes in Orwell's novels (Winston in *1984* is a good example) as precursors of Osborne's Angry Young Man, for they tend to be rebels, outsiders, disfigured misfits who are angry about society and about their lives and protesting loudly against them. So there were a lot of cultural currents in the mid-1950s which would certainly encourage a film version of *1984*.

Unfortunately, the 1955 film had all the impact of a cold pudding. Two things in particular went wrong. Like the film of *Animal Farm*, it imposed a defiant and affirmative ending that seemed even more incongruous than in the Halas–Batchelor cartoon. Also the odd casting of Americans in the leading roles (Edmond O'Brien as Winston, Jan Sterling as Julia) robbed it of authenticity: only Michael Redgrave as the interrogator O'Brien makes any impression. Strange that an actor called O'Brien should have a key role in *1984*, and an actor called McCarthy, in the following year, should play the lead in Don Siegel's distinctly McCarthyist *Invasion of the Body Snatchers* (1956). I only mention this because these two films might have more in common in terms of political attitude than the specific elements Orwell had in mind. His novel is certainly a satire of the Soviet system, but Orwell also said he got his sense of how a totalitarian society is run by remembering the structure of his old prep school, St. Cyprians. *1984* is a general warning about baffling bureaucracy; the increasing estrangement between state and people; of the possibilities of an England divided into two nations of leaders and led; and of the dull conformity that goes with illiteracy and an unblinking acceptance of the apparatus and information system of the state, be it communist or capitalist. However, by casting two Americans as lovers struggling against oppression, this *1984* film becomes merely a pro-American contribution to Cold War rhetoric — a travesty of Orwell, in fact, since he was equally suspicious of both superpowers.

At this stage, it might be worth emphasising the significance of the novel *1984* in Orwell's work. It was his last novel and the culmination of his creative credo: *1984* is not a prophecy but a warning, a taking to extremes of some of Orwell's most deeply felt fears about modern civilisation. First, there is the corruption of language: 'Newspeak' is the ultimate manifestation of Orwell's fear — expressed in 'Politics and the English Language' — about political euphemisms that defend the indefensible. Then there is the ruthless pursuit of absolute power: O'Brien and Big Brother in *1984* are the embodiments of Orwell's apprehensions about totalitarian personalities, as voiced in his essay 'Wells, Hitler and the World State'. The destruction of the past in *1984*, the rewriting of history, is the dramatisation of a fear Orwell expressed in his essay 'Looking Back on the Spanish War': that the concept of objective truth was fading out of the world, that history is in danger of being rewritten by the winners, a prospect that, as Orwell says, 'frightens me much more than bombs — and after our experience of the last few years, that is not a frivolous statement'.[22] The noble working classes of *Wigan Pier* and *Homage to Catalonia* have become the bovine proles of *1984*, decent but inarticulate, unable to rebel until they become conscious but who will not become conscious until they rebel. In *1984*, Orwell shows the destruction of literacy and the book by a totalitarianism of technology, represented by surveillance and the omnipresent telescreen that will eventually spy out Winston and Julia's hiding place above a decaying junkshop. At the end of 'Looking Back on the Spanish War', Orwell wrote an optimistic poem in tribute to an Italian soldier whom he had met only once during their common fight against Fascism. It concludes: 'But the thing that I saw in your face/No power can disinherit:/No bomb that ever burst/Shatters the crystal spirit.' In *1984*, the arrest of Winston and Julia is accompanied by the smashing of their beloved glass paperweight ('The fragment of coral, a tiny crinkle of pink like a sugar rose-bud from a cake, rolled across the mat. How small, thought Winston, how small it always was!').[23] It is the terrifying moment in Orwell when the crystal spirit is shattered.

Like *Coming Up for Air*, *1984* is poised between nostalgia and nightmare, and the grim vision does not preclude a certain black humour. It prophesies the banalities of breakfast television and the pap of Bingo Lottery; it makes jokes about the forthcoming Europeanisation and Americanisation of Britain as the pint disappears as a unit of measurement and decimalisation comes along with the twenty-four-hour clock ('It was a bright cold day in April, and the clocks were striking thirteen' is the novel's ominous opening line). One can see its influence on such novels as Anthony Burgess's *A Clockwork Orange* (the fascination with language, the 'normalisation' of the hero) and Ray Bradbury's *Fahrenheit 451* (the destruction of books and a fear that the mass media of today will lead to the doublethink of tomorrow). The American equivalents would probably be *All the President's Men* (a vision of totalitarianism and fabrications of past and present that has a happy ending, though visually the film remains extremely dark and paranoid); and *The Day After* (like *1984*, raising the big political issue of the day in *emotional* more than political terms, aiming for the heart and for the reverberations of nightmare, and having the courage to go through with the bleakness of its conclusions). The relevance of Orwell's message has not lessened, only intensified, over the years. It was inevitable that, come the year itself, the cinema would have to have another shot at doing justice to this unnerving work.

For producer Simon Perry, his new film of *1984* was to be a 'cautionary tale, a high quality weepie and a wicked satire'.[24] For director Michael Radford, who had previously made the highly acclaimed *Another Time, Another Place* (1983), *1984* was to be 'a naturalistic science-fiction movie'. Like Radford's previous film, *1984* is about prisoners, a forbidden, destructive passion, and the impact of war on the mentality of the 1940s. The challenge of the new film was to make it look like a 1948 vision of the 1984 world, a vision that seems freshly influenced by the recent struggle against Nazism, the menace of Stalinist Russia, the drabness of an exhausted postwar Britain. Of Big Brother, Perry said he wanted him 'nationless, stern, benevolent, reassuring, the kind of face you see on secretarial advertisements, essentially *not* Stalin'. By not limiting the novel to a Stalinist critique, the film becomes a more universal look at media manipulation and the effect ruthless power-seekers have on other people's lives. Roger Deakin's photography has a muted melancholy that gives *1984* the look of an Eastern European film, but the association that comes to mind is not so much with a picture of Eastern European society but with an impression of those national cinemas in Eastern Europe (Poland, Hungary) that have the courage to criticise their society and the determination to make the cinema and the film-artist part of their country's conscience. Not many English films do that, but *1984* belongs in that category. In every sense, it is the British film of the year.

Michael Radford's adaptation is concise and intelligent. It cuts through the novel's pamphleteering, and the Goldstein manifesto comes over less as surrogate Trotskyism but as the voice of Orwell himself, the beleaguered but determined truth-teller in defiance of an authoritarian society which always needs an enemy, a scapegoat, and so is happy to give him his head. Radford makes more of the dream atmosphere in the novel than Orwell, even though the visual imagination has to be appropriately limited. Unlike the novel, Winston's fear of rats is revealed in a dream connected with the death of his mother, so that O'Brien's knowledge of this for Room 101 is truly terrifying. In the novel, Winston's expression of his fear has been overheard (anticipated by that grim pun, 'I bet that particular picture's got bugs behind it').[25] In the film, it is not overheard, but intuitively understood: O'Brien really can get inside people's heads.

The world of the film has been thought through visually, from the ersatz meat ('I don't think there's a single piece of meat in this stew' is said in a tone of approval) to the omnipresent propaganda that is even displayed on the label of a bottle of gin. There are two particular visual motifs: the stare through the window at an external world that is yearned for but denied (for example, Winston's vision of the prole immediately before his capture); and the track forward into darkness towards a door that might open into release or oppression, wish-fulfilment or ultimate nightmare, a beautiful English landscape that might at any moment dissolve into Room 101. The torture room is chillingly bare — a timeless, almost medieval set, with the victim on the rack, and with stray, subliminal details (a hose pipe, broken glass) that convey the horrific chill that all this has happened many times before. The interrogation scenes, alternating between menace and embrace, show John Hurt, as Winston, and Richard Burton, as O'Brien, at their finest. Subtly visualised moments seem precisely to mirror one's imagination of the corresponding event in the novel: when Winston literally sees five fingers and not the four O'Brien is holding up (the ultimate doublethink brainwash, where the victim is persuaded and convinces *himself* of the validity of something that part of him knows is an objective falsehood); or when Winston sees himself in the mirror, a rotting, decaying symbol of the Last Man on Earth, with a horribly distorted curvature of the spine that gives a gruesome twist to that throwaway remark early on in the novel in a quite different context: 'Even a back can be revealing.'[26]

Of course, the film cannot hope to replicate the extensive political analysis of the novel, though it is a sign of Orwell's own difficulty with that aspect of the novel that the crucial political arguments — Goldstein's book, the Dictionary of Newspeak — are the parts that structurally do not fit into the narrative. Yet the film makes more of the romantic relationship. Suzanna Hamilton's touching performance as Julia gives the relationship a heart and vibrancy it does not possess in the novel, assisted by Radford's decision to conflate Winston's dream about Julia and the love-making into one scene that gives a degree of concentration and intensity. The scenes of propagandist rabble-rousing are highly effective, a reminder not only of May Day parades but of the crude appeal to an audience's lowest instincts that characterises too much of the mass media. 'The horrible thing about the Two Minutes Hate,' says Orwell, 'was not that one was obligated to act a part but, on the contrary, that it was impossible to avoid joining in.'[27]

In addition to Radford's excellent recreation of Orwellian nightmare, there have been several other recent British films that seem to have expressed an Orwellian perception of the contemporary world. Roland Joffe's *The Killing Fields* (1984) is a film about a war between superpower ideologies in which the individual is of no account and the year is zero (a dark echo of the Party slogan in Orwell's *1984*: 'Who controls the past controls the future: who controls the present controls the past'). Ken Loach's film about the 1984 miners' strike, *Which Side are You On?*, is an Orwellian vision of an English police state, consisting of the oppression of the proles and of media distortion in favour of the Established Order (the extreme reluctance of British television to show the film only serving to emphasise the validity of its Orwellian paranoia). Terry Gilliam's eccentric fantasy, *Brazil* (1985), has Jonathan Pryce as a modern Winston Smith hounded by the Secret Police. His idyll with his girl is shattered in precisely the same way as Winston's and Julia's in *1984*; the surrounding slogans are effective imitation Orwell — 'Suspicion Breeds Confidence', 'Loose Talk is Noose Talk'; the use of pastoral imagery and sinister children is distinctly Orwellian; and the name of the film's hero, Lowry, is almost an anagram of Orwell. The whole structure of *Brazil* is informed by a fundamental Orwellian conception: that one cannot escape a totalitarian society by creating a fantasy world of one's own imagination — sooner or later the oppression of the real world will be too strong. There is also a fundamental Orwellian conception behind Richard Eyre's *The Ploughman's Lunch* (1983), a glum but interesting study of an upwardly mobile history man (Jonathan Pryce again) progressing in Thatcher's Britain. The Orwellian concepts are first of all implied by the title: the pub food that represents a plastic fabrication of the past to be sold to the public; and, connected with this, the strategy of setting the action against the background of the 1982 Conservative Party Conference where politicians crow over their victory in the Falklands. It is no accident that Pryce's character has been assigned to write a book about Suez that shows the Conservatives in a favourable light, at a time when the Falklands victory is also being moulded into Tory mythology. (In parenthesis, one might say that the continuing controversy over the sinking of the *General Belgrano* is a fundamental debate between the concept of 'objective truth' on the one hand, and that of 'history being rewritten by the winners', on the other.) In the light of these films, one can see that the styles one can operate in recreating an Orwellian 1984 are many and varied: science-fiction naturalism (Radford); documentary polemic (Loach); modern epic (Joffe); narrative realism (Eyre); surrealism (Gilliam). As one can also see, the *1984* world these films depict have as much reference to Western society as to that behind the Iron Curtain.

This last point is important, for Orwell is not simply criticising one particular political system but a global tendency in power politics that implicates and affects us all. Really, *1984* is the culmination of something which Hardy's *Jude the Obscure* had begun nearly a century earlier, with his talk of 'a coming universal wish not to live' and his proposition about the future — particularly the twentieth-century future — as something to be feared. By the time of *Coming Up for Air*, Orwell's apprehensions seem to have solidified into traumatic certainty. 'It's all going to happen,' says the narrator–hero of the novel. 'All the things you've got at the back of your mind, the things you're terrified of, the things that you tell yourselves are just a nightmare or only happen in foreign countries. The bombs, the food queues, the rubber truncheons, the barbed wire ... There's no escape.'[28] If you corrupt the idea of equality, this is bad enough for Orwell's utopian socialism, which hinges on this concept: the famous catchphrase in *Animal Farm* that 'all animals are equal but some are more equal than others' is not witty in Orwell's eyes but profoundly disturbing. But if your faith in the future is destroyed, then Orwell's brand of democratic socialism becomes impossible. For if there is no future, what is the point of sacrificing what you have for the sake of someone else? If there is no future, what is the point of trying to attain power (it cannot change anything) *unless* you believe in power for its own sake — which will only let in again the brutes, the selfish, the dispassionate and the fascistic, with the result that the only growth industries will be despair and hopelessness? This is really the significance of *1984* as a post-*nuclear* novel, and an argument Orwell anticipates in his important, depressing 1947 essay, 'Toward European Unity', which predicts the division of the world among two or three superstates, unable to conquer one another or to be overthrown by internal rebellion; with a hierarchical structure of 'a semi-divine caste at the top and outright slavery at the bottom'; with continuous phoney wars against rival states; and with 'the crushing out of liberty' that 'would exceed anything that the world has yet seen'.[29] Is *1984*, finally, a warning against, or a manual on, totalitarianism? A shield against such things happening, or an unwitting revelation of how they can be achieved? Given the possibilities now for total global annihilation, total technological surveillance, total state control of the media, those who work in the fields of television and film — as entertainers or educators, practitioners or pedagogues — have an awesome responsibility in the images they project of the modern world. One of Orwell's main achievements is to have made that responsibility frighteningly clear. The year of 1984 has now safely passed us by. Nevertheless, for the atmosphere, the apparatus, and the apprehension of Orwell's *1984*, one only needs to look around.

Notes

1. George Orwell, *The Collected Essays: Journalism and Letters*, vol. 2 (Penguin edition, 1970), p. 25.

2. Ibid., vol. 3, p. 39.

3. Ibid., vol. 4, p. 92.

4. George Orwell, 'Why I Write' (1947), *Collected Essays* (Secker & Warburg, 1961), p. 442.

5. George Orwell, *1984* (Penguin, 1984), p. 5.

6. For a useful summary of Grierson's ideas about documentary, see Alan Lovell's essay in *Studies in Documentary* (Secker & Warburg, 1972), pp. 9-35.

7. Orwell, 'Why I Write', pp. 440-1.

8. Quoted in 'Realism and the Problem of Documentary', *BFI Distribution Catalogue*, edited by Julian Petley (British Film Institute, 1978), p. 6.

9. Charles Barr, *Ealing Studios* (David & Charles, 1977), p. 7.

10. Orwell, *Collected Essays* vol. 2, p. 88.

11. Ibid., vol. 4, p. 218.

12. 'The English People', *Collected Essays*, vol. 3, p. 22.

13. The speech is quoted in full in Chaplin's *My Autobiography* (Bodley Head, 1964).

14. Orwell, 'Looking Back on the Spanish War', in *Homage to Catalonia* (Penguin, 1966), p. 245.

15. Letter to George Orwell, 13 July 1944.

16. *Collected Essays*, vol. 4, p. 138.

17. See Pare Lorentz's review of *Snow White* (February 1938), in *Lorentz on Film* (Hutchinson & Blake, 1975), pp. 148-51.

18. Orwell, *Animal Farm* (Penguin, 1951), p. 120.

19. Orwell, *Homage to Catalonia*, p. 81.

20. Quoted in *Daily Mirror* (7 December 1954).

21. See Robert Conquest's preface to the poetry collection *New Lines* (Macmillan, 1956).

22. Orwell, 'Looking Back on the Spanish War', *Homage to Catalonia*, p. 236.

23. Orwell, *1984*, p. 177.

24. All quotations from Simon Perry and Michael Radford are taken from comments made by them in the BBC documentary *Designing a Nightmare*, a film about the making of *1984*, transmitted in October of that year.

25. Orwell, *1984*, p. 120.

26. Ibid., p. 6.

27. Ibid., p. 15.

28. Orwell, *Coming Up for Air* (Penguin, 1962), pp. 223-4.

29. Orwell, 'Toward European Unity', *Collected Essays*, vol. 4, p. 424.

Chapter Five

Pinter's *Go-Between*

How faithful is Harold Pinter's screenplay for *The Go-Between* to L.P. Hartley's novel? The plot is adhered to fairly strictly and Pinter has kept close to Hartley's original dialogue — so much so that Hartley allegedly was rather piqued that Pinter was given the credit for lines that are actually his. However, a close consideration would reveal that there have been significant changes of emphasis in the translation from novel to screen. As well as being appreciated for the considerable cinematic merits of Joseph Losey's direction, the film can be approached as an intriguing addition to Pinter's own literary output and as a perceptive and acute interpretation of the novel: it is this latter approach I wish to pursue in this essay.

Although the film follows the novel's narrative quite closely (with some significant exclusions and alterations, as we shall see), it becomes clear that the two works build to different points of climax. Hartley's climax is in the past, with Leo's discovery, with Mrs Maudsley, of Burgess and Marion in the outhouse, a discovery which results in Leo's nervous breakdown: the present serves as a prologue and epilogue to the main tale. The film, on the other hand, builds to the final shots of the face of Leo as an adult, where the past is felt as a profound, destructive influence on the present: the elder Marion's romantic vision of it contrasts with the haggard face of a 60-year-old Leo still haunted by dark and dreadful memories.

Another difference of emphasis between novel and film is the treatment of Burgess's suicide. In the film it could almost go unnoticed. It is never mentioned and the shot of Burgess dead is held only momentarily, with Burgess in darkness and the camera at some distance from him. (In the film this image of darkness and death contrasts powerfully with the image of Marion in the hammock, content and in sunlight, which is also recalled at this juncture by Leo, and which encapsulates the polarities within which the story moves — deceptive innocence and destructive violence.) It is possible that the film is attempting to reflect Leo's subjective reaction to that event: even as an adult, the memory is still too painful for him to think about for very long. But two other explanations are also possible. The first is that the shot is deliberately mystifying and consciously invites close scrutiny: as will become clear, the film continually compels a viewer to ponder what he is seeing, and the notion of the film as mystery (rather than as, say, tragic love story) seems a crucial clue to its whole style. The second explanation might be that this detail, along with Leo's breakdown, is not dwelt on because neither Pinter nor Losey found it entirely convincing. A film adaptation of a novel, inevitably in the process of selection and emphasis, becomes implicitly a form of criticism as well. Pinter and Losey have gone beyond mere slavish adherence to the original by attempting to offer alternative explanations for some of the events in the work that critics have either found puzzling or unconvincing.

This raises the question of what it was that drew Pinter and Losey to *The Go-Between* in the first place. Joseph Losey has said that he originally wanted to make *The Go-Between* immediately after his collaboration with Pinter on *The Servant* (1963) but had not been able to obtain the rights until some years later.[1] Between *The Servant* and *The Go-Between*, Pinter and Losey worked together on *Accident* (1967), adapted from Nicholas Mosley's novel. The three films taken together make up a kind of unofficial trilogy about English class and hypocrisy, in which the implications of anxiety in Losey's lucid camerawork trigger the tension throbbing beneath the urbane civilities of Pinter's prose. If one wants an explanation of their fascination with *The Go-Between* and the particular themes of the novel, one might find it in the nature of their collaboration and the elements it shares with *The Servant* and *Accident*.

Thematically, all three films are about destructive relationships ending in tragedy. In each case, hypocrisy plays an important part, characters being torn apart through acting out a role in their public lives that bears no relation to their private desires. 'If I have one theme,' said Losey, 'it is the question of hypocrisy: the people who condemn others without looking at themselves.'[2] The pessimism of the films stems from their dual sense of the necessity yet the impossibility of fundamental emotional and social change, and each film has its own distinctive statement to make about the hypocrisies of English society. *The Servant* is a bracing black comedy about the country's declining moral leadership, particularly after the Profumo affair. The authority of James Fox's languid and licentious master is completely undermined by a demonic peasant's revolt unleashed by Dirk Bogarde's servant; and, in a remarkable final orgy scene, which involves all strata of society, the film offers a contemptuous image of 1963 England as a brothel in which everybody comes to know his vice. By contrast, *Accident* is an elegantly ironic movie about the middle-class Oxford intelligentsia, who have all the answers to complex philosophical questions but are completely at sea in their own emotional lives. *The Go-Between* is probably the most brilliantly malevolent of them all in its evocation of a turn-of-the-century England grappling tremulously with the deceits of its own social and sexual attitudes.

If one wishes to narrow these attitudes down further, one might say that Pinter and Losey focus on two particular aspects of social and sexual relationships: class attitudes, and infidelity. All three films communicate their tensions through acts of sexual infidelity, in each case intensifying the shock with a moment when a character comes upon or interrupts a moment of forbidden sexual contact which shatters that character's illusions. (One might add that in each film a character is put in the situation of acting as a go-between for two lovers, a role which, in Leo's case in *The Go-Between*, is also a metaphor for his social alienation: wandering helplessly back and forth between two distinct social orders whilst belonging to neither.) These relationships are violations of a conventional social order: between master and servant (in *The Servant*); between teacher and student (in *Accident*); between aristocratic lady and farmer (in *The Go-Between*). There is an element of social revenge in the way in which Pinter and Losey show their fair-haired aristocrats — James Fox in *The Servant*, Michael York in *Accident*, Edward Fox in *The Go-Between* — being victimised by events. But there is also an element of misogyny in the way they show their enigmatic *femmes fatales* — Sarah Miles in *The Servant*, Jacqueline Sassard in *Accident*, Julie Christie in *The Go-Between* — blithely surviving the destruction they cause.

The three films also have certain stylistic features in common. All are characterised by spatial compression. In each of them, houses are very important, territories in which the characters become confined. This sense of imprisonment is reinforced by the photographing of characters through bars: like the shot of the prostrate master through the stair-rails, a complete prisoner of his obsessions, which ends *The Servant*; or the way the first meeting between Leo and Burgess in *The Go-Between* is shot from behind a closed gate, an early warning of their entrapment within this relationship. This motif gives particular force to the moment in *The Go-Between* when Leo writes to his mother for permission to come home early and she refuses: he must remain a prisoner in the house until his dreadful destiny is completed. It is a motif which would appeal equally to both Pinter, who so often writes dramas about rooms and intruders who shatter the status quo, and to Losey, who so often made films about seemingly impregnable fortresses — both physical and psychological — that are nevertheless invaded from outside.

Intriguingly also, all three films begin with an approach to a house which is to play a crucial part in the drama: all end on a virtual reprise of the opening, in a way that forces an awareness of the changing situation between these two events. At the beginning of *The Servant*, the servant approaches his master's house, which at that stage is in need of furnishing and decoration. The process by which the servant dresses and vulgarises the house echoes the process by which he asserts his own personality over that of his master, and by the end of the film he is in charge of both the house and the master. The last shot of the don's house in *Accident* is an exact reversal of the first, but although the façade remains the same, we hear over the soundtrack the sound of a car crash: the accident of the title that has jolted the stability of his inner life and which will remain for ever in his memory. *The Go-Between* begins and ends with an approach to Brandham Hall: in between are fifty years and what has changed Leo from the enthusiastic 12-year-old to the joyless adulthood he projects in the closing shots of the film. This cyclical structure is not simply symmetrical but chillingly claustrophobic. In fact, it might make Leo's birthday gift of a cycle a more deadly symbol than has often been acknowledged. Leo has never escaped from his past and at the end is going on 'another errand of love' for the older Marion. 'The last time I shall ever ask you to be our postman,' she says, just as the young Leo, almost on an impulse in his final meeting with Burgess, has asked, 'Shall I take one more message for you?' — the message that is to precipitate the tragedy. The cycle is never-ending.

If the material of *The Go-Between* seems closely bound to the concerns of the other Pinter–Losey collaborations, there are also certain elements in it which seem specifically to link it to aspects of Harold Pinter's writings, and would explain Pinter's fascination with the work. For example, it is a commonplace of criticism to suggest that Pinter in his plays uses game as a metaphor for, amongst other things, competitiveness, power, sexual relationships. In *The Servant* there is the ball game on the stairs between master and servant which becomes a metaphor for their imminent reversal of roles. In *Accident*, Dirk Bogarde's middle-aged don plays a game in the young aristocrat's home in which he is compelled to strain every fibre to defend his territory against the aggressive surge of youth — again, the game motif underlines one of the film's main themes. There are a number of games in *The Go-Between*. There is the early contrast in the film between the adult game of croquet (representing the grace of the upper classes) and the boyish game of hide-and-seek (the release of youthful instinctive energies). Later in the tale, the game of hide-and-seek is to take on increasingly disturbing overtones, when Trimingham employs Leo to find Marion (does he already suspect something?), and above all, when Mrs Maudsley dementedly drags Leo along to seek out Marion in the outhouse. As a cricket fanatic, Pinter would also have been drawn to the cricket match in *The Go-Between*, a highly significant set-piece in which the two levels of society are brought together and in which Leo is to catch Burgess out (as he is later, tragically, in the outhouse — 'I never thought I'd be caught out by our postman').

Another Pinteresque feature of *The Go-Between*, which Pinter's adaptation particularly emphasises, is the unusual time-structure of the work. The past is seen from the perspective of the present and hence coloured by reverie, retrospection and hindsight; but, as we have seen, the present is also seen as having been determined by the past. 'I think I'm conscious of a kind of ever-present quality in life,' Pinter has said. 'I certainly feel more and more that the past is not past, that it never was past. It's present.'[3] It is worth recalling that *The Go-Between* screenplay comes during a period in Pinter's development when he is preoccupied with the theme of the complex intermingling of past and present — his play *Old Times*, for example, first performed in 1971, and his adaptation of Marcel Proust's *A*

La Recherche du Temps Perdu, which Pinter wrote in 1972 for a film with Joseph Losey that, alas, was never made. In his introduction to the Proust screenplay, Pinter comments: 'The subject was Time. In *Le Temps Retrouvé*, Marcel, in his forties, hears again the garden bell of his childhood. His childhood, long forgotten, is suddenly present within him, but his consciousness of himself as a child, his memory of the experience is more real, more acute than the experience itself.'[4] There are echoes of this in the screenplay of *The Go-Between*, notably in the bold time-shifts between past and present. The present is represented in the film by a mysterious figure, only later identified as an adult Leo, who stalks disruptively through the narrative on an overcast day, in so doing imparting a sense of ominousness and unforeseen dread to the events of 1900. In a way, these disruptions of time force on one's attention the importance of time in the main narrative, and the way significant moments are carefully marked in time: the clocks in the Maudsley's dining-room beginning to chime as Leo says, 'Well, it wasn't a killing curse, you see. There are curses and curses. It depends on the curse'; the clock striking when Leo comes out into the cathedral square and sees Marion and Burgess together for the first time and does not realise what he has seen. The tragedy in the past is ultimately to hinge on time: Burgess fixes his meeting with Marion at a time when she is due at Leo's birthday party, her broken appointment with Leo having fateful consequences.

More generally, the material of *The Go-Between* shares with Pinter's work a fascination with trust, loyalty and betrayal, which would explain Pinter's imaginative identification in his screenplay with L.P. Hartley's world. The theme of loyalty and betrayal in Pinter's work warrants more discussion than is possible here, but some examples should suffice to show its importance: Aston in *The Caretaker* undone by people he trusted to understand; Davies in the same play whose problem is an inability to trust anyone; Mick who is almost too loyal to his brother; the two assassins in *The Dumb Waiter* whose blind loyalty to an organisation is to be tested; the betrayals of which Stanley is accused and of which he is a victim in *The Birthday Party*; the leitmotif of infidelity which runs through *The Collection, Tea Party, Betrayal*, and so many of his film scripts; the very subject of spying in his screenplay for *The Quiller Memorandum* (1966). In *The Go-Between* Leo betrays Marion and Burgess, and also betrays Trimingham in his collusion in the lovers' relationship; but, in a more fundamental sense, it is Leo himself who is the most deeply betrayed of all. 'We trusted you with our great treasure,' says the adult Marion, failing to comprehend what this contaminated trust has done to him. 'Can I trust you?' asks Burgess of Leo in their first meeting, wondering whether to give him the letter to Marion. 'I'll trust you,' he decides, and in a master stroke, the film cuts immediately to a shot of Burgess's handkerchief, stained by Leo's blood, in Marion's hand: the trust is to lead to blood, to the destruction of both Burgess and Leo at the hands of Miss Marion Maudsley. Leo is the outsider, a figure who comes into a strange society and destroys its stability, in the process destroying himself. This kind of structure — the disruptive influence of the outsider on a situation or relationship which is already fraught with undisclosed tensions — forms the dramatic pattern of most of Pinter's plays: *The Room, A Slight Ache, The Birthday Party, The Caretaker, The Homecoming, Old Times*. Mick's final tirade against Davies in *The Caretaker* ('Ever since you come into this house there's been nothing but trouble ...')[5] is astonishingly similar to Marion's outburst against Leo in the novel of *The Go-Between*, when he is refusing to deliver her letter ('You come into this house, our guest ... we take you in, we know nothing about you ...').[6] Anyone who doubts Pinter's affinity with Hartley need only compare these two passages.

This brings me to a closer consideration of the film itself, and here more than just the specific contributions of Pinter and Losey should be taken into account, even though these other contributors are moulded by director and writer to reinforce a consistent interpretation. To do full justice to the skill of the film's adaptation of Hartley, credit should be paid to a wide range of technical excellence. But I would like to concentrate attention for a moment on two particular areas, which seem crucial to an understanding of the film's interpretation of the work: the music; and the performances of Michael Redgrave as the older Leo, and Margaret Leighton as Mrs Maudsley.

One of the most controversial areas of the film has always been the background score of Michel Legrand, which has often been attacked for being insistent, portentous, obtrusive and anachronistic. 'The turn-of-the-century, East Anglian setting during a summer heat wave ... seems to have eluded Legrand's muse,' commented a critic, reviewing Legrand's symphonic suite drawn from his score. 'This is an instance where the producer of the film might well have drawn on the work of a contemporary composer, say Delius, for his picture.'[7] But it is clear that the wrong question is being asked: the point is not whether the music reflects the England of 1900 but why it so obviously refuses to do that. Why is the music so dramatically drawing attention to an atmosphere of ominousness that is not apparent in the images? The reason is that the score is conceived retrospectively, in the full knowledge of disaster. It has the foreknowledge of the camera, which also evokes an air of unease which eludes the characters (for example, the menacing swoop of the camera behind Leo as he sees Marion and Burgess in Norwich, the shot infusing the moment with a tension that is not immediately discernible from the context). The music's traumatic, passionate chords underneath the film alert an audience to the suppressed passion underneath the surface of this society which is ultimately to erupt into hysteria and tragedy. The insistence of the music prevents a spectator at a very early stage from being lulled by the surface attractions of the society. It also draws attention to the discordance between soundtrack and image, which is a pronounced characteristic of the style of the film and highly appropriate for people whose faces betray a meaning their words conceal. 'Of course you may go,' says Mrs Maudsley, agreeing to Marion's trip to Norwich but revealing a face tight with displeasure. 'I may look hot, but I'm really quite cool underneath,' says young Leo in the same scene, perspiring profusely in his Norfolk jacket and yet ashamed to admit that he has nothing more suitable to wear. The remark sets him apart from the Maudsley household, which may look cool but is simmering underneath.

As mentioned earlier, Losey and Pinter seem to have planned the film almost as a suspense film rather than as a tragic love story. The music; those strange flash-forwards of Leo as an adult which, for a long time in the film, are left unexplained (and have been known to try an impatient cinema audience); the inexplicit shot of Burgess's death — all these impart a palpable sense of mystery. There is a scene in the smoking-room — wonderfully acted by Edward Fox, Michael Gough and Dominic Guard — when Trimingham and Mr Maudsley, in the presence of Leo, talk about Ted Burgess ('He wouldn't exactly be a loss to the district') and one wonders how much each of them knows. But the two major mysteries are contained in the uncommonly powerful performances of Michael Redgrave as the older Leo and Margaret Leighton as Mrs Maudsley, and what the power of these performances actually portends. Redgrave's face in the closing stretches of the film — alternately strained, frightened, spiteful, shattered — carries the whole tragic weight of the work. Why has the experience had such a demoralising effect on Leo? The answer is not only to be found in his disillusionment with Marion and Burgess, whom he has elevated to the level of gods and become — like Mercury — their messenger. It is also to be found in the demonic behaviour of Mrs Maudsley, the clues to whose extraordinary actions are contained in a performance of quite unnerving intensity by Margaret Leighton. We know that Mrs Maudsley suspects a relationship between Marion and Burgess, which would violate her sense of propriety. But this in itself does not adequately explain the sense of impending mental breakdown signalled by the performance, nor does it explain the maliciousness of her behaviour towards Leo on his fateful thirteenth birthday (when, like another Pinter character, he is to have a singularly traumatic birthday party). Why does she take Leo with her to the outhouse? Around the birthday table, Mrs Maudsley, hearing from the butler that Marion has not visited Nanny Robson as she has said, suddenly rises, and we have the following section from the screenplay:

Mrs Maudsley's chair scraping back. Her skirt.
Close-up of Mrs Maudsley.

Mrs Maudsley: No, we won't wait. I'm going to look for her. Leo, you know where she is. You shall show me the way.

Long shot. Room.
Mrs Maudsley seizes Leo's hand. A chair falls. She takes him to the door.
Close-up of *Mr Maudsley.*

Mr Maudsley: Madeleine![8]

Her explanation for taking Leo, then, is that she needs him to show her the way. But it is clear from what follows that she does not need Leo for this purpose: she is leading and he is following, with the utmost reluctance. How does she know exactly where to go? The novel has offered an explanation for this ('Marcus it must have been who told his mother that I knew something of Marion's whereabouts when she gave out that she was with her old Nannie ...').[9] This explanation is not offered by the film and the moment remains inexplicable until one pieces together a series of implications in the film about the real cause of Mrs Maudsley's emotions. Does not the powerful impression of neurotic intensity and limitless ache in Mrs Maudsley here imply the abuse of sexual as well as social feelings? For if Mrs Maudsley's motivation is sexual jealousy as well as class outrage, then her extraordinary behaviour at this juncture with Leo becomes more comprehensible. Her impulse to take Leo to the outhouse with her becomes the irrational act of a rejected woman, avenging herself on the boy for his connivance in a relationship which has destroyed her own sexual hopes ('No, you *shall* come,' she says, pulling him after her, as if this were a kind of punishment). Further, if she knows exactly where to go, could it not imply that she has been in that outhouse with Ted Burgess herself?

It is here that one regrets not having immediate access to the film since so much of the evidence for this is embodied in looks, gestures and tone. But once the idea is grasped, then everything about Margaret Leighton's performance (and indeed Michael Gough's performance as Mr Maudsley) falls into place. Her tense behaviour at afternoon tea, or at the village concert, seems excessively overwrought if it is only her social feelings that have been offended. It would also explain certain calculated visual arrangements in the film which are otherwise puzzling: the fact that one can mistake Mrs Maudsley for Marion in long shot; the fact that they are seated at the cricket match, one behind the other, as if mirror extensions of each other (and both ducking simultaneously to get out of the way of Burgess's fiercely struck cricket ball); the fact that the cricket match closes with a shot of Marion in a state of nervous tension that reminds one of her mother. At the village concert, when Burgess asks for an accompanist, we do not actually see Marion rise to assist him. At that moment, the camera rests pointedly on Mrs Maudsley as she hears the sound of a chair moving behind her (an anticipation of her own intemperate rise from Leo's birthday party) and she knows without looking what is happening, her face registering all the anguish of an older woman's rejection. When she notices the letter to Burgess which Marion and Leo have dropped when playing outside, the impression is that she knows instantly what this means and what this letter contains. One notices how, in Margaret Leighton's performance, she dwells on the phrase 'She is certainly growing old, poor Nanny Robson,' in a way which seems to draw attention to her own age and sorrow. When demanding the letter from Leo, she does seem quite prepared to have it delivered to Nanny Robson, an action inconceivable from a woman supposedly attempting to suppress a social scandal at all costs but not at all surprising from one in the grips of a desperate jealousy.

Her behaviour throws fresh light on Mr Maudsley's. Throughout the film he has seemed much less concerned about Marion's behaviour than his wife's. At morning prayers, Mr Maudsley has read out the text 'See that you walk circumspectly ...' in a pointed manner that is directed less at his daughter than at his wife, who looks down in a state of tension. There are two interesting differences in the film from the published screenplay which would tend to confirm this. In the film, during the interval of the cricket match, Mr Maudsley turns to Burgess and says bluntly, 'And now ... what are we going to do about you?' as if the rivalry between these two men is more immediate than has hitherto been acknowledged. Also, at the village concert, when Burgess is singing 'Take a Pair of Sparkling Eyes' to Marion's piano accompaniment, particular visual prominence is given to Mr Maudsley's walking forward and throwing a pointed look not at Trimingham (as originally directed in the published screenplay)[10] but at his wife, who seems to be swooning in a cocoon of private pain. In retrospect, the scene between the men in the smoking-room takes on a darker perspective. The two men, Trimingham and Maudsley, converse insinuatingly over their cigars about Ted Burgess, each wishing Burgess away from the district because he is threatening the woman they love. Leo's first entry into the man's room, into the realm of adult experience — with his query about honour — could hardly be charged with greater tension.

What do Pinter and Losey intend by their addition of this new dimension to the material? Part of the reason is probably to extend the view of marriage which is offered in the novel. Marriage is seen in the film as something horrible and restrictive, Marion being impelled towards a marriage to a man she does not love (and having the insensitivity to ask the elder Leo why he never married); Mrs Maudsley trapped in her marriage to the arid Mr Maudsley. As in *Accident*, and in much of Pinter's work, passion is stifled by conventional marriage and can only be inflamed outside its boundaries or (as in *The Lover*) by ingenious arrangements from within.

Another reason is to strengthen Mrs Maudsley's motivation in taking Leo with her to the outhouse, which, as handled by L.P. Hartley, is not totally convincing. In the original novel, one could see why, in plot terms, Leo had to be there and be able to account for what had happened; and yet one was a little puzzled by the detail, the act having a twisted cruelty that could not be adequately accounted for by Mrs Maudsley's outraged sense of social decorum. The explicitly sexual revelation suggests a sexual motive, which the film deftly supplies. Mrs Maudsley's strategy is not only a punishment of Leo; his presence is a humiliation for Burgess and Marion. The scene is so powerful because it represents a hideous and perverted acting out of Leo's own suppressed desire for Marion and Mrs Maudsley's for Burgess — a scene whose tension is released by Mrs Maudsley's anguished groan, and Leo's cry as she seizes him, in her confusion instinctively protecting him from a sight she has actively brought him out to see.

This gesture is echoed by Marion, who pulls Burgess towards her, and mother and daughter face each other in mutual sexual enmity.

The final effect is to enlarge the horror of the situation and to trap Leo in a web of human corruption that is even larger than he comprehends, since more than one generation is now involved. The sense of tainted blood — the fear of Burgess's grandson, whom Marion wants Leo to reassure — is thus given more power and resonance. It also makes Mrs Maudsley's encouragement of Trimingham's relationship with Marion not simply a social move, but a tactic of active sexual spite. If Hartley's intention were to make it a story of innocence betrayed and corrupted, the film extends it into an attack on the tremulous hypocrisy, corrupt sexuality and poisoned continuity of a whole society, with Mrs Maudsley unnervingly representing a social and a sexual nemesis.

Ultimately, the film's central theme is not Leo's loss of innocence as a child: it is the traumatisation of Leo as an adult. One of the finest parts of the film is the moment when young Leo sings his song:

Angels ever bright and fair
Take, oh take me to your care.
Speed to your own courts my flight
Clad in robes of virgin white
Clad in robes of virgin white.

The red, white and blue of the Union Jack is behind Leo, but the shot is compressed so that all we can see is the column of red. This blood-like column behind him is an ominous portent of the blood-letting to come, and the blood-red in the context of 'virgin white' is a powerful image of loss of innocence (one thinks of the similar colour imagery in Hardy's *Tess of the d'Urbervilles*). The 'virgin white' recalls not only the flannels of the cricketers in whose match Leo has excelled and which has led to this invitation for him to sing. It also evokes the white dresses of both Marion and her mother, whose virtue is to come under scrutiny; and it sadly predicts the virginity to which Leo will be consigned because of the effect these events have had on him, his idealisation of figures who are to prove all too fallible fallen angels.

Leo finally becomes a spectator of life, a man who wants to be involved but is afraid of involvement. 'Why are you bringing your bathing suit if you're not allowed to swim' is a recurrent refrain, and Leo is carrying his bathing suit, which is perfectly dry, in his last meeting with Ted Burgess when he is to carry the one more message that will consign Leo to an arid future. He becomes a man whose disappointed idealism will find the greatest difficulty in adjusting to the imperfection of human contact. Leo is constantly being touched in the film and himself starts grabbing at Burgess when he demands to know what 'spooning' is; and the film builds to the moment when Leo apprehends the meaning of the most intimate physical contact, a knowledge so warped by its context as to sour his view of sexual contact for the rest of his life. It is significant that Leo's first sight of Marion in the hammock has been followed immediately by his discovery of the deadly nightshade which, like Marion, is beautiful but poisonous to the touch. The whole work has this sense of lifting a beautiful stone and finding a serpent underneath. Pinter's adaptation for Losey has brought out all — and more — of its sting.

Notes

1. Michel Ciment, *Conversations with Losey* (Methuen, 1985), p. 239.
2. Tom Milne, *Losey on Losey* (Secker & Warburg, 1967), p. 128.
3. Mel Gussow, 'An Interview with Harold Pinter', *Performing Arts*, vol. 6, no. 6 (June 1972), pp. 25-6.
4. Harold Pinter, *The Proust Screenplay* (Grove Press, 1977), p. x.
5. Harold Pinter, *The Caretaker* (Methuen, 1960), p. 73.
6. L.P. Hartley, *The Go-Between* (Penguin edition, 1958), pp. 166-7.
7. Adrian Edwards, *Gramophone* (January 1980), p. 1203.
8. Harold Pinter, *Five Screenplays* (Methuen, 1971), p. 363.
9. L.P. Hartley, *The Go-Between*, p. 266.
10. Pinter, *Five Screenplays*, p. 333.

Chapter Six

The Camera Eye of James Agee

In 1955, James Agee died of a heart attack in the back of a New York taxi-cab at the age of forty-five. His Pulitzer Prize-winning novel, *A Death in the Family*, was unfinished at the time of his death, and he also never lived to see Charles Laughton's magnificent realisation of his screenplay for *The Night of the Hunter* (1955). As with comparable self-destructive literary figures like Scott Fitzgerald and Truman Capote, there is a sense of incompleteness about Agee's achievement, for all the individual flashes of brilliance that illuminate his extraordinary versatility as novelist, poet, screenwriter, film critic. Yet the sum of these things is probably more important than considerations of the aesthetic value and endurance of individual works. What comes through is not so much a body of work as the unmistakable voice of a complete and complex personality who belongs to that category of writers who, as Lionel Trilling said of Orwell, '*are* what they write'.[1] Speculation about what he might have accomplished if he had lived longer is probably fruitless. Like one of his literary heroes, Stephen Crane, Agee seems to have been fated to die a young man's death. One could not imagine the urgent and lacerating sensitivity that one feels in the writing being allowed to mellow and grow old gracefully.

Agee's reputation as a writer mainly rests on the film criticism he wrote for *Nation* and *Time* during the 1940s. For W.H. Auden, who was a fan neither of the cinema ('I do not care for movies and rarely see them') nor of critics ('pedants without insight, intellectuals without love'), Agee's criticism belonged to 'that very select class — the music critiques of Berlioz and Shaw are the only other members I know — of newspaper work which has permanent literary value'.[2] There is no question that, for Agee, film criticism was essentially a creative act. He brought to it the same kind of care and fastidious attention to detail and style that a serious writer would have brought to a more respected literary form. The film journalist Ezra Goodman has written about finding a massive pile of writing paper in the cinema reviewer's office at *Time*, which consisted of over thirty hand-written drafts by Agee of the opening paragraph of his review of Olivier's *Henry V*: 'It was an extraordinary series of documents, almost blood-chilling in their near microscopic intensity, and all the more forbidding because all this labor had been lavished on a product for a weekly news magazine.'[3] But Agee had been labouring towards this position for a long time. Film reviewing was no routine chore for him, but the culmination and fullest expression of his maturity as a writer. The film criticism of the 1940s is the heart of Agee's achievement, with his work in the following decade developing out of it and his work in the preceding decade seeming an important preparation for it.

Agee's writing in the 1930s can roughly be grouped under three headings: poetry, film treatments, and narrative and documentary prose work. The poetry consists mainly of the volume *Permit Me Voyage* (Yale University Press, 1934) and an uncompleted narrative poem, 'John Carter', which is a formal and thematic imitation of Byron's *Don Juan* in the American vernacular. (Agee's later poetic output includes a fine poem on the ending of the Second World War, 'We Soldiers of All Nations Who Lie Killed' and interesting, unused draft lyrics for the Lillian Hellman–Leonard Bernstein musical, *Candide*; but the major poetic achievement is in the 1930s.) Agee's poetry comprises personal love poems, verse-form imitations and celebrations of nature. Stylistically old-fashioned, they reveal a lyrical and emotional sensibility, infused with a sensitive feeling for the love of the land. Part of the interest of the poetry is the way it anticipates important aspects of Agee's future film criticism. It foreshadows his preference for a certain kind of lyrical film-maker who seems close to the soil and has a sense of the poetry of ordinary life. Agee's admiration for directors like Dovzhenko, Flaherty, Pare Lorentz and Jean Vigo would stem directly from this feeling. Also it anticipates the way Agee will write about film, not as a dry impressionistic recorder of personal response but as a uniquely sensitive observer who has filtered his impressions through an essentially poetic sensibility. It was John Huston who said of Agee's writing that 'in a sense it was *all* poetry'.[4] Two examples from this film criticism will suffice. There is this description of a Buster Keaton performance, full of vivid imagery and metaphoric elaboration:

> When he moved his eyes it was like seeing them move in a statue. His short-legged body was all sudden machine-like angles, governed by a daft aplomb. When he swept a semaphor-like arm to point, you could almost hear the electrical impulse in the signal block. When he ran from a cop his transitions from accelerating walk to easy jogtrot to brisk canter to headlong gallop to flogged-piston sprint — always floating, above this frenzy, the untroubled, untouchable face — were as distinct and as soberly in order as an automatic gearshift.[5]

Equally vivid in a different vein is his description of a murder scene in Huston's *We Were Strangers* (1949): 'What seems to be hundreds of young men and women, all in summery whites, throw themselves flat on the marble stairs in a wavelike motion as graceful as the sudden close swooping of so many doves.' This is followed by a concise cogent analysis of the shot's meaning: 'By their trained, quiet unison in falling, these students are used to this. They expect it any average morning. And that suffices, with great efficiency, to suggest the Cuban tyranny.'[6] Perception and analysis are presented in a unique combination of poetry and precision: it is the essence of Agee's style, and no film critic since has ever come near it.

Agee's two film script outlines of the 1930s — his 'Notes for a Moving Picture: "The House"' (1937) and his screen storyboard for a sequence out of Malraux's *Man's Fate* (1939) — are further examples of Agee's cinematic potential. His visual precision is indicated by his description of the opening three shots of 'The House', in which not only camera position but length and rhythm of shots are indicated.[7] A description of an imagined shot from *Man's Fate* instructs the cameraman as follows: 'every possible trick of lighting and depth and focus must be used to give two impressions to the maximum: that the men are thrown down here like straws; and that they are pressed so utterly into the floor, the earth, that they are almost printed on it'.[8] Such passages not only anticipate Agee the film critic or screenwriter, but suggest the potential of Agee the film director. The *Man's Fate* treatment concludes with notes on the photographic and editing style intended, with photography that would avoid the 'smooth and lyric fog', as he says, of Rowland Lee's *Zoo in Budapest* (1932) and John Ford's *The Informer* (1935), and with editing as 'dry and dynamic' as Dovzhenko's *Arsenal* (1930). If he had lived longer, Agee might well have been compelled to try direction, as not many directors relish a writer whose perceptions are so forceful as to reduce the director's importance. 'I feel sure you will forgive me if as the writer I infringe on other territories, including those of the director,' Agee wrote innocently in a letter to Fred Zinnemann in January 1954.[9] It is not certain that many directors would have forgiven him for that.

Prior to his film criticism, Agee's most considerable work is *Let Us Now Praise Famous Men*, a record of the lives of three families of tenant farmers in the Southern states of America during the Depression. The text, augmented by Walker Evans's eloquent photographs, was researched and written in 1936 but not published until 1941. It is an almost unclassifiable work. On the one hand, it is intended as a piece of honest journalism ('whatever that paradox may mean,' as Agee says) in which details of education, money and clothes of a working family are precisely recorded. It is also a loose-limbed symphony of country life, in which documentary observation is punctuated by idealistic artistic cadenzas from Agee, and ordinary people are scrutinised for symptoms of what Agee calls 'human divinity'. 'If complications arise,' says Agee about his and Evans's enterprise, it is because they 'are trying to deal with it not as journalists, sociologists, entertainers, humanitarians, priests or artists, but seriously.'[10] It is a work very much of its period, burning with commitment, anger and social concern. One is reminded of Orwell's roughly contemporaneous *Road to Wigan Pier* (1936) and *Homage to Catalonia* (1937) which are also odd baggages of essay, polemical philosophising and first-hand observation; also autobiographical plunges into the depths; and were also derided on first appearance by both publishers and public and are now indisputable classics. (I have not traced any reference to Orwell in Agee's writings, but there are curious parallels in their work from time to time: for example, Agee's 1952 short story, 'A Mother's Tale', is an animal allegory that has much in common with Orwell's *Animal Farm*.) The blaze of Agee's social and aesthetic fervour can be felt in a passage such as this: 'In every child who is born, under no matter what circumstances, and of no matter what parents, the potentiality of the human race is born again: and in him too, once more, and of each of us, our terrific responsibility towards human life; towards the utmost idea of goodness, of the horror of error, and of God.'[11] Small wonder that the text is a Bible to educationalists and teachers.

At one stage in the book, Agee writes: 'The camera seems to me, next to unassisted and weaponless consciousness, the central instrument of our time, and is why in turn I feel such rage at its misuse.'[12] The text and the wonderful Walker Evans photographs prophesy not only the direction of Agee's future involvement with film, but the style of his criticism: the social concern in his reviewing; his sensitivity to photographic evidence; and his overriding commitment to realism, which makes him harder on Hollywood's falsifications of realism than on the industry's more overtly fantastical and escapist product. Agee's basic aesthetic credo, as critic and creator, involves a kind of welding together of poetry and realism, towards a *heightened* reality, a *relevant* poetry. 'The artist's task is not to alter the world as the eye sees it into a world of aesthetic reality,' he once said, 'but to perceive the aesthetic reality within the actual world, and to make an undisturbed and faithful record of the instant in which this movement of creativeness achieves its most expressive crystallisation. Through his eye and through his instrument the artist has thus a leverage upon the materials of existence which is unique.'[13] It has perhaps not been sufficiently observed how close this is to the aesthetic credo of the film theorist, André Bazin, and to Bazin's insistence on the film artist's respect for, rather than distortion of, the appearance of the real world. Both Bazin and Agee found something of their ideal in the Italian neo-realists, and both tried to find it in favoured directors whom they overpraised so eloquently that these directors have tended to be undervalued ever since: in Bazin's case, William Wyler; in Agee's, John Huston.

In his opening film column for *Nation* magazine, Agee set forth his credentials as a critic. Describing himself as 'an amateur critic amongst amateur critics', with little or no knowledge of how films are made but a great deal of experience watching them, Agee went on to make claims about the advantages of his amateur status. He would not be distracted by technical matters but be able to judge directly how effectively a film communicated. Certain implications arise from Agee's stated position. He emphasises the importance of intelligent *response*, which is an obligation on an audience as well as on a film-maker. Later he will castigate audiences for their insensitive response to Chaplin's *Monsieur Verdoux* (1947), the masses' 'spoiled eyes' preventing them from recognising Chaplin's 'swiftness and uninsistence', his 'genius for mood', his 'visual wit' and 'the bracing absence of fancy composition and prettiness'.[14] In his essay on John Huston, he will castigate movies for being made 'in the evident assumption that the audience is passive; every effort is made to do all the work — the seeing, the explaining, the understanding, even the feeling'.[15] Agee's self-professed amateur status is neither sycophantic, inactive, nor vaguely impressionist. He is very specific about where films go wrong; and when, for example, criticising Billy Wilder's portrayal of the alcoholic in *The Lost Weekend* (1945), Agee will be stirred into suggesting alternative scenes and approaches, undoubtedly suggested by his own first-hand experience of alcohol abuse. At moments like this, he is no longer a critic but a kind of co-writer. For all his pleas of amateurism, Agee had a definite concept about the kind of film he wanted to see. He believes the two primal requirements of the camera are 'living — rather than imitative — visual, aural and psychological authenticity, and the paralyzing electric energy of the present tense'.[16] From this perspective, he dismisses the humanist sentiments of Ford's *The Grapes of Wrath* (1940) and Renoir's *The Southerner* (1946), because he feels that the people look so inauthentic that it devalues and sentimentalises their experience. Alternatively, he embraces the war documentaries of Huston and Wyler, and the early neo-realist exercises of de Sica and Rossellini.

Agee's sense of the responsibility of the film camera would unquestionably be heightened during wartime, when the cinema's capacity to inform, encourage and enlighten the people is particularly put to the test. He reviews newsreels and documentaries, and the films that fascinate him most at this time are realist war movies like William Wellman's *The Story of G.I. Joe* (1945). Even *Bataan* (1943) and *Objective Burma* (1945) (British sensitivities to this film are not considered) received more attention than classics like *Casablanca* (1943) and *Brief Encounter* (1945) because they are closer to what Agee feels the cinema should be doing at this time.

This raises the question of how far Agee was misled by this particular critical obsession and how far his judgements have stood the test of time. Partly, of course, this is a matter of personal opinion, and one ought also to acknowledge the pressures of weekly reviewing and of space which can distort particular preferences (my comments are also confined to the reviews contained in the collection *Agee on Film,* rather than the whole corpus of work, because this is the collection on which his reputation is based). Overall, it would be fair to say that some of his judgements (on the almost forgotten *Farrebique* and *To Live in Peace,* for example) seem inflated because of the films' realist content. Conversely, the importance of convention, of cycles and genres in film, tended to have eluded Agee. For example, he reviews *The Killers, Black Angel* and *Dark Corner* in the same week (14 September 1946) without noticing striking existential and *film noir* motifs in each, though at a later stage, he does include those films with *The Big Sleep* (1946) in a defence of their presentation of violence and their less than glamorous portrayal of postwar America. Although the 1940s are now often regarded as a golden age of film music, with some of the finest scores of Bernard Herrman, Franz Waxman, Miklos Rozsa and Hugo Friedhofer, Agee rarely mentions film music except to condemn it (justifiably so in the case of *The Clock* and *The Treasure of the Sierra Madre*). Bernard Herrman's description of film music as 'the connecting tissue between the screen and the audience, reaching out and enveloping all into one single experience' is neither acknowledged nor understood by Agee. Film music leads an audience too much, he feels, and is anti-realistic. He would probably echo Hitchcock's reluctance to have a score for *Lifeboat* where the entire action takes place on a cramped lifeboat adrift on the ocean, because an audience might ask: 'Where does the music come from?' (But as composer David Raksin pointed out, one could equally retort: 'Where did the camera come from?')

As far as directors are concerned, Agee's judgements are not too different from the norm. He remains perceptively loyal to Hitchcock during the decade, preferring *Shadow of a Doubt* and *Notorious* to *Spellbound* and *Lifeboat* (nowadays this seems more obvious than it must have seemed at the time, *Spellbound* being Hitchcock's most commercial film of the decade and *Lifeboat* being his single Oscar nomination of the 1940s after *Rebecca*). Interestingly, Agee responds to Hitchcock's realism and his psychological perception rather than his mastery of technique and suspense. He likes the 'real attention to what people and places look like' in *Shadow of a Doubt* and Cary Grant's American agent in *Notorious* 'has almost precisely the cultivated, clipped puzzled-idealist brutality of a man whom I knew in a roughly equivalent job.'[17] On John Ford, Agee is generous about *They were Expendable* (1945) and even *The Fugitive*, which now seems to be liked only by Agee and Ford himself. However, he is curt and dismissive of the story, love interest and Irish humour of *Fort Apache* (1948) and, in general, he has little to say about Ford's westerns of the period, including the classic *My Darling Clementine* (1946), or indeed about any westerns (he does not like *The Oxbow Incident* that much and the critical volume contains not a single reference to the biggest box-office hit of the decade, Selznick and Vidor's *Duel in the Sun*). On Hawks, he is less impressed by any anti-Fascist theme in *To Have and Have Not* (1944) than by Lauren Bacall, which seems eminently sensible. He is properly sceptical about Renoir's American films, though the best, *Diary of a Chambermaid* (1945), is not mentioned in the collection. He has hardly anything to say in favour of the work done during the decade by Fritz Lang, though some would argue that *Hangmen also Die* (1943), *The Woman in the Window* (1944) and *Scarlet Street* (1945) are amongst his finest achievements. He is less generous towards those directors who are to be championed by auteurist critics in the following two decades than to those who will fall out of critical favour: Stevens, Wyler, Wilder.

The film-makers Agee champions during this period are Chaplin, Preston Sturges, Val Lewton and John Huston. Agee's admiration for Chaplin runs through all his writing. Quite apart from the film criticism, Agee celebrates him in his letters to Father Flye; in his introduction to *Permit Me Voyage*; and in the early chapters of his novel, *A Death in the Family*. His homage to and defence of *Monsieur Verdoux* is one of Agee's noblest and most incisive pieces of writing, as is his tribute to Chaplin in his essay 'Comedy's Greatest Era'. Chaplin's autobiography salutes Agee's brave support of the comedian when he was being hounded by the American press during the McCarthyist period. Val Lewton is congratulated for his tasteful, literary and visually imaginative contribution to a derided form, the low-budget horror film; Sturges for his outrageous, courageously tasteless assault on American sacred cows during a period of comic corn and conventionality; and Huston for his visual craftsmanship and his iconoclastic moral allegories. His tastes might not have been the same, but Agee might be said to have anticipated auteurist criticism. (Andrew Sarris has said that he felt he was both the beneficiary and the victim of the intellectual vacuum that occurred in film reviewing after Agee's death.)[18] His longer pieces do tend to be on directors, and his Freudian interpretation of the films of Sturges and Huston in terms of their lives is very much an anticipation of auteurism.

Overall, Agee's weaknesses as a critic can be quickly summarised. He is properly attentive to the contribution of stars towards the appeal of a film, but certain treacly tributes to June Allyson, Olivia de Havilland, Ingrid Bergman and Jean Simmons (who was to play Agee's mother in *All the Way Home*, the film version of *A Death in the Family*) seem closer to crushes than criticism. His embarrassing effusions about Elizabeth Taylor's 'mock-pastoral simplicity' in *National Velvet* (1945) have drawn the wrath of fellow-critics like Theodore Strauss, who accused Agee of believing that a sentence is the longest distance between two points. Agee's crushes, though, are balanced by his aversions to performers like Irene Dunne, who made his skin crawl, and Jean Arthur, who reminded him of a cute monkey not only holding out its hat for a penny but insisting that it was working its way through Harvard. Agee sometimes succumbs to a common danger of weekly criticism, which is to miss the excellence of the mainstream in his longsighted pursuit of masterpieces on the horizon, so films as varied and as pleasing as *Build My Gallows High* (1947), *I Walk Alone* (1947) and even *Citizen Kane* are rather curtly dismissed. The biggest fault perhaps is sentimentality and the overwriting this engenders. Pauline Kael feels that: 'His excessive virtue may have been his worst critical vice. Agee's demands were, in some ways, both impossibly high for the movie medium and peculiarly child-like.'[19] Molly Haskell feels his criticism suffered from a touch of 'Hemingway; it is ... an infatuation with the masculine mystique, the pale-faced New York intellectual's compensation for life in a cubicle'.[20] It is true that Agee seems to have preferred male-oriented films and to have had little of substance to say on the period's popular 'women's pictures' like *Random Harvest* (1942) and *Mildred Pierce* (1945), which stand the test of time very well (though he is very good on the money theme of *Mildred Pierce* even if its implications about the role of women in postwar America pass him by).

His strengths can be summarised as follows: his visual sensitivity and his descriptive powers; his moral commitment, which compels him to attack the mindless violence of the 1945 movie *Passage to Marseilles* (he would concur with George Eliot's belief that if art does not enlarge men's sympathies, it does nothing morally); his insistence on fitting the column to his preferences and prejudices when the occasion demands, as in his three-part rave for *Monsieur Verdoux*; his revival of interest in silent comedy, which did more than anything at the time to resuscitate the career of Buster Keaton, leading to his reappearance in *Sunset Boulevard* (1950) and *Limelight* (1952); and, above all, his ability to write criticism which expresses the whole man. Few writers better fulfil D.H. Lawrence's prescription for good criticism: 'A critic must be able to *feel* the impact of a work of art in all its complexity and its force. To do so, he must be a man of force and complexity himself, which few critics are.'[21]

The final thing which distinguishes Agee as a critic is the quality of his wit. I am not thinking of the pay-off lines to his reviews of *The Lost Weekend* and *I Walk Alone* which, in contrast to the opinion of critic Manny Farber,[22] seem to me the most heavy-handed examples of his comic timing. Much better to my mind, because more vivid and pertinent, is his devastating exposure of the evasions of the film of *For Whom the Bell Tolls* ('you may easily get the impression that Gary Cooper is simply fighting for the Republican Party in a place where the New Deal has got particularly out of hand').[23] Equally sharp is his summary of the limited appeal of *Mrs Skeffington* (the theme of 'a woman is beautiful only when she is loved' as relayed to an audience 'which, I fear will be made up mainly of unloved and not easily lovable women');[24] his characterisation of Joan Fontaine's portrayal of the adulteress in *Frenchman's Creek* ('She never once suggests a woman in love or even in confusion; but she does constantly suggest a Vassar girl on a picket line');[25] his comment on the casting of Katharine Hepburn, Walter Huston and Agnes Moorehead as Chinese in *Dragon Seed* ('I've never seen another picture so full of wrong slants');[26] and his endearing, semi-serious suggestion, built up from her performance in *Mrs Miniver, Madame Curie* and *Random Harvest*, that Greer Garson might make a very good Lady Macbeth.

His influence on subsequent film criticism, particularly American film criticism, has been enormous. Andrew Sarris has already been mentioned. Pauline Kael has certainly imitated Agee in the cultivation of *personality* in the film critic, insisting on the 'I' of criticism and eschewing theory, science and objectivity in favour of a dialogue with the readers and a genuine appreciation for the low-brow energy of Hollywood. She also shares a lot of Agee's dislikes, like the western and British films (Agee was not as Anglophobic as Kael and he likes British realism and Olivier, but he is not bowled over by Lean or Reed, not at all by Powell and Pressburger and surprisingly not by Humphrey Jennings); and she feels herself so attuned to his sensibility as proprietorially to predict his tastes ('It's a pity James Agee didn't live to see the films of Satyajit Ray which fulfil Agee's dreams').[27] Robert Warshow in *The Immediate Experience* (1962) and David Riesman in *The Lonely Crowd* (1961) intelligently assimilate Agee's influence in their critique of American popular culture. In *Negative Space* (1971) Manny Farber expresses his reservations about Agee's style in a style that, as Lawrence Alloway has pointed out, [28] is remarkably close to it. In England, Kenneth Tynan's theatre criticism of the 1950s, advocating a drama of realism and commitment away from bourgeois angst and facile escapism, seems a continuation of Agee's ideas in the 1940s, whilst the influence of Agee is openly acknowledged by English critics of the *Observer* newspaper like Penelope Gilliat (an influence fruitfully applied) and Penelope Mortimer (an influence crassly abused, as particularly revealed by her philistine review of Pasolini's *Pigsty* and her astonishing ignorance of the career of Alfred Hitchcock).

Agee might also have been an inspiration in another direction, because he is one of the comparatively few critics who have gone on to become a screenwriter. Before him, one can think of Graham Greene and John Ford's excellent writer, Frank Nugent. After him, one thinks of Penelope Gilliat, Paul Mayersberg, Paul Schrader, Chris Petit and Paul Zimmermann. As his scenarios for 'The House' and *Man's Fate* in the 1930s reveal, screenwriting was one of Agee's main artistic aspirations and, in the late 1940s, he was particularly encouraged in this endeavour by John Huston.

Agee wrote five feature film screenplays, of which the unfilmed 'Noa-Noa', based on the life of Gauguin, is perhaps the most ambitious. Typically with Agee, the script is full of precise, complicated, visual instructions: the cutting of a scene to Chopin's 'Funeral March'; a love scene that dissolves between the characters and Gauguin's paintings; a very precise sequence of images for the part where Gauguin paints *Where Do We Come From? What Are We? Where Are We Going?* and Agee attempts, in his words, 'to involve us deeper than ever before in films in the work of painting a masterpiece';[29] precise instructions on the gradual withdrawal of colour from the frame to signify Gauguin's enveloping blindness and his oncoming death; and a remarkable image when a blood-red flower is placed at Gauguin's graveside and a bee suddenly dives into it like a bullet. It is a long script in three parts, centring on Gauguin's relationship with Van Gogh, and on his experience in Tahiti. One suspects that Agee saw in it a kind of self-portrait of the artist as a driven, self-destructive and isolated individual, who alienates himself from people in pursuit of an elusive artistic ideal. It was to have been directed by David Bradley but production negotiations were interrupted by Agee's death. In the meantime, MGM stepped in with their heavyweight production of the life of Van Gogh, *Lust for Life* (1956), which conclusively upstaged the Agee script.

Agee also did two adaptations of short stories by Stephen Crane, 'The

Blue Hotel' and 'The Bride Comes to Yellow Sky'. The latter was filmed by Bretaigne Windust for RKO in 1952 and released with another short picture (an adaptation of Conrad's 'The Secret Sharer') under the title of *Face to Face*. Crane's story is a comic study of the coming of civilisation to the West, reducing the old conflicts and confrontations to an archaic irrelevance. Scratchy Wilson challenges the marshal to draw: the marshal says he cannot because he is, for the first time, unarmed, and, what is more, he is married. Wilson wanders off disconsolately, his feet making 'funnel-shaped tracks in the heavy sand' (the last sentence of both story and screenplay). With hindsight, the screenplay reads almost like a humorous anticipation of *High Noon* (the fateful arrival of a train — except the marshal is coming, not the outlaw — and an impending showdown), *Shane* (a gunman called Wilson) and a whole host of 1960s westerns about the transition from wilderness to civilisation in late-nineteenth-century America. Agee renders the story very faithfully with one brilliant visual addition that absolutely encapsualtes the theme: the deputy tearing up old outlaw handbills to scatter as improvised confetti as the marshal carries his bride over the threshold.

'The Blue Hotel' is a more expansive adaptation of a more elaborate and interesting tale. Crane's story tells of a frightened Swede who, when forced to fight a Westerner he has accused of cheating at cards, unexpectedly wins. Walking to a nearby town with newfound confidence in his masculine strength, he pressurises a gambler to join him in a drink, and is stabbed to death for his pains. Both story and screenplay draw attention to the cash register at this point, as it reads: THIS REGISTERS THE AMOUNT OF YOUR PURCHASE. (In other words, the Swede has, perhaps, got what he asked for.)

Agee's screenplay faithfully reproduces some of the most vivid detail of the story — the furious fight, the Swede's joyous walk to town on a stormy night — and interestingly elaborates other moments, such as the memory flashes of the Swede on the point of death, including hints about a harsh childhood that are not contained in the story. However, the screenplay makes two significant shifts from the original. In the story, the revelation that the Swede was right and that the cowboy was cheating is saved until the end, when the Easterner claims that they are therefore all responsible for his death. In the screenplay, this revelation comes immediately after the Swede has left the hotel for the town, affording a premonition of what is to follow and a sense of the Swede as a man in danger. 'Any man is in danger,' says Agee's Easterner, embroidering the theme, 'who has spent a lifetime in fear and humiliation, and then suddenly finds his right to be alive. He's a danger to others, too. He doesn't know any better yet how to handle his power than a child with a loaded gun.'[30] This shift in position of the main events in the narrative has the effect of changing the perspective and tone. Crane's story is one of ironic fatalism: no one is really responsible and it is a mistake to assign responsibility; it is simply an example of the irrationality of life where an accidental chain of events is set in motion (the fight is described as a perplexity of flying arms 'like a swiftly revolving wheel') and must be allowed perforce to career to its crazy conclusion. Agee, however, turns it into a moral tale of courage, cowardice, conscience and collaboration (as Agee's Easterner says in the screenplay's final line of dialogue: 'Every sin is a collaboration. Everybody is responsible for everything').[31] If the Easterner had spoken up sooner, this might have been avoided. Why this change of emphasis, and the insistence on the theme of the cowardice of the man who does not speak up against a wrong? Perhaps because of the time Agee wrote it, which was between 1948 and 1949, the period of the House of UnAmerican Activities Committee, the hounding of Chaplin, the beginnings of the Hollywood blacklist and the odious political career of Senator McCarthy.[32]

Agee's most famous screenplay is for John Huston's *The African Queen* (1951). In a letter to Father Flye in December 1950, Agee wrote: 'If everything works out right, it could be a wonderful movie. If much works out wrong, it can be lousier than most. I think most likely it will wind up as good, maybe even very good, but not wonderful, or lousy.'[33] This seems a fair enough description. Agee's screenplay has fun in describing Allnutt's stomach growl that so discomfits Rosie and her brother round the dinner table ('a sound like a mandolin string being plucked ... He glances up quickly and slyly — hopeful they've missed it — to find the eyes of both still fixed on him. The instant their eyes meet they bounce apart like billiard balls').[34] There is a memorable description of the collapse of the brother, 'sprawled out on the floor as ill-shaped as a wounded bat'.[35] The romance is sensitively written and the film plays up the comedy much more than the novel. During the writing, Agee suffered his first heart attack, and the script was completed by Huston and Peter Viertel. This is the reason that the final part of the published screenplay does not have Agee's usual detailed camera instructions; and perhaps one of the reasons that the film at this point loses some of its grip and becomes not so much comic as facetious (like the moment when, after the sinking of the German ship, a German sailor insists on saluting his commanding officer whilst they are both still floating in the water).

If *The African Queen* is the most famous of the films on which Agee collaborated, *The Night of the Hunter* is undoubtedly the finest. Davis Grubb's novel has such a clear and exciting narrative line that the task of the screenwriter is basically one of compression rather than adaptation: Agee, with the help of Grubb and Charles Laughton, ensures that the most vivid details are included intact — the Love/Hate tattoos on the preacher's fingers; the gruesome description of the slashed throat of the murdered Willa as being 'like an extra mouth'. Other events are dramatically telescoped. The opening of the story has been considerably tightened in adaptation, with the film contriving an entrance for the demonic Preacher Powell (Robert Mitchum) that is one of the most electrifying entrances of any screen character. It was Agee himself who had described a Robert Mitchum performance in the 1940s as 'so sleepily self-confident that when he slopes into clinches with the women you expect him to snore in their faces'.[36] There is nothing sleepy about Mitchum's magnificent performance here as the self-appointed preacher on the hunt for some stolen loot. The money is hidden on the premises of an unsuspecting widow (Shelley Winters), and there is a particularly telling effect when a conversation suggesting that the widow should remarry is crosscut with two ominous shots of a train hurtling down the track, tansporting Powell who, of course, is determined to make the widow marry *him*. The train belching out black smoke serves as a highly effective demonic symbol in the manner of the arrival of the uncle in Hitchcock's *Shadow of a Doubt*. Similarly, the moment when the evil preacher reaches for the children as they try to escape from him across the lake is one of the classic horror moments of the cinema. It should be said that the effectiveness of both these moments is only hinted at in the screenplay: Laughton's direction brings an extra dimension of menace in the first instance and extraordinary slapstick suspense in the second.

The writing is throughout enhanced by the exceptional quality of the music, photography and direction. Walter Schumann's score is a masterly blend of original material, lullaby, nursery rhyme and revivalist hymn tune that expertly extend the atmospheric tapestry of the film. Stanley Cortez's chiaroscuro photography is his finest film work outside of his work on Orson Welles' *The Magnificent Ambersons* and he has described in fascinating detail[37] the lengths to which he and the director went to gain certain effects, like the extraordinary shot of the murdered woman in the car under water, her hair streaming. The murder scene is even more striking, with lighting as sharp as a knife, movement choreographed to a waltz rhythm in the manner of Sibelius's 'Valse Triste', and the actual stabbing suggested by a slashing vertical wipe from right to left of the screen at the conclusion of the scene. Agee's screenplay indicates a dissolve at this point, but Laughton's solution is much more dramatic, indeed one of the most inventive uses of this device I have ever seen in a film. Laughton's work overall on the film constitutes one of the great directing debuts of the cinema. Not everything he does in the film is original, to say the least, but just about everything he does in the film seems right. Andrew Sarris described the style, which he admired greatly, as 'semi-Germanic Griffith'.[38] The phrase 'semi-Germanic' draws attention to the Expressionist play of shadow, of light and dark, which is so striking a feature of the film's look. It also implicitly likens the hypnotic powers of the preacher with the title character of the supreme example of Expressionist cinema, *The Cabinet of Dr Caligari*. The reference to D.W. Griffith calls attention to Laughton's use of old-fashioned devices such as the 'iris', which again is used as well as ever I have seen it (particularly the moment when the preacher is searching for the children and the shot closes in on their frightened faces at the window of the cellar). Also, like Griffith, the theme of the film is essentially a study of Good and Evil, represented in stark outlines to suggest the point of view of the children. Mitchum's preacher is described at one point in the screenplay as 'Big Bad Wolf' and he seems a terrifying, nocturnal cartoon depiction of Evil, like Ted Hughes's Crow. On the side of Good is Mrs Cooper, powerfully embodied by Griffith's favourite actress, Lillian Gish. Out of a host of powerful moments, perhaps none is more haunting and hair-raising than the startling duet they sing together, 'Leaning — Leaning — Leaning on the Everlasting Arms': she indoors with a shotgun at dead of night protecting the children, he on the outside biding his time. It symbolises to perfection their wedded conflict, the desire of both of them to have the children to themselves.

The novel's quirky humour, its sense of dream and deadly games, its natural imagery and religious atmosphere have all been faithfully caught. It is an atmospheric tale rather than crudely shocking, lyrical as well as nightmarish. The children's escape along the river has something of the quality of Twain and, with animals prominent in the frame, also the quality of children's illustration. In the final resort, it is probably impossible to say how much of the extraordinary achievement of the film can be attributed to Agee. From his point of view, perhaps the most congenial aspect of the story is in the child's viewpoint of the action. *Night of the Hunter* deals with the mysteries and terrors of both childhood and fatherhood in a highly poeticised manner. By a curious coincidence, both his novels — *The Morning Watch* (1951) and the magnificent posthumously published work, *A Death in the Family* (1958) — deal with exactly the same themes.

To do justice to these two novels would require a separate essay and take us away from the specific focus of Agee's work for the cinema. But perhaps the flavour of both can be briefly conveyed. *The Morning Watch* can be succinctly stated: it is Agee's *Portrait of the Artist as a Young Man*, a kind of homage to Joyce (whom Agee revered) but also a novel steeped in autobiography. The story is about one night in the life of a 12-year-old boy, Richard, boarding at a Catholic school, who stands his watch before the altar on Good Friday and later goes swimming with two friends in a nearby river. This slight tale of 110 pages took Agee five years to write, partly because of the interruption of other projects, and partly because of a very Joycean perfectionism bordering on the pernickety. The Catholic background is similar to Joyce, as is the fascination with language, the portrayal of the sensitive outsider (with his two, very different, friends) who both does and does not want to belong, and the theme of spiritual pride. There is an echo of the stream-of-consciousness technique and the twenty-four-hour structure of *Ulysses* in the novel's intense use of internal monologue and the way Agee takes 80 pages over an hour of the boy's life to give a sense of what is going through his head. However, although both *Portrait* and *The Morning Watch* are semi-autobiographical, there is a different stance towards the material. Agee's intense identification with Richard contrasts with Joyce's detachment and irony towards Stephen Dedalus. In the latter part of the book, there is an enormous sense of release when the boys leave the church and move into the open air, a relief that seems partly to do with Agee's being able to throw off the Joycean influence. Richard's dangerous swim and his encounter with the snake actually suggest two other influences on Agee: John Huston (Huston's famous story of his secret nocturnal swims as a sickly young boy which, he told Agee, he is convinced saved his life), and D.H. Lawrence (a snake that, as in Lawrence's poem, emerges as both a lord of life and as a sense of Richard's vitalising subconscious, and ultimately a test of his courage). It is in this final part that, after the turgidity of some of the early pages, Agee the novelist begins to find himself, just as his young hero begins to acquire a new self-esteem and self-awareness.

Agee's potential as a great novelist is indicated by *A Death in the Family*, the uncompleted but still magnificent work Agee was engaged on when he died. It is an autobiographical depiction of Agee's own family, brought together when they hear about the fatal car crash of Agee's father, which occurred when Agee was a young boy in Knoxville in 1915. The novel is a massive leap forward from *The Morning Watch*, for it is not limited to one particular point of view and this allows for greater variety and colour in characterisation and development. The family — the boy's religious mother, his cynical uncle, his fatalistic grandfather — are all brought vividly to life. The early scenes between the young boy Rufus (Agee's own middle name) and his father are affectionately done. The two enjoy the picture-show together (Agee doing another lively description of a Chaplin performance) and the father later shows off his son at the public bar. Even better is a tender leave-taking of father and mother. Ironically, he is having to leave because he fears his own father is on the point of death. Agee's lingering over precious detail gives a tense yet treasurable sense of dramatic irony ('In the single quiet light in the enormous quietude of the night, all the little objects in the room looked golden brown and curiously gentle. He was touched, without knowing why. Home. He snapped off the light').[39] 'I almost wish I could come with you,' says his wife. The long night where the family gathers to comfort the new widow, with its range of sorrow, spirituality and the odd ungainly bursts of slapstick, is a *tour de force* of sustained tenderness. The description of the burial — a magnificent butterfly lands on the coffin, stays there all the way down, and then flies out as the sun suddenly bursts through the clouds — is poetically imagined but narrated in such a way as to avoid all traces of sentimentality. In the midst of this moving study of the human capacity to absorb and transcend grief is a delicate portrayal of the hypersensitive child who is groping his way towards some accommodation into a baffling and often cruel adult world. The publishers incorporated Agee's prose piece, 'Knoxville: Summer of 1915' to serve as a sort of prologue, a beautiful poetic fragment which was later to be set to music by Samuel Barber.

Agee's overall achievement is difficult to assess. If there is a sense of disappointment, it is perhaps simply that so much was projected and relatively little completed. He was obstructed in this by an intense perfectionism, an enormous capacity for critical self-analysis, and a morbid streak of self-destruction which he never entirely overcame. At the same time, the writing reveals a rounded personality, often roused to fury by cruelty to animals or prejudice against people ('I feel that any human being has the right not to be discriminated against in order to indulge somebody's right to hate, for instance, Jews or Negroes. I feel it the more strongly because I don't regard that right to hate as a right at all but as a deadly wrong').[40] At times during the 1940s — in his defence of Chaplin, in his anguished piece for *Time* after the dropping of the bombs at Hiroshima and Nagasaki[41] — he seems something like the conscience of his country, his generation and his age. In artistic terms, he has something of the prolixity of an O'Neill, the glorious free-form expansiveness of a Mahler, and the freshly burning intensity of a Stephen Crane and a D.H. Lawrence. He also falls into the trap that seems to be the constant peril of the American artist: the temptation to disperse rather than develop his natural talent. But he could not have done otherwise and remained the same man. John Huston has written gracefully about Agee on several occasions — about Agee's carelessness over his own appearance, his gentle smile, his regard for other people's feelings, his talent which made his death, in Huston's view, one of the biggest blows the film world ever had. In his autobiography Huston concludes his portrait of Agee like this:

Jim Agee was a Poet of Truth — a man who cared nothing for his appearance, only his integrity. This he guarded as something more precious than his life. He carried this love of truth to the point of obsession. In *Let Us Now Praise Famous Men* his description of objects in a room is detailed to the point of being an homage to truth. For one fraction of eternity those objects existed in a given arrangement within a circumscribed area; that was truth. Truth was worth telling.[42]

We could do with much more of James Agee's brand of perceptiveness and luminous idealism — and not only in the field of film criticism.

Notes

1. Quoted in Richard Hoggart's *Speaking to Each Other*, vol. 2, (Chatto & Windus, 1970), p. 126.
2. W.H. Auden, letter to *The Nation* (16 October 1944).
3. Ezra Goodman, *The Fifty Year Decline and Fall of Hollywood* (Macfadden Books, 1962), p. 153.
4. Foreword to *Agee on Film*, vol. 2, (Peter Owen, 1965).
5. 'Comedy's Greatest Era', in *Agee on Film*, (Peter Owen, 1963), p. 15.
6. *Agee on Film*, vol. 1, p. 329.
7. *The Collected Short Prose of James Agee* (Calders & Boyars, 1972), pp. 152-3.
8. Ibid., p. 207.
9. Quoted in Tom Dardis's *Some Time in the Sun* (André Deutsch, 1976), p. 243.
10. *Let Us Now Praise Famous Men* (Panther edition, 1969), p. xv.
11. Ibid., p. 263.

12. Ibid., p. 11.
13. Agee, *Collected Short Prose*, p. 34.
14. *Agee on Film*, vol. 1, p. 255.
15. Ibid., p. 329.
16. Ibid., p. 25.
17. Ibid., pp. 26, 214.
18. Andrew Sarris, *Confessions of a Cultist* (Simon & Schuster, 1971), p. 15.
19. Pauline Kael, *Going Steady* (Temple Smith, 1970), pp. 49-50.
20. Molly Haskell, *From Reverence to Rape* (New English Library, 1974), p. 159.
21. D.H. Lawrence, 'John Galsworthy' (1928), in *Selected Literary Criticism* (Heinemann, 1956), p. 118.
22. Manny Faber, 'Nearer My Agee to Thee', in *Negative Space* (Studio Vista, 1971), pp. 84-8.
23. *Agee on Film* vol, 1, p. 46.
24. Ibid., p. 96.
25. Ibid., p. 121.
26. Ibid., p. 110.
27. Pauline Kael, *Reeling* (Warner Books, 1976), p. 203.
28. Lawrence Alloway, *Violent America* (Museum of Modern Art, 1971), p. 74.
29. *Agee on Film*, vol. 2, p. 111.
30. Ibid., p. 469.
31. Ibid., p. 487.
32. Agee's script for *The Blue Hotel* was to have been filmed by John Huston (an ideal choice) but it was never made as a feature. NBC did an adaptation of it for its *Omnibus* series and, more recently, Jan Kadar directed a version of the Crane story for the *American Short Story* television series, with David Warner as the Swede, though this was not based on Agee's adaptation.
33. *Letters of James Agee to Father Flye* (Peter Owen, 1964), p. 183.
34. *Agee on Film*, vol. 2, p. 157.
35. Ibid., p. 166.
36. Ibid., vol. 1, p. 301.
37. Charles Higham, *Hollywood Cameraman* (Thames & Hudson, 1970), pp. 111-15.
38. Andrew Sarris, *The American Cinema* (Dutton, 1968), p. 215.
39. Agee, *A Death in the Family* (Panther edition, 1967), p. 31.
40. Agee, *Letters to Father Flye*, p. 141.
41. Quoted in *Collected Short Prose of James Agee*, p. 51.
42. John Huston, *An Open Book* (Macmillan, 1981), p. 190.

Chapter Seven

Kindred Spirits:
Analogies between the
Film and Literary Artist

Back in 1969, the film theorist Peter Wollen claimed: 'We need comparisons with authors in the other arts: Ford with Fenimore Cooper, for example, or Hawks with Faulkner.'[1] Such comparisons have not happened, for the most part, and this chapter is an attempt to follow through Wollen's idea by perceiving some connections between Dickens and Chaplin, Twain and Ford, Greene and Hitchcock, and Conrad and Welles.

Such comparisons might be of particular interest to teachers who wish to devise an integrated Film and Literature programme, but who wish to avoid the conventional 'film of the book' or 'theme' strategy. With the 'film of the book' approach, the difference between the way film and prose communicates can be too easily elided. Also the teacher is often in a defensive position regarding the film, being expected to share a Leavisite antagonism to popular culture and approaching the film as either a crass simplification or, at best, a mere memoir of the book. (I am speaking here particularly of the English situation and from first-hand experience of almost unbelievably reactionary attitudes to the media which still widely persist across the whole educational spectrum.) In some cases, anyway, the film version of the book might not actually be the best choice of cinematic equivalent: Billy Wilder's *Kiss Me, Stupid* (1964) is much closer in feeling to Nathaneal West's novel *The Day of the Locust* than is John Schlesinger's wretched film version; the same can be said of the relation of Robert Altman's iconoclastic film *M*A*S*H* (1970) to the spirit of Joseph Heller's novel *Catch 22*, Altman's work being far more authentic in feeling than Mike Nichol's cautious film adaptation of Heller. An analogous approach allows the teacher to respect the specificity of film and literature, giving him room to treat them as separate entities and to choose when to make particular parallels between the two media (in a consideration of narrative structure, for example).

In making analogies of this kind, one is not necessarily making qualitative comparisons. Film purists and literary specialists were a little hard on critics like Robin Wood in the 1960s for invoking Keats in a discussion of *Vertigo* or Mozart in a discussion of Howard Hawks.[2] The film specialists thought it constructed another form of cultural elitism; the literary scholars felt it was a critical sleight-of-hand to upgrade the status of cinema. In retrospect, it seemed a valid and valuable strategy for breaking up narrow specialisation. Film-makers should not be seen in a vacuum, and the best of them have never seen themselves so. It is not only exciting but necessary to understanding to follow through the references to Thoreau's *Walden* in Douglas Sirk's *All That Heaven Allows* (1955), for example, or the legend of Bluebeard's Castle as a structural motif in Michael Powell's *Peeping Tom* (1959) (small wonder that Powell was shortly to make a film of the Bartók opera). The richness of Val Lewton's low-budget horror classics has much to do with the wide-ranging literary, philosophical, and artistic references that underpin them, like the John Donne quotation in *Cat People* (1942) or the *Jane Eyre* sub-text of *I Walked with a Zombie* (1943), a sort of precursor of Jean Rhys's novel *The Wide Sargasso Sea.*

The critic Raymond Durgnat once called the cinema a 'mongrel muse',[3] but not enough has been made of its literary, musical, painterly, theatrical qualities as well as its specifically cinematic ones. 'The best way to "know" a thing, is in the context of another discipline,' said Leonard Bernstein.[4] Film's crucial relationship with the other arts is one area of film studies that has hardly begun.

Charles Dickens and Charlie Chaplin

> Although we were aware of the shame of going to the workhouse, when Mother told us about it both Sidney and I thought it adventurous and a change from living in one stuffy room. But on that doleful day I didn't realise what was happening until we entered the workhouse gate. Then the forlorn bewilderment of it struck me; for there we were made to separate, Mother going in one direction to the women's ward and we in another to the children's.[5]

When one reads the above passage from Charles Chaplin's autobiography, or indeed any of the first hundred pages, one epithet comes repeatedly and insistently to mind: 'Dickensian'. The element of pathos, the workhouse experience, the point of view of the bewildered child in Chaplin are all features that one recognises from Dickens's view of the world. Dickens's descriptive powers transform documentary record into nightmarish art that stands as an enduringly blistering critique of the cruelties of the Victorian age.

Dickens and Chaplin are artistic giants of their respective centuries, in remarkably similar ways and for remarkably similar reasons. Coincidentally, they were even physically rather similar: both small and wiry. Their childhoods were similarly traumatic, Chaplin being indelibly marked by his experience of poverty and the workhouse, Dickens affected by the spectre of the debtors' prison and the horrors of child labour. Dickens's working experience in a blacking factory (to support his family after the imprison-ment of his father) was so terrifying that he could not bring himself even to speak about it until well into his adult life. As children, both found compen-sation and relief in performance and theatrical art. Dickens used to console himself when a boy by impersonating favourite characters from his read-ing, like Tom Jones or Roderick Random, and, as a young man, he seriously contemplated a career on the stage. At an early age, Chaplin was entranced by the actor Bransby Williams's imitations of Uriah Heep and Bill Sikes, which impelled him to buy a copy of *Oliver Twist.* One of his earliest stage appearances consisted of his impression of Williams as the old man in Dickens's *The Old Curiosity Shop* who cannot recognise the death of his Little Nell.

During their lifetimes, both Dickens and Chaplin were popular enter-tainers on an almost unprecedented scale, cutting across country and class. Professor Arnold Kettle commented on Dickens: 'Millions of people all over the world (including many who've never read a word of Dickens) can tell you what happened in Oliver Twist's workhouse: comparatively few can tell you what happened at Box Hill.'[6] André Bazin made a similar observation of Chaplin: 'In less than fifteen years, the little fellow with the ridiculous cutaway coat, the little trapezoid moustache, the cane, and the bowler hat, had become part of the consciousness of mankind. Never since the world began had a myth been so universally accepted.'[7] G.K. Chester-ton thought Dickens's characters were mythological personages, like Father Christmas or Punch; James Agee thought Chaplin's tramp as many-sided and as centrally representative of humanity as Hamlet. Need-less to say, this popular admiration stirred up a degree of critical resent-ment, particularly after their deaths, resulting in a temporary drop in esteem. But if the academics and the critics had their doubts, they were not shared by fellow-artists. Barry Norman, Robin Wood and Stanley Reynolds might not have been overwhelmed by Chaplin's art, but Buster Keaton, W.C. Fields and Woody Allen were. A young Henry James and, later, an older F.R. Leavis might have serious reservations about Dickens,[8] but they were not shared by, for example, Dostoevsky, Joyce and Kafka. The scenes between Marmeladov and Sonia in Dostoevsky's *Crime and Punishment* have an unmistakable Dickensian feeling (compare the scenes between father and daughter in *Little Dorrit*); Jingle's stagecoach journey in *Pickwick Papers* is a remarkable anticipation of Joycean stream-of-consciousness; the Circumlocution Office in *Little Dorrit* and the laby-rinthine Jarndyce case in *Bleak House* are a stunning precedent of Kafka's *The Trial.*

Of course, neither artist is without his faults. What is remarkable is the similarity of their faults: an inability to create well-rounded female charac-ters (perhaps relating to an innate misogyny in both and difficulties in their own lives with women); a tendency to sentimentality, melodrama and narcissistic self-pity. Chaplin sometimes goes down on his knees to make you laugh, or cry. Dickens summons up an armoury of biblical effusions when he wants to wring your heart. 'Only a heart of stone,' said Oscar Wilde about the death of Dickens's Little Nell, 'could read it without laughing.' Film critics have also been derisive about the final close-up of Charlie in *City Lights* (1931), when the blind girl recognises that her benefactor is a tramp, or the death of Calvero in *Limelight* (1952). Both seem occasionally too frenetic about wringing the heart of a society which has, in the past, been unfeeling to them. It becomes a sort of social revenge — they want too much to make society weep for having made them weep. Critics would say they see life too much in terms of black and white. Dickens finds infinite gradation within the colour black, very little within white, and that is almost the range of his palette; Chaplin's one colour film is a flop.

Yet these vices are inseparable from their virtues and, indeed, in the final analysis, completely subsumed by them. They do not aspire to the analytical complexity of a George Eliot or a Henry James, in one case, or an Antonioni or Resnais, in the other. They are popular artists not intellectuals and their appeal is emotional not analytical, stemming not only from their sympathy for the common man but their identification with him. In fact, Dickens and Chaplin share an intensity of sympathy for the same three persecuted categories of individual: children, criminals and commoners. *Oliver Twist, Great Expectations* and *Little Dorrit* are terrifying studies of how children are at the mercy of the prejudices and bigotries of the adult world; in their different way, so too are Chaplin's *The Kid* (1921) and *A King in New York* (1957). Magwitch in *Great Expectations* and even Bill Sikes on the run in *Oliver Twist* are tremendous revelations of a common humanity that still beats within the heart of men whom society has condemned as criminals; Chaplin finds similar humanity in his depiction of the thieves in *Modern Times* (1936) and, overwhelmingly, in his magnificent characterisation of the Bluebeard-type murderer in *Monsieur Verdoux* (1947). If, as James Agee claimed, Chaplin 'of all comedians, worked most deeply and most shrewdly within a realisation of what a human being is, and is up against',[9] Dickens is similarly perceptive about what, in *Hard Times*, he calls 'society's quiet servants', fighting for survival in a hostile world. Henry James might have found it inconceivable that love can be expressed so deeply by simple Joe Gargery at his forge in *Great Expectations*, but Dickens would not, and nor would Chaplin — see how insistent he is at the end of *The Gold Rush* (1925) that success and wealth have not alienated Charlie from his basic feelings.

Politically, their sympathies are remarkably alike. They are not political theorists, nor men of ideas: they are detached socialists, old-fashioned radicals. Carlyle summed up Dickens's political ideas thus: 'He thinks men ought to be buttered up, and the world made soft and accommodating for them, and all sorts of fellow have turkey for their Christmas dinner.'[10] When *Modern Times* was reissued in 1972, a number of critics (notably George Melly in the *Observer*) made a similar point about Chaplin's politics: that his only proposed alternative to inhumanity is more kindness, and that his social aspirations are basically petit-bourgeois. (When the tramp leads a communist march against unemployment in *Modern Times*, he does so entirely by accident.) Nevertheless, if Lenin was reputedly appalled by Dickens's bourgeois sentiment, George Bernard Shaw claimed that *Little Dorrit* alone had converted him to socialism. If Chaplin's social critique is not much more controversial than the Queen's Christmas Day broadcast, it was considered sufficiently dangerous to have him branded a communist and forced out of America for twenty years. Both men would shrink at the thought of social revolution (look at Dickens's ambivalence to the French Revolution in *A Tale of Two Cities*) and both struggle to reconcile in their minds a contradictory image of the lower classes: on the one hand, miserable and degraded; on the other, noble and dignified. In Dickens, the lot of the poor is sometimes redeemed by good and rich benefactors, like Brownlow in *Oliver Twist* and Jarndyce in *Bleak House*, who help without dirtying their fingernails. As Orwell suggests, there is an air of unreality about these figures: 'Even Dickens must have reflected occasionally that anyone who was so anxious to give his money away would never have acquired it in the first place.'[11] (Actually, Dickens did reflect on this occasionally, as his cynical comment in *Hard Times* shows: 'The Good Samaritan was a bad Economist.') Chaplin is more cynical of such figures. The benefactor in *City Lights*, who, when drunk, treats Charlie like a prince and, when sober, treats him like a pestilential pauper, is viciously satirised. In Chaplin the poor must, in all senses, help themselves.

If Dickens and Chaplin do not want revolution, they are remarkably consistent in their perception of what is wrong with the world. *Hard Times* is an attack on the repression of the human spirit brought on by a mechanistic, materialistic, depersonalised industrial society; *Modern Times* mimics that theme precisely. Both are attacks on the mechanisation of the individual; both see the only release in imagination. Neither of them identifies the forces of law with the forces of good. Dickens has greater contempt for law-administrators than law-breakers (Fagin and company are seen more sympathetically in *Oliver Twist* than the hypocritical workhouse authorities); Chaplin's tramp has a similar running battle with the police and the courts, the two detectives in *Modern Times* being real Dickensian, unfeeling bureaucrats. The Artful Dodger makes the processes of justice look cumbersome and ludicrous in *Oliver Twist*; Verdoux does the same, in a more seriously sardonic way, in *Monsieur Verdoux*.

As both men developed as artists, their visions seemed to grow darker. When Chaplin's tramp in *Modern Times* is threatened by a machine, his days are truly numbered, for how can you argue with or outwit a machine? A similar depersonalisation is at work in *Little Dorrit*, notably in a Circumlocution Office that is strangling the whole country in red tape. Their contempt for politicians increases; their concept of city as prison becomes obsessive; and their vision of evil intensifies. Dickens always had such a vision, as the character of Orlick in *Great Expectations* or the infinite variety of wickedness in *Bleak House* exemplifies, and critics like Lionel Trilling have seen the madness and malevolence in Dickens's world, often attacked for melodramatic excess, as being made terrifyingly credible by modern history and by the rampages of megalomaniacs like Hitler and Mussolini on the world stage. For someone with so Dickensian a temperament as Chaplin, it would be inevitable that he too would be drawn to the evil of the modern world in his work. Chaplin's later work is fired by his anger at the absurd horrors of Nazism in *The Great Dictator* (1940), by a post-atomic-bomb despair at indiscriminate mass slaughter in *Monsieur Verdoux*, by a disgust at the lynch-mob mentality of McCarthyist America in *A King in New York*.

Both Chaplin and Dickens found their equilibrium through comedy, and through the creation of character. Their genius made a singular contribution to the recognition of their respective popular entertainments as art forms. However, both ultimately transcend even a recognition of their artistic greatness. Dickens and Chaplin belong not simply to art, but to history, and to everyone.

Mark Twain and John Ford

Mark Twain's real name was Samuel Clemens; John Ford's real name was Sean O'Feeney. Two names: dual personalities. Clemens played the role of Mark Twain, the celebrity writer, crackerbarrel philosopher and humorist. O'Feeney played the part of John Ford, celebrity film director, the gruff, instinctive professional who was equally the scourge of interfering studio bosses as of theorising critics ('I'm a hard-nosed director; I get a script — if I like it, I'll do it').[12] Both Twain and Ford cultivated a strong streak of anti-intellectualism which was partly a blind (there are potent allusions to *Hamlet* in both Twain's *Huckleberry Finn* and Ford's *My Darling Clementine*, for example), but also a genuine dimension of their 'ornery' individualism, extrovert Americanism, and of their hostility to Eastern snobbery. Paradoxically, no American writer or American director has been the subject of greater or more intense speculation about their work. 'All modern American literature,' said Ernest Hemingway in *The Green Hills of Africa* (1935), 'came from one book by Mark Twain called *Huckleberry Finn* ... There was nothing before. There has been nothing as good since.' 'There's one general premise,' said director Sidney Lumet in a *Films and Filming* interview (October 1964), 'almost anything that any of us has done you can find in a John Ford film.'

Both Twain and Ford cultivated a manner of irreverence and liked to see themselves as entertainers, not artists. Orson Welles described Ford as 'a poet, a comedian — not for women, of course, but for men'.[13] Welles's characterisation of Ford as a man's director seems equally applicable to Twain as a writer: neither of them gets much beyond an idealised maternity in their portrayals of women, and they scarcely have created a single memorable female character between them. They were poets because of the way their work transcends its immediate realism into a universal statement about the relationship between man and Nature: one needs only think of the symbolic dimension Twain instils into the Mississippi river and Ford into Monument Valley without either seeming to strain for poetic effect. They are comedians, for Twain's work is rarely without a satirical or ironic dimension (his attempt to master gun and horse in his experience of the Wild West in *Roughing It* is a masterly exercise in humorous self-deprecation), and Ford's films function best with a strong influx of humour. 'I did it for my own amusement,' 'I tried to make the character as humorous as possible' are common refrains in his published interview with Peter Bogdanovich: by common consent, his overtly serious movies, like *The Informer* and *The Fugitive*, are the ones that wear least well. This sense of play in both their works often comes out in the form of digression and episodic structures — a sense of the artist enjoying and indulging himself rather than submitting to the severe formal rigours of 'art'.

Yet, in both cases, the humour often has a darker edge to it. Twain's satirical irony in *Pudd'nhead Wilson* only just keeps ahead of the story's appalling tragedies. Before starting his masterpiece, *The Searchers* (1956), Ford commented: 'I should like to do a tragedy, the most serious in the world, that turned into the ridiculous.'[14] The comedy in their work seems to conceal as much as it expresses — perhaps a basically tragic vision of life. Mary Astor thought Ford 'a dark personality' when she worked with him on *The Hurricane* (1937), and readers of Twain's final works, such as *The Man that Corrupted Hadleyburg* (1900) and his treatise *What is Man?* (1906), could hardly fail to come to the same conclusion.

Ostensibly, the works of Twain and Ford that have most in common are Twain's *Life on the Mississippi* (1883) and Ford's *Judge Priest* (1934) and *Steamboat Round the Bend* (1935), in both of which Will Rogers adopts a persona that is very like Twain's — philosophical, mischievous, comical but fundamentally wise. In the latter film, Rogers plays a steamboat captain, just as Twain was a pilot of steamboats before the Civil War: indeed, Ford once told Lindsay Anderson that 'I want to be a tugboat captain.'[15] However, a more relevant fundamental and wide-ranging comparison would be with the works that are the highest achievements of both men — Twain's *The Adventures of Huckleberry Finn* (1884) and *Pudd'nhead Wilson* (1894), and Ford's *The Searchers* and *The Man Who Shot Liberty Valance* (1962).

Firstly, all of them raise the question of Twain's and Ford's attitude to race. For a long time, certainly prior to the American Civil War (in which he had sided with the Confederates), Twain's attitude to the Negro was strictly in accordance with his Southern upbringing. He assumes an instinctive superiority on the part of the white man, though as his auto-biography reveals, this did not preclude friendly relationships with the Negro. By the time of *Huckleberry Finn*, however, he is beginning to worry about racism. That great moment in the novel when Huck tears up the letter to Miss Watson, telling her where her runaway slave Jim is, is a triumph of conscience over convention, of instinct above social law. But there is a certain ambivalence about Huck's cry when he tears up the letter ('All right, then, I'll *go* to hell'):[16] he still thinks he is doing wrong even when his feeling for Jim overrides his obedience to social prejudice. The racial theme of *Pudd'nhead Wilson* is handled with remarkable candour, but in that novel too, there is an element of ambiguity. On the one hand, we have Tom's soulful 'Why were niggers *and* whites made? What crime did the uncreated first nigger commit that the curse of birth was decreed for him?'[17] — a sentiment somewhat modified by Tom's own self-pity. On the other hand, we have Roxana's attack on her good-for-nothing son, an attack that seems part character, part Twain: 'It's de nigger in you, dat's what it is. Thirty-one parts of you is white, en only one part nigger, en dat po' little part is yo' soul. 'Tain't wuth savin', 'tain't wuth totin' out in a shovel en throwin' in de gutter.'[18] Twain might have campaigned against the persecution of Chinese immigrants, but his Negro characters seldom rise above the level of Noble Savage, and the critic Leslie Fiedler has accused Twain of a real hatred of Indians.[19]

Ford's films reveal a similar ambivalence. The cute cavortings of Stepin' Fetchit in a film like *Judge Priest* are embarrassing to watch nowadays. In films like *Stagecoach* (1939) and his cavalry trilogy — *Fort Apache* (1948), *She Wore a Yellow Ribbon* (1949), *Rio Grande* (1950) — the Indians are mainly used either as a symbol of chaos, or as Noble Savages who would benefit from a dose of paternal white kindness. In *My Darling Clementine*, there is an uncomfortable scene when Wyatt Earp roughs up Indian Joe, who has run riot after getting drunk, and demands to know why Joe has been allowed out of the reservation. As Robin Wood comments astutely on this scene: 'in racial terms the scene is obviously very unpleasant, but in mythic terms very meaningful, civilisation conceived as demanding the rigorous suppression of the untamed forces Indian Joe represents'.[20] Like Twain, however, Ford's attitudes begin to modify and deepen as he moves into the later phase of his career. Like *Pudd'nhead Wilson*, *The Searchers* boldly confronts the theme of miscegenation (less boldly, so does Ford's 1961 film, *Two Rode Together*). *Sergeant Rutledge* (1960) is an overtly sympathetic study of a Negro soldier, though within very conservative boundaries. In *Cheyenne Autumn* (1964), it is the cavalry who whoop like savages and it is the Indians who are the civilised people. Like the Okies in *The Grapes of Wrath*, they have been deprived of their land by decisions taken far away by faceless bureaucrats.

The works of Twain and Ford that seem to have most in common are *Pudd'nhead Wilson* and *The Man Who Shot Liberty Valance*. Both have a significant racial sub-theme: in Ford's film, this is represented by Woody Strode's role as Pompey, John Wayne's Negro 'boy' who drifts over to attend James Stewart's classes on the American Constitution but cannot remember the part about all men being created equal. Both are detective stories of an individual and eccentric kind, with a twist in the dénouement. Pudd'nhead not only unmasks a killer but a Negro through his fingerprinting expertise in the trial; in Ford's film, the senator discovers that, contrary to legend, he is not the man who shot Liberty Valance.

The closest connection between the two works, however, is in the progress of the major characters — Wilson in Twain, James Stewart's Ranse Stoddard in *Liberty Valance* — neither of whom seems to be the main character when the narratives begin. Both Wilson and Stoddard are dudes from the East who are treated as outsiders and even ridiculed by the townspeople at the outset of the story: hence Wilson's nickname, and Stoddard's nickname of 'Pilgrim'. By the end, however, they have moved centre-stage and it is the old Westerners who are left seeming old-fashioned and slow-witted. Pudd'nhead's triumph in the courtroom — 'for all his sentences were golden now, all were marvellous' — leads to a recognition on the part of the townspeople that Wilson has resigned from the position of pudd'nhead but that 'we're elected'.[21] Similarly, Stoddard's movement from newpaper office to schoolroom to political eminence is a progress which shows his integration into the community, his movement from outsider to leader, and the triumph of literacy, law and civilisation. In the last twenty minutes, *Liberty Valance* is a political film, not a western, and the most powerful instrument becomes the courtroom gavel, not a gun. Intriguingly, however, what is equally true of both works is that, as this progress begins to take shape, the spirit of the works sours; the tone grows more bitter; the faces of the two authors seem to cloud over. What is staring both of them in the face is the twentieth century — and neither of them likes what he sees. Both Ford and Twain are men whose hearts are with the pioneers and with the adventurist America of the nineteenth century.

The penultimate sentence of *Huckleberry Finn* is: 'But I reckon I got to light out for the Territory ahead of the rest, because Aunt Sally she's going to adopt me and civilise me and I can't stand it.'[22] One's mind flashes forward to two key moments in Ford. There is the doctor's comment on the escape of Ringo and Dallas at the end of *Stagecoach*: 'Well, they're saved from the blessings of civilisation.' Even more strikingly, there is the great, much discussed ending of *The Searchers*, when Ethan Edwards (John Wayne) chooses not to follow the people into the protective bosom of home and family but turns back towards the wilderness as the door closes. Like Twain, Ford's darkening vision of America was especially linked to his developing concern with racial injustice and his disturbing second thoughts about the encroachments of civilisation on freedom. 'Our ancestors would be bloody ashamed if they could see us today,' said Ford in an interview towards the end of his life.[23] One might compare that with the very last entry in Pudd'nhead Wilson's calendar: 'It was wonderful to find America, but it would have been more wonderful to miss it.'[24]

Graham Greene and Alfred Hitchcock

Graham Greene's connection with the cinema dates from the 1930s when he was amongst the best of our film critics, his most notorious review bankrupting the magazine for which he worked because of his libellous remarks about Shirley Temple. His novels were quickly turned into films and, as he has wryly noted, unquestionably the worst films were made by the best directors. Fritz Lang personally apologised to Greene for his version of *The Ministry of Fear* (1943); John Ford's film of Greene's *The Power and the Glory*, entitled *The Fugitive*, is, by general repute, one of the worst films of his career; Joseph Mankiewicz's film of *The Quiet American* (1957), to Greene's utter chagrin, reversed the anti-American theme of the novel; George Cukor's *Travels with my Aunt* (1972) was, in Greene's estimation, 'intolerably bad'; and Greene's response after seeing Otto Preminger's bedevilled production of *The Human Factor* (1979) was to 'thank God Preminger did not make *A Burnt-Out Case*'. The only director he fully trusted was Carol Reed, with whom he worked on *The Fallen Idol* (1947), *The Third Man* (1949) and *Our Man in Havana* (1960). Surprisingly, and certainly unfashionably in the 1930s, Greene had a poor opinion of Alfred Hitchcock. In his review of Hitchcock's *The Secret Agent* (based on Somerset Maugham's *Ashenden*) in the *Spectator* of 15 May 1936, he complained of Hitchcock's 'inadequate sense of reality ... he has no sense of life. His films consist of a series of small "amusing" melodramatic situations ... they mean nothing: they lead to nothing.' Although he later confessed to a liking for Hitchcock's *Notorious*, he basically held to this opinion. In 1958, when Hitchcock tried to acquire the rights to *Our Man in Havana*, Greene refused to sell them to him: 'I felt the book just wouldn't survive his touch.'[25]

Just as Greene had close contact with the film world, Hitchcock also had an interesting relationship with the world of literature. As well as adapting for the screen writers like Conrad, Maugham and O'Casey, he also collaborated with such esteemed authors as Thornton Wilder on *Shadow of a Doubt*, John Steinbeck on *Lifeboat*, Raymond Chandler on *Strangers on a Train* (1951) and Brian Moore on *Torn Curtain* (1966). François Truffaut has compared Hitchcock's films with 'such artists of anxiety as Kafka, Dostoevsky and Poe'[26] but the literary comparison that always insistently suggests itself is that with Graham Greene, in spite of Greene's disclaimers. It might be that Greene saw the comparison with himself at an early age and wished to distance himself and the critics from it: we know that, acknowledging the profound influence of Conrad on his early fiction, Greene dedicatedly refused to read Conrad for the next thirty years. But the Hitchcock comparison will not go away.

Firstly, their development is rather similar. During the 1930s, both made their respective reputations with quirky, characterful explorations of British crime. Greene establishes his reputation as a master with *Brighton Rock* (1938); Hitchcock confirms his status as Britain's finest director with *The Thirty-nine Steps* (1935) and *The Lady Vanishes* (1938). During the 1940s and 1950s, they both acquire celebrity status and their work expands into an international phase. Greene explores exotic locations and political themes in works like *The Heart of the Matter* (1948) and *The Quiet American*

(1955); Hitchcock ranges across the American psyche in films like *Notorious*, *Rear Window* (1954) and *Vertigo*. In the 1970s, both revisit the England of their past, recreating a kind of anachronistic thriller in the style of the 1930s but tinged with a modern harshness — in Greene's case *The Human Factor* (1976), in Hitchcock's case *Frenzy* (1972).

Three other minor parallels between them can be mentioned. Graham Greene was fond of listing some of his novels as 'entertainments' (that is, novels with a spanking combination of plot, melodrama and suspense, rather than a more serious purpose): it was not until 1970 and *Travels with my Aunt* that he discontinued this practice. It would not be hard to divide Hitchcock's work in a similar way — the 'entertainments' including most of the British films and American works like *To Catch a Thief* (1955), *The Trouble with Harry* (1956) and *North by Northwest* (1959), the serious including more sombre psychological explorations like *I Confess* (1953), *The Wrong Man* (1957) and *Vertigo*. Graham Greene relaxes in his short stories; Hitchcock relaxes in his short TV films; nevertheless, in both cases, characteristic themes and flourishes emerge. Finally, one might add that the development of their reputations has been similar. Patronisingly referred to as 'old masters' by the critical establishment, there is still the nagging sense of a certain underestimation, of being taken for granted, of their greatness and intensity being ignored. If Hitchcock is the greatest director never to win a directing Oscar, Graham Greene is the greatest modern novelist never to win the Nobel Prize.

There are other connections one could mention and develop. *The Third Man* has at least two similarities to Hitchcock. There is a situation in which the hero is required to give an unexpected lecture, as in *The Thirty-nine Steps* (Greene's treatment is certainly closer to the moment in the Hitchcock film than in the Buchan novel). Also the use of the Great Wheel in Vienna as a metaphor for the wheel of modern history against which the individual looks small and puny has a symbolic similarity to Hitchcock's use of the windmill in his anti-Nazi melodrama *Foreign Correspondent*. Greene writes train novels, like *Stamboul Train* (1932); Hitchcock makes train movies, like *Strangers on a Train*. Greene has a 'blinding terror of birds';[27] Hitchcock makes *The Birds*. Greene is much inspired by his dreams;[28] several Hitchcock films, like *Spellbound* (1945) and *Marnie* (1964), are intensely dream-like. Greene's anti-Americanism is certainly more corrosive than Hitchcock's, but in Hitchcock films — *Notorious* and *North by Northwest*, for instance — one can sense a Greene-like critique of the secret service and a fear of the kind of global conspiracy that renders the individual helpless. Greene's political sensibilities are more radical and finely tuned than Hitchcock's, and his nose for the next political trouble-spot is unrivalled ('when I hear that Graham is going off to visit some part of the globe,' said Alec Guinness jokingly, 'I will avoid the place like the plague because that means that a revolution or a war is bound to break out there soon').[29] But Hitchcock's political films are a sub-genre of their own that might require closer attention — the two versions of *The Man Who*

Knew Too Much (1934 and 1956), *Sabotage* (1937), *Foreign Correspondent,
Lifeboat, Torn Curtain* (a strange Faustian allegory of American meddling
abroad, made at the time of the Vietnam War) and his account of the
Cuban missile crisis, *Topaz* (1969). Also some of their dramatic situations
are similar. Donald Spoto has usefully compared *Shadow of a Doubt* with
Brighton Rock,[30] suggesting that Hitchcock's heroine, Charlie, and Green's
heroine, Rose, are similar characters — untempted and untried individuals
forced to undergo a moral education by confronting a 'double' figure,
Hitchcock's Uncle Charlie and Greene's Pinkie, who are both 'guiltless'
killers, at once demons and lost souls. An equally potent parallel to *Brighton Rock* is *Strangers on a Train*. Hitchcock's Bruno has all of Pinkie's
puritanism and instinctive equation of sexuality and evil; and the film
shares the novel's metaphor of the fairground as a potential site of libidi-
nous chaos.

Above all, there are two fundamental parallels between Greene and
Hitchcock. The first is that, in their respective fields, they are incomparable story-tellers. For Hitchcock, the *raison d'être* of the cinema is the
telling of stories. One of the mysteries of Greene on the screen is: why are
his novels so compulsively readable, yet the films of these novels so listless
and lacking in narrative vitality? Greene believes it is because 'one cannot
tell a story from the single point of view of one character in a film as one
can in a novel. You cannot look through the eyes of one character in a
film.'[31] Because of this, he believes, coherence and concentration are dissi-
pated. The ironic thing about this comment is that this is precisely the kind
of filming of which Hitchcock is a master. The first third of *Psycho*, the
first two-thirds of *Vertigo*, the whole of *Rear Window* are the greatest
examples of 'single point of view' filming in the history of the cinema.

The second fundamental connection is their Roman Catholicism. One
scarcely need mention how strong is the religious current that runs through
Graham Greene novels like *The Power and the Glory, The Heart of the
Matter* and *The End of the Affair* (1951), so strong that when Greene felt he
ought to drop God from his novels, Evelyn Waugh strongly counselled him
against it ('It would be like P.G. Wodehouse dropping Jeeves'). Hitchcock
also was a deeply religious man, and this shows in the imagery at moments
of great intensity in some of his films. For example, one thinks of the
moment in *The Wrong Man* when Manny (Henry Fonda) prays for relief
from his troubles, and at this moment, the real criminal 'miraculously'
steps forward to superimpose his presence on Manny's face (as Truffaut
said: 'it seems unlikely to me that anyone but a Catholic would have
handled Henry Fonda's prayer scene as you did').[32] There is the terrifying
appearance of the nun that causes the guilty woman to fall to her death at
the end of *Vertigo*, and whose words seal the theme of Hitchcock's supreme
masterpiece — 'God have mercy on us.' The whole dramatic structure of *I
Confess* is built around the confidentiality of the confessional, which seems
slowly and perversely to be tightening a noose around a priest's neck. If, in
general terms, one had to define the influence of Catholicism on the work

of Greene and Hitchcock, one might echo Truffaut's feeling that Hitchcock's work is 'strongly permeated by the concept of original sin, and of man's guilt', and echo Gavin Lambert's feeling that Greene has a Catholic 'fascination with the ignoble'.[33] Both artists see the demon of sex as the root of all evil but also the root of all that is most tantalising, intoxicating, exciting in life. Greene's choice of an epigraph to all his novels were these lines from the Robert Browning poem 'Bishop Blougram's Apology':[34]

Our interest's on the dangerous edge of things.
The honest thief, the tender murderer,
The superstitious atheist, demi-rep
That loves and saves her soul in new French books —
We watch while these in equilibrium keep
The giddy line midway.

Murder, theft, danger, religion, love, vertiginous morality — the lines, with their perverse tone and tantalising emotional range, could equally serve as an epigraph for Hitchcock's films.

Perhaps the works of each that are closest to each other, however, are the nearly contemporaneous *Our Man in Havana* and *North by Northwest.* They are both light in tone, with darker colourations, and both about ordinary men in increasingly extraordinary and dangerous situations. In Greene's *Our Man in Havana,* a vacuum-cleaner salesman, Wormold, is exploited by MI5, represented in the film by Noël Coward; in *North by Northwest,* Roger Thornhill is exploited by the CIA, represented by Leo G. Carroll ('FBI, CIA — we're all part of the same alphabet soup'). For financial reasons, Wormold prolongs his deception as a spy by submitting drawings of suspicious military installations that are actually vacuum-cleaners. For survival and romantic reasons, Thornhill continues his deception by assuming the identity of someone who does not exist but who *does* have dandruff. Curiously, Carol Reed's film of Greene's novel was rather heavy and humourless, whereas Hitchcock's film was spry and sparkling. Contary to Greene's view, the Hitchcock touch was precisely what the film of *Our Man in Havana* needed. But in denying this, Greene was characteristically, enigmatically, still refusing to accept what the evidence now overwhelmingly suggests: that Greene and Hitchcock were made for each other.

Joseph Conrad and Orson Welles

It is well known that, prior to *Citizen Kane,* Orson Welles's original idea for his feature film directing début was an adaptation of Conrad's *Heart of Darkness.* What has not been perceived is the pervasive influence of *Heart of Darkness* on the whole structure and idea of *Citizen Kane.* Welles has transferred the Conradian themes to an American context (as Coppola was to do, most ingeniously, in his 1979 movie, *Apocalypse Now*), but the shadow of Conrad's novella over the film is quite remarkable.

Both Welles's film and Conrad's story are about the deaths of men who have turned themselves into kings, into self-proclaimed gods. In the shooting script of *Citizen Kane*, the approach to Xanadu on the night of Kane's death is described thus: 'The dominating note is one of almost exaggerated tropical lushness, hanging limp and despairing — Moss, moss, moss. Angkor Wat, the night the last king died.'[35] In the film, after the election defeat that signals Kane's disillusionment with democracy, Leland (Joseph Cotten) ironically suggests that Kane should 'sail away to a desert island and lord it over the monkeys': it is an image strongly reminiscent of Conrad. A shot of Orson Welles's Kane in his tent during a party — face half in shadow, bald skull gleaming like ivory in the dark — is similar to one's mental image of Kurtz in his hut in the Conrad story, both men listening to the beat of drums outside.

Kane and Kurtz are both men of limitless but frustrated potential. Kane has infinite promise, ambition and riches that refuse to work for him or satisfy him; Kurtz could have been a great writer, politician, philosopher. Both men are disappointed with the world they find and compensate by building their own isolated monarchies. Both are damned or deified according to the point of view of the person who is speaking, the multiplicity of voices and narrators on the subject of the main character being a feature of both works (in Conrad's novella, we have interpretations of Kurtz from Marlow, the Harlequin, Kurtz's fiancée, among others; in Welles's film, Kane is seen through the eyes of Bernstein, Thatcher, Leland, Susan Alexander). Both works are dominated by the meaning of the dying god's last words, which are felt to hold the key to their existence. In *Heart of Darkness*, they are 'the horror, the horror'; in *Citizen Kane*, it is 'Rosebud'.

Finally, the structure of both works is remarkably similar. Both are built around the concept of interior journeys. The search for Kurtz in *Heart of Darkness* is also a search for understanding Kurtz, bringing enlightenment out of the jungle. The search for 'Rosebud' in *Citizen Kane* is also a search for the explanation of Kane's character, bringing truth from out of the shadows. In both cases, these become metaphysical journeys, a movement away from realism and towards myth — towards Kurtz as the savage god who must be sacrificed; towards Kane as Kubla Khan in his own Xanadu.

Although Welles's main literary adaptations for the screen have been of Shakespeare and Kafka, the literary spirit whom one senses most behind his work is Conrad. One can see it in small details at first, like Welles's symbolic use of the sea, in *Lady from Shanghai* (1948), *Othello* and *The Immortal Story* (1968), which is so fundamental a symbol — of Nature, of Fate, of Eternity — in Conrad's work. One can also sense a kinship in the accumulation of comparable figures and images: the black-clad, doom-laden, cackling harpy figures in the trial scene of *Lady from Shanghai* who seem so much like those ominous women knitting black wool outside the Company's office in *Heart of Darkness*; Conrad's Harlequin figure in *Heart of Darkness* and Dennis Weaver's unnerving 'night man' in Welles's *Touch of Evil* (1958), who both seem atmospheric additions more than narrative necessities, in works totally dominated by pervasive nocturnal imagery out of synchronisation with a strict chronological realism. One can even sense a kinship in the personalities of Conrad and Welles themselves, not so much in their characters as in their artistic situations: both giant exiles, compelled to create away from the countries that had nurtured them, both creating a kind of unique international language forged from their individual vacuums, both operating uneasily in the commercial world (Conrad tries and fails to sell a story to *Tit Bits*, Welles keeps going — and growing — through advertising sherry and lager). Welles seems to accept his fate ('I have always felt isolated, I believe that any good artist feels isolated');[36] for Conrad, isolation is not only his main artistic theme, but the fundamental fact of man's tragic existence ('Who knows what true loneliness is — not the conventional word, but the naked terror? ... No human being could bear a steady view of moral solitude without going mad').[37]

The main analogies between Conrad and Welles can be grouped under three headings: style, characterisation and theme. Stylistically, both make imaginative use of fallible narrators, like Marlow in *Heart of Darkness*, a language teacher in *Under Western Eyes*, O'Hara in *Lady from Shanghai*, the multiple narrators of *Citizen Kane*, all of whom reveal as much about themselves through their narration as about the ostensible events they describe. Both also have distinctive, personal languages. Welles's elaborate visual style, his inability to make one forget the presence of the camera, corresponds to the kind of verbal circumlocutions characteristic of Conrad: in both cases one is aware not only of the experience depicted or described, but of the particular consciousness through which it is being filtered. In both cases, the style has been dismissed as empty rhetoric, Welles, accused of a flashy flamboyance out of all proportion to his subject-matter, H.G. Wells accusing Conrad of writing 'despicably ... so as to mask and dishonour the greatness that is in him'.[38] But Conrad's style, like Welles's, reflects with artistic exactitude his sense of life. It is his means of deflecting by irony, of subduing by stoicism, a gigantic despair bubbling away in his subconscious which would engulf him utterly if allowed to rise to the surface. 'Droll thing life is,' says Marlow in *Heart of Darkness*, 'that mysterious arrangement of merciless logic for a futile purpose.'[39] It is the ironic tone that keeps the tragic vision at arm's length, as it does also when Marlow sees those disembodied heads staked out in front of Kurtz's hut and his convoluted description so eloquently conveys the sense of a man attempting to adjust to and play down the horror of something that has scared him out of his wits. Welles's restless camerawork in a film like *Touch of Evil* has something of the same implication, the *mise-en-scène* corresponding to what Welles calls 'my vision of the world; it reflects that sort of vertigo, uncertainty, lack of stability, that *mélange* of movement and tension that is our universe'.[40] Both styles give one the sensation of spiralling down into an abyss.

In terms of characterisation and theme, the similarities are striking.

Neither Conrad nor Welles shows any interest in the psychology of women. F.R. Leavis observes correctly of Conrad: 'About his attitude towards women there is perceptible, all the way through his literary career, something of the gallant simple sailor.'[41] With similar accuracy, Robin Wood observes of Welles that women 'are almost never central to his films and their roles are usually passive; the real tensions are between men'.[42] What are these tensions? There is the situation of the innocent who crosses the border into an unfamiliar, frightening and guilty world. Marlow, Razumov in *Under Western Eyes*, O'Hara in *Lady from Shanghai*, Vargas in *Touch of Evil* all come into the category, and are tainted by that contact, revealed in such details as Marlow's blood-stained socks in *Heart of Darkness* as he gets nearer to the source of evil, and Vargas's being covered in slime in *Touch of Evil* as he descends to Quinlan's level. Both are touched by evil. Both Conrad and Welles are fascinated by the situation of the 'double', what the critic Douglas Hewitt in his book on Conrad defined as 'the recurrent situation of the ostensibly "good" man who is confronted by a "double" whom he cannot repudiate and who makes him aware of evil or equivocal qualities in himself which he would rather not see'.[43] In Conrad's *Lord Jim*, this connection exists between Lord Jim and Gentleman Brown when, in that great confrontation between them and to the torment of the hero, there runs through the rough talk of the latter 'a vein of subtle reference to their common blood, an assumption of common experience; a sickening assumption of common guilt, of secret knowledge that was like a bond of their mind and hearts'.[44] In the similar confrontations between Marlow and Kurtz in *Heart of Darkness*, or the serene d'Hubert and the ferocious Feraud in *The Duel*, a hero seems to confront his satanic opposite, an adversary who might actually be revealing a suppressed side of himself: what Marlow in *Heart of Darkness* calls 'the fascination of the abomination'.[45] Welles's films often follow the same pattern. The demonic spells cast by Quinlan over Vargas in *Touch of Evil*, Iago over Othello in *Othello*, Bannister over O'Hara in *Lady from Shanghai* are also a recognition by the heroes of a potential darkness within themselves as they feel their antagonists' dreadful attraction. One might add to this list Welles's characterisation of Harry Lime in *The Third Man* and his impact on his simple and staid friend, Holly Martins (Joseph Cotten). Lime is the suppressed Dionysiac side of Martins's inhibited personality, representing an outlawed vitality which Martins both envies and fears and a temptation to irresponsible licence that is to be rooted out in an exciting and symbolically appropriate final confrontation between the two men in a sewer.

The writer of *The Third Man*, Graham Greene, used the following Conrad idea as epigraph to his novel *The Human Factor*: 'I only know that he who forms a tie is lost. The germ of corruption has entered into his soul.' Conrad's 'germ of corruption' is the equivalent of Welles's 'touch of evil' (indeed, in *Touch of Evil* we see Akim Tamiroff's character quite literally forming a tie, with which he is later to be strangled). Conrad believed that the world rested basically on the idea of fidelity, but the theme to which he obsessively returns is that of betrayal: betrayal of one's country (*The Secret Agent*), betrayal of one's friends (even Marlow believes he has let Kurtz down in *Heart of Darkness*), betrayal of oneself (*Lord Jim*). Perhaps the greatest moment in the whole of Conrad is the moment, in *Under Western Eyes*, when Razumov's uneasy justification of why he must surrender the anarchist Haddin to the police is followed immediately by the one word 'betray': almost a jump-cut from the conscious to the subconscious, from rationalisation to conscience. The whole future development of the novel is in that single moment. By way of comparison, one might note that the strongest, most memorable moments in Welles are acts of betrayal — the shooting of Quinlan by his best friend Menzies in *Touch of Evil*; the betrayal of Harry Lime by his best friend in *The Third Man*; the rejection of Falstaff by his closest companion, the King, in *Chimes at Midnight*; the realisation of Othello that his only trusted confidant, Iago, is the man working hardest for his destruction. *Lady from Shanghai* is an orgy of betrayal from start to finish; one might say that Charles Foster Kane exemplifies self-betrayal every bit as much as Conrad's Lord Jim or Razumov. There is a strong streak of nihilism in both artists. The face they show to the world is very different, for Welles's bright acknowledgement of the world's guilt contrasts with Conrad's consistent premonition of catastrophe, life felt as a 'dangerous walk on a thin crust of barely cooled lava which at any moment might crack and let the unwary sink into fiery depths'.[46] Basically, however, Welles's decadence and Conrad's despair are the two sides of the same coin.

Notes

1. Peter Wollen, *Signs and Meaning in the Cinema* (Thames & Hudson, 1st edn 1969), p. 115.

2. Robin Wood, *Hitchcock's Films* (Tantivy, 1965) and *Howard Hawks* (Secker & Warburg, 1968).

3. Raymond Durgnat, *Films and Feelings* (Faber, 1967), p. 19.

4. Leonard Bernstein, *The Unanswered Question* (Harvard University Press, 1976), p. 3.

5. Charles Chaplin, *My Autobiography* (Bodley Head, 1964), p. 26.

6. Arnold Kettle, *An Introduction to the English Novel*, vol. 1 (Hutchinson, 1967), p. 117.

7. André Bazin, *What is Cinema*, vol. 2, translated by Hugh Gray (University of California Press, 1971), p. 105.

8. Henry James's most famous negative critique of Dickens is his 1865 review of *Our Mutual Friend* (see *James: Selected Literary Criticism*, edited by Morris Shapira, Heinemann, 1963). F.R. Leavis's strictures on Dickens are to be found in his chapter on *Hard Times* in *The Great Tradition* (1948). With typical controversial belligerence, Leavis was later to revise his assessment in Dickens's favour, without acknowledging his earlier error and attacking critics for holding views on Dickens that were remarkably similar to those he had previously held himself. See F.R. Leavis and Q.D. Leavis, *Dickens the Novelist* (Chatto & Windus, 1970).

9. *Agee on Film*, vol. 1 (Peter Owen, 1963), p. 9.

10. George Ford, *Dickens and his Readers*, p. 91. Quoted in Edward Buscombe's interesting article, 'Dickens and Hitchcock', *Screen* (July/October 1970).

11. George Orwell, 'Charles Dickens', *Collected Essays* (Secker & Warburg, 1961), p. 35.

12. Peter Bogdanovich, *John Ford* (Studio Vista, 1967), pp. 99-100.

13. *Interviews with Film Directors*, edited by Andrew Sarris (Avon Books, 1967), p. 533.

14. Joseph McBride and Michael Wilmington, *John Ford* (Secker & Warburg, 1974), p. 147.

15. Quoted in Andrew Sarris's *The John Ford Movie Mystery* (Secker & Warburg, 1976), p. 12.

16. Mark Twain, *The Adventures of Huckleberry Finn* (Penguin, 1966), p. 283.

17. Mark Twain, *Pudd'nhead Wilson* (Penguin, 1969), p. 117.

18. Ibid., p. 157.

19. Leslie A. Fiedler, *The Return of the Vanishing American* (Jonathan Cape, 1968), p. 124.

20. *Theories of Authorship*, edited by John Caughie (Routledge & Kegan Paul, 1981), p. 90.

21. Twain, *Pudd'nhead Wilson*, p. 224.

22. Twain, *Adventures of Huckleberry Finn*, p. 369.

23. Quoted in 'Ford's Lost World' by Jeffrey Richards, *Focus on Film*, no. 6 (Spring 1971), p. 30.

24. Twain, *Pudd'nhead Wilson*, p. 224.

25. Quoted in Quentin Falk's *Travels to Greeneland* (Quartet Books, 1984), p. 145.

26. François Truffaut, *Hitchcock* (Secker & Warburg, 1968), p. 20.

27. Graham Greene, *A Sort of Life* (Bodley Head, 1971), p. 19.

28. Ibid., p. 30.

29. See Gene D. Phillips, *Graham Greene: The Films of his Fiction* (Teachers' College Press, 1974), p. 85.

30. Donald Spoto, *The Art of Alfred Hitchcock* (W.H. Allen, 1977), p. 139.

31. Phillips, *Graham Greene: The Films of his Fiction*, p. 175.

32. Truffaut, *Hitchcock*, p. 266.

33. Gavin Lambert, *On Cukor* (W.H. Allen, 1973), p. 129.

34. Greene, *A Sort of Life*, p. 115.

35. Pauline Kael, Herman J. Mankiewicz, Orson Welles, *The Citizen Kane Book* (Paladin edition, 1974), p. 83.

36. Sarris (ed.), *Interviews with Film Directors*, p. 547.

37. Joseph Conrad, *Under Western Eyes* (Penguin, 1969), p. 40.

38. *Saturday Review*, vol. 81 (16 May 1896), pp. 509-10.

39. Joseph Conrad, *Heart of Darkness*, (Bantam edition, 1960), p. 85.

40. Sarris (ed.), *Interviews with Film Directors*, p. 537.

41. F.R. Leavis, *The Great Tradition*, p. 203.

42. Robin Wood, *Personal Views* (Gordon Fraser, 1976), p. 138.

43. Douglas Hewitt, *Conrad: A Reassessment* (Bowes & Bowes, 1952), p. 127.

44. Joseph Conrad, *Lord Jim* (Penguin, 1969), p. 291.

45. Conrad, *Heart of Darkness*, p. 5.

46. An image used by Bertrand Russell of Conrad in *Portraits from Memory and Other Essays* (1956), p. 85. Quoted in Jocelyn Baines, *Joseph Conrad: A Critical Biography* (Weidenfeld & Nicolson, 1969), p. 448.

Chapter Eight

Adaptation as Criticism: Four Films

When defining his approach to adapting a literary work for film, screenwriter Daniel Taradash said: 'What I try to discover is the basic premise, the basic idea, the basic theme behind a particular piece of writing and to try to dramatise that without making it obvious.'[1] Two things are especially interesting and revealing there: the stress on 'the basic theme'; and the implied emphasis on personal interpretation ('What I try to discover ...'). There is no reference to the novelist's declared intention, nor to fidelity to the original, nor inclusiveness. Clearly, Taradash's conception of the role of the screenwriter is one of interpretation more than reproduction. This is possibly the reason why he has been so successful at streamlining lengthy novels like *From Here to Eternity* and *The Other Side of Midnight* into coherent screen shape.

Taradash's comment underlines what has been a leitmotif of this book — the proposition that the best adaptations of books for film can often best be approached as an activity of literary criticism, not a pictorialisation of the complete novel, but a critical essay which stresses what it sees as the main theme. Like a critical essay, the film adaptation selects some episodes, excludes others, offers preferred alternatives. It focuses on specific areas of the novel, expands or contracts detail, and has imaginative flights about some characters. In the process, like the best criticism, it can throw new light on the original.

The following four films seem to me particularly interesting examples of film adaptation. They bring the novels to vivid visual and dramatic life. But they are also not afraid to kick the novels around, to take liberties with character and structure when they feel they have more convincing readings to offer than the original, to emphasise some features and disregard others. In other words, they go for intensity of illumination more than a shapeless inclusiveness. It is easy to pick on film adaptations for omitting this or that aspect of a favourite novel: it is also often pedantic and pointless, and done in a tone of academic superiority and condescension towards the newer art form that is actually a thin mask for ignorance. The best film adaptations provide a critical gloss on the novels and a freshly imagined cinematic experience that enrich the appreciation of anyone sincerely devoted to film and literature and not insistent on seeing them as antagonistic poles.

Great Expectations

'Imagine,' said David Lean, 'that as the lights go down, a member of the audience strikes up a match in order to light his cigarette. The task of the film-maker is to ensure that that cigarette remains unlit, because the spectator cannot lower his eyes from the screen.'[2]

David Lean is one of the great narrative masters of the screen, specialising in the ability to relate sprawling and complicated stories like *Oliver Twist* (1948), *Dr Zhivago* (1965), and *Ryan's Daughter* (1970), in a single narrative sweep. *Great Expectations* is a good example of his skill and the opening is justly famous. As the first words of the novel are narrated off-screen, a wind seems to blow the pages forward, and there is a cut to a chilling long shot of an isolated figure, Pip, running across the bleak and windy marshes to the graveyard of his parents. Kneeling by their headstone, he is frightened by the sound of the wind as it strikes the creaking branches (very characteristic of Lean to expand an emotional mood by the sound of nature: the young Zhivago's fears are amplified in that way, as is the love scene in *Ryan's Daughter*). As he moves to run away, a black shape from the left of the frame springs out at him, seen by the audience fractionally before Pip sees him. Pip's attempt to scream is silenced by Magwitch's hand over his mouth, the shock effect clinched by the jump from medium shot to close-up, the contrast in the size of the image seeming to magnify Pip's fear. 'At the preview,' recalled Lean, 'when Magwitch appeared from nowhere to grab Pip, the audience leaned back in a wave — when that happened, I knew I was halfway there.'[3] A dramatisation of *Great Expectations*, like a performance of a Bruckner symphony, stands or falls on the shaping of its opening. If it does not have the requisite narrative sense of 'great expectations' — of an extraordinary world in the making — then it will never recover, as Joseph Hardy's sorry 1974 remake amply confirms.

Inevitably, Lean's adaptation has simplified the novel. The film's structure is linear and nothing deflects from Pip's progress, whereas Dickens is a digressor of genius who, without including anything strictly irrelevant in *Great Expectations*, occasionally gives himself room to breathe and relax in comical incident or colourful character. Lean's tactic of simplification is justifiable, in one sense, because it highlights the particular aspects of *Great Expectations* which interest him (and, by contrast, the omissions are equally revealing about what does not concern him). Cavalcanti's version of *Nicholas Nickleby* (1947) might be more inclusive in incident and have its intelligent touches, but the overall effect is rather muffled and cluttered, precisely because there seems no single central idea about the text the film wishes to carry through. Its overall fidelity simply produces a peculiarly faded reproduction. By contrast, Lean's *Great Expectations* offers an incisive critical gloss on certain aspects of Dicken's tale, and is not afraid of tinkering with narrative details.

One of the most striking changes concerns the death of Mrs Gargery. In the film, it is conveyed in one shot of a funeral procession, accompanied by Pip's brief commentary: 'Three months later, my sister became ill ... and was later laid to rest.' In the novel, the violent attack on Mrs Gargery, from which she never recovers, is a mystery that occupies many pages until the assailant is revealed as the malevolent journeyman, Orlick, who is envious of being displaced by Pip as Joe's apprentice. Orlick is a remark-able inspiration of Dickens, a free-ranging agent of chaos, who seems determined to bring down the structure of the novel. The force of the character stems from the sense that he represents a terrifying image of Pip's repressed shadow side, Orlick's attack on Mrs Gargery being an extension of Pip's own repressed wish to avenge himself on his sister (Orlick strikes her with the leg-irons from which Pip had freed Magwitch). One of the strangest developments in the novel is the peculiar attachment the stricken Mrs Gargery forms for Orlick after the attack, an attachment that is very hard to rationalise. Is it a kind of perverted admiration for the extreme contrast the brutal Orlick offers to her husband, the kindly but impotent Joe? It might be remembered that Joe is this way because of his memory of the brutality of his father towards his mother. This whole section of the novel takes it into Freudian areas (before Freud) which is simply not part of Lean's scheme. There is no suggestion in the film that Pip feels guilty about his sister's death, which means inevitably that there is no room for a character like Orlick. Mrs Gargery is primarily of interest to Lean simply because of the pressure she puts on young Pip, and the sympathy which accrues to Pip as a result. She is one of the three women to treat Pip harshly or deceptively (the others being Estella and Miss Havisham) and, in the novel, this pattern contributes to a strange echo of the structure of *Macbeth*, which Pip has been to see in the theatre two nights before he sees Jagger's housekeeper (Estella's mother). Pip, like Macbeth, is given great expectations, which turn out to be false trails: the story is similarly full of ghosts, of the male being manipulated by the female, and with the three women becoming, like the three witches, the complex agents of Pip's doom. None of this finds its way into Lean's film, for whom the grotesque, caricatured, subconscious side of Dickens — perhaps the most original aspect of his art — has no real interest.

Lean basically approaches Dickens as a realist. In a way, the film antici-pates F.R. Leavis's notorious essay on Dickens in *The Great Tradition*, where Leavis rejects the flamboyant aspects of Dickens's art in favour of the concise sobriety of something like *Hard Times*. Lean is similar: he has no room in his film for Trabb's boy, or the eccentric side of Dickens. Also he clearly wishes to make Pip more sympathetic than he is in the novel. There is no room for Orlick because there is no room in Lean's interpreta-tion for that black side of Pip. Similarly, when Joe comes to visit Pip in his London lodgings, the scene which follows is an odd piece of Chaplinesque pantomime that seems to divide sympathy equally between Joe and Pip rather than indict Pip's snobbery: we are equally amused and touched by Pip's social embarrassment as by Joe's social awkwardness. Implicit in this is Lean's criticism of Dickens for being too hard on Pip: Lean has a lot of time for him, perhaps because Lean himself has professed a lifelong feeling of inferiority to intellectuals, and consequently shares some of Pip's fears, awkwardness, and hopes in his strange, new, elevated society. (Lean's sympathy for Pip in that situation might go some way to explaining the film's great popularity at the time, Britain's newly elected socialist government offering the prospect of more social mobility and 'greater expectations' for a wider range of people than ever before.)

If the character of Pip is one of the attractions of the novel for Lean, the other is the theme of romantic repression and sexual frustration, which has run right through Lean's work, from *Brief Encounter* (1945), through *Hobson's Choice* (1954) and *Summer Madness* (1955), to *Ryan's Daughter* and *A Passage to India* (1984). Lean's ostensible suburban sobriety in his films conceals a remarkable perceptiveness and obsession with sexual feelings and with the passion that lurks beneath a surface primness. One of the differences between the film of *Great Expectations* and the novel is the greater emphasis on sexuality than on society. Martita Hunt's Miss Havisham is by far the most powerful creation of the role one has seen because of the weight Lean gives to her and the decaying monument she has erected to her destroyed romantic hopes. Just as Pip is Magwitch's creation, so Estella is hers. A key moment in the film, as in the novel, is that when she sees in Pip's grief for his unsuccessful love of Estella something of her own suffering and dashed romantic expectations (in the novel she says: 'I saw in you a looking glass that showed me what I once felt myself').[4] In the film, everything — Pip's becoming a gentleman, his initial horror at the revelation of Magwitch as benefactor, his softening towards the old man as he begins to suspect that he is Estella's father — is generated by Pip's love for Estella. Lean had just made the greatest love story of the British cinema, *Brief Encounter* — typically a story of unrequited passion. *Great Expectations* is a continuation of that theme. In the film, one feels that Pip's expectations are exclusively romantic, not social.

A discussion of the romantic theme in *Great Expectations* inevitably leads to a discussion of the ending, which has been criticised in both novel and film. The pressure on the nineteenth-century novelist to provide an uplifting ending cannot have been too different from that on the modern filmmaker. Not many novels of the period — exceptions would be *Wuthering Heights* and *Jude the Obscure* — have the courage to follow through the pessimism of their arguments to their logical conclusion. Some, like *Mansfield Park* and *Middlemarch,* have happy endings so unconvincing that they seem to fly in the face of all the other elements that have made the remaining seven-eighths of the novel so interesting. As George Eliot said: 'Conclusions are the weak points of most authors, but some of the fault lies in the very nature of a conclusion, which is at best a negation.'[5] It is well known that in Dickens's original ending of *Great Expectations*, Pip was not to be united with Estella, but was to go abroad and become a clerk to Herbert Pocket. However, on the advice of his friend, the novelist Bulwer Lytton, he changed it to allow the possibility of Pip's future happiness with Estella. The final paragraph now reads: 'I took her hand in mine, and we went out of the ruined place; and, as the morning mists had risen long ago when I first left the forge, so, the evening mists were rising now, and in all the broad expanse of tranquil light they showed to me, I saw no shadow of another parting from her.'

Given the limitations of Pip's subjective view, and the ominousness of shadow elsewhere in the novel, that final phrase ('I saw no shadow of another parting from her') has a subdued and rather tentative sense of affirmation, which clearly represents Dicken's attempt to reconcile the exigencies of the 'happy ending' with aesthetic sense. It is still not very satisfactory. As has been much remarked, if the novel is being narrated in retrospect, with the knowledge that Pip is to win Estella at the end, why is the tone of the novel so mournful, melancholy, and full of self-reproach? The ending that Dickens has contrived negates the whole movement of the narrative and the novel's emotional sense.

Lean comes at the same problem (for truly happy endings are as unusual in his films as they are in Dickens's novels) from a somewhat different angle, and attempts to solve it in a highly ingenious way. Pip is sitting out on the grass with Joe and Joe's new wife, Biddy, and telling Biddy that he will never marry. 'That poor dream, Biddy,' he says, 'has all gone by.' It is an interesting scene because it matches a scene on the grass between young Pip and Biddy much earlier in the film, when Pip has told her of his feelings of social inferiority and hinted at his desire to become a gentleman. His ambition — his 'poor dream', if you like — has been realised, but, as this later scene stresses, it has brought him even more misery. We now hear Pip over the soundtrack resolving to revisit Satis House 'that evening' one last time. As he goes through the gate and ascends the stairs of the old house, he hears voices from the past: it is as if he is retracing the steps of his youth. The voices stop when he opens the door of Miss Havisham's room to see Estella seated there. She is now separated from her husband, Bentley Drummle ('when Mr Jaggers disclosed to Bentley Drummle my true parentage, he no longer wished me to be his wife ...'), and she is settling into the Miss Havisham role of the lonely and disillusioned spinster. But Pip refuses to accept this. In an act of defiance against the ghost of Miss Havisham, he tears down the curtains, letting the sunlight into the room. 'Come with me out into the sunlight,' he says to Estella, and together they run from the house.

The sunlight imagery is very interesting here. 'You're not afraid of a woman who has never seen the sun since you were born?' Miss Havisham has asked the young Pip in their first meeting. Letting in the sunlight at the end is a final exorcism of that fear and the dead hand of Miss Havisham on his life. When he tears down the curtains, the sun's rays strike across

Estella's face in an image that has startling reminiscences of a horror film, as if a mummified figure is being brought to life. It is a reminder of an interesting horror motif in the novel, when Pip compares his relationship with his benefactor, the convict Magwitch, with that of Dr Frankenstein and his monster; 'The imaginary student pursued by the misshapen creature he had impiously made was not more wretched than I, pursued by the creature who had made me . . .'[6] Miss Havisham has created a monster out of Estella, Magwitch a monster out of Pip. For different motives, Magwitch and Miss Havisham both take revenge on the world for their own thwarted ambitions by projecting them on to their adopted children, and, in both cases, the children are twisted and deformed as a result. It is only by letting in the sunlight (in contrast to Miss Havisham's self-imposed gloom and Magwitch's self-protective lurking in shadows) that the holds of these parent figures can at last be lifted.

However, the question one asks of the film's ending is: does David Lean, any more than Dickens, really believe it or intend us to believe it? There are several strange things about the staging of this last scene. Firstly, one can hardly fail to be struck by a sudden break in style. For a film that is relatively subdued and quiet in its presentation of emotion, Pip's defiance, vibrance and assertiveness — plus the sunny imagery and rousing music — is nothing less than a violent switch from realism to melodrama. Also there is a peculiar question-mark about continuity. It is stressed that Pip arrives at the house 'in the evening' and yet, during the scene with Estella, he keeps insisting on coming out 'into the sunlight'. My feeling is that the 'unlikelihood' of this happy ending is precisely the feeling that Lean intended. It becomes self-alienating in the way that Douglas Sirk was to perfect in so many melodramas of the following decade in which he exploited the irony of the happy ending ('It makes the crowd happy. To the few it makes the aporia more apparent').[7] Like so many other characters in Lean, Pip has transformed reality into wish-fulfilment in which he, as a knight in shining armour, can at last irradiate and claim his forlorn and abandoned princess. In other words, the final scene of the film — from the point when Pip enters Miss Havisham's room — is pure dream. It is precisely an imagination, a dramatisation, of the 'poor dream that has all gone by' — the dream he was talking about to Biddy, and which has provided the preface to a final scene of subjective fantasy.

Lean, then, has chosen to concentrate on *Great Expectations* as a romantic rather than social tragedy, and the film as an essay on that theme is an extremely powerful one. Some of the performances — Alec Guinness as the delightful Herbert Pocket, Martita Hunt as the haunted Miss Havisham, Francis L. Sullivan as the sinister Jaggers, Finlay Currie as the imposing Magwitch — are as near definitive as one could hope. The children — Anthony Wager as the young Pip, and Jean Simmons as Estella — are also exceptionally sensitive, and it is a pity that their elder selves are not as well cast. John Mills is never too convincing in his working-class roles, so that the actual transition of Pip to gentleman lacks a sense of development. Valerie Hobson is so much less lively and alluring than the young Jean Simmons that Pauline Kael's observation that 'it's inconceivable one could grow into the other'[8] seems quite justified.

Dickens's social range and his sense of evil are quite outside Lean's world. We see the famous casts of condemned men hanging in Jaggers's office, and Sullivan's splendid performance suggests the cold arrogance of the man, but his powerful symbolic function in the novel — a symbol of the law's dehumanised attitude to life — is not really felt because not enough of the social context is sketched in. Compeyson's evil is only hinted at, and in the film, he tends to play the same role in Magwitch's life as Bentley Drummle does in Pip's: the shadow, the gentleman spoiler, the nightmare obstruction who, at the most inopportune moment, will stand between his rival and what that rival most desires.

Some of the elements are reproduced with great effectiveness. The opening, up until the departure of Magwitch from the narrative (a wonderful shot as he looks round in the boat at Pip, as his face disappears into the shadow), is tremendous. The voices in Pip's head, the emphasis on guilt and fear, the moment when even a cow seems to be speaking a reproach, are imaginatively visualised from the original, dramatising what Dickens describes in the novel as the 'secrecy there is in the young, under terror'.[9] As in the novel, Pip is repeatedly being grabbed and struck in the early stages of the film, and a shot of him around the dinner table, compressed between fearful elders, whose voices are heard off-screen, is an eloquent enough image on the key Dickensian theme of the horrifying intimidation of the child in a frightening adult world.

The critic Richard Winnington commented about the film that one of the things he admired was that it seemed to get the weather right.[10] From the opening wind which blows Pip to that fateful graveyard on that fateful day, from the wind and rain that blows Magwitch to Pip's apartment to reveal his identity, to the draught that will blow out the smouldering log that will roll on to Miss Havisham's dress and consume her in fire, the film's narrative is a kind of continuous wind, with hero and heroine being buffeted by forces and feelings over which they have no control.

The middle section of the film is the weakest, largely because Pip's progress is seen in terms of dancing, fencing, boxing and archery; but there is no real sense of the society in which he moves. A montage of dance, archery, skating and then dance again has a symmetrical structure that eloquently indicates the kind of enchanted but malevolent web that Estella is casting around Pip (she does dance a circle around him at one point). However, Magwitch's reappearance rejuvenates the drama. The death scene is poignantly done. Pip goes into the kind of delirium that afflicts so many characters in Lean's films (Laura in *Brief Encounter*, Nicholson in *The Bridge on the River Kwai*, Lawrence of Arabia, Adela in *Passage to India*). He is certainly in a ripe state for the dream-image finale.

In a generally favourable review, James Agee regretted the 'smooth, middle-distance narrative style which so often merely illustrates the story nicely' instead of a style contorted into something 'much more subjective and more visually expressive'.[11] There is something to be said for that. Lean's pictorialism is imaginative within fairly strict, tasteful bounds: Dickens's vulgarity is not for him, but nor is his extraordinary, exciting, bizarre visual invention. Of all our novelists, Dickens is the most pictorial. He is not analytical in the manner of George Eliot, but his visual sense is so vivid that he can convey the quality of a person's mind through visual analogy. Think of his description of Miss Havisham's wedding table:

> The most prominent object was a long table, with a table-cloth spread on it, as if a feast had been in preparation when the house and clocks all stopped together. A centre-piece of some kind was in the middle of the cloth; it was so heavily overhung with cobwebs that its form was quite indistinguishable; and as I looked along the yellow expanse out of which I remember its seeming to grow, like a black fungus, I saw speckled-legged spiders with blotchy bodies running home to it and running out from it.[12]

After a description like that, one hardly needs an analysis of Miss Havisham's thoughts: that table is a metaphor for her diseased mind and all part of the imaginative process by which Dickens transforms the stock character of the jilted bride into the most famous jilted bride in all literature. The trial of Magwitch is also a wonderfully visualised scene in the novel, the crowd complacently watching the prisoners as if they were watching a play, the sunlight uniting both accused and spectators in a single beam of common humanity (simultaneously sentimental and ironical) and Pip emphasising his recognition of society's responsibility for the criminals by the simple gesture of holding Magwitch's hand across the partition. Dickens's imagination of that scene is profoundly critical of society, potentially subversive. Lean reduces it to a bare panning shot across the accused — poignant, but hardly very radical, since no audience is seen.

Lean, then, has responded to Dickens's realism and romanticism, and has duplicated something of his story-telling verve. This is still probably the best film treatment of Dickens to date. Yet the element of 'grotesque tragicomedy', which Dickens saw himself in the material, is missing. The phantasmagoric nature of Dickens's inspiration, his inspired melodrama, is studiously and discreetly put to one side. Nevertheless, there is a famous film which, unexpectedly, analogously and in a completely different context, comes very close to the spirit as distinct from the content of the Dickens original.

'A neglected house gets an unhappy look — this one had it in spades. It was like that old woman in *Great Expectations*, that Miss Havisham and her rotting wedding dress and her torn veil, taking it out on the world because she'd been given the go-by.' The speaker is the B-picture writer–hero of Billy Wilder's *Sunset Boulevard* (1950), narrating (as we learn later, from beyond the grave) his first impression of the mansion which he discovers is occupied by the old movie star Norma Desmond. The reference to *Great Expectations* here is clearly very calculated. The film had been popular in America, so Wilder would expect an audience to pick up the reference, whether they were Dickens fans or not; and Wilder has not been averse to paying due homage to a director he greatly admires, David Lean (*Brief Encounter* is affectionately satirised in *The Seven-Year Itch* and provided the inspiration for *The Apartment*). But Wilder's baroque black comedy is actually closer to a Dickensian view of the world than to that of David Lean. The film's outrageous melodrama and decadence has a true Dickensian spirit and flair. Like Dickens's *Great Expectations, Sunset Boulevard* is a grotesque tragi-comedy if ever there was one.

The plot and imagery of *Sunset Boulevard* have definite Dickensian echoes. An ambitious young man who is floundering in his society (Hollywood rather than Victorian England) acquires a benefactress. Like Miss Havisham, Norma Desmond lives in a world of the past, jilted not by her lover but by her audience (which is all she truly loves). Miss Havisham has spiders running out of her wedding cake, signifying a decaying dream; Norma Desmond has rats in her swimming pool to suggest a similarly satisfying and luxurious life that has gone to seed. Pip compares Miss Havisham to a 'waxwork' in the novel;[13] Joe refers to Norma and her friends as 'the waxworks'. In extolling Dickens's use of external detail to signify inner states, the critic Mario Praz has particularly singled out the author's description of 'Miss Havisham's house with its walled-up windows and gratings and its front door barred with chains, symbol of its owner's spiritual confinement'.[14] Similarly, Norma Desmond's mansion is expressive of her personality — expansive, decrepit, full of bric-à-brac for which no one can find a use. The Hollywood writer, Joe Gillis (William Holden), describes it as 'stricken with a kind of paralysis, out of beat with the rest of the world' — which could equally apply to Satis House in *Great Expectations*. Like Dickens's Pip, Joe will have great expectations that are to be unfulfilled. As with Pip, the expected fortune from his benefactress is to take a cruel and ironic form. Like Miss Havisham with Pip, Norma takes on Joe to help her but gradually sees in him an echo of her own loneliness. A frustrated romance leads to a kind of dream ending, happy but bizarre, grotesque. If Miss Havisham is consumed by flames, Norma Desmond will be consumed by her illusions. Pip cannot give up 'Estella' in the novel, the star of his life, any more than Norma Desmond can surrender Joe — 'No one deserts a star. That's what makes one a star.' There is even a curious resemblance between some of the names of the characters — Joe Gillis/Joe Gargery, Betty/Biddy (as, in both narratives, the girl that got away).

In *Sunset Boulevard,* Hollywood has a similar function to that of Victorian London in Dickens's *Great Expectations*. It is a hard, ruthless uncaring society, consumed entirely by the pursuit of money and success and complacent about suffering: the 'heartless so-and-sos' who flock to Norma Desmond's mansion after the murder are not very different from the crowd at Magwitch's trial. David Lean's film might be a skilful para-phrase of *Great Expectations*, but Wilder's *Sunset Boulevard* is an imagina-tive transformation of it, converting it into the currency and imagery of modern popular art but having that cheeky confidence, risk-taking fear-lessness, narrative ingenuity and blackly bizarre invention that also charac-terise Dickens at his best.

Death in Venice

The film of *Death in Venice* (1971) represents a meeting of minds of three of the great European artists of the twentieth century: writer Thomas Mann, composer Gustav Mahler, and film-maker Luchino Visconti. The conjunction is almost too rich, a well-nigh indigestible cultural pudding from a writer who, in D.H. Lawrence's phrase, 'feels vaguely that he has in him something finer than ever physical life revealed';[15] from a composer who felt he was carrying the whole history of music on his shoulders; and from a massively cultured and aristocratic director seeking to make the ultimate art movie in an industry given over to commerce. Consequently, we have a movie almost insufferable in its self-importance, top-heavy with significance, which somehow compels respect and attention because the artists involved have the genius to justify their massive pretensions.

Written in 1911, Thomas Mann's *Death in Venice* tells the story of an esteemed author, Gustav von Aschenbach, who, holidaying in Venice, becomes slowly obsessed and infatuated with an adolescent boy, Tadzio, who is staying with his family at the same hotel as Aschenbach. The development of Aschenbach's love for the boy, which sweeps over him like a contagion, is paralleled by the slow spread of plague in Venice itself.

Mann originally planned the novella as a tale centrally concerned with 'the fascination of death, the triumph of extreme disorder over a life founded upon order ... a droll conflict between macabre adventure and a bourgeois sense of duty'.[16] It is intended to some extent as an ironic attack on an excessively inhibited and ordered man whose renunciation of what he calls a 'sympathy with the abyss' is presented as a failure of self-knowledge and a measure of his moral arrogance. Mann's presentation of Aschenbach undoubtedly owes much to the increasing influence at that time of the ideas of Freud, to whom Mann was to pay tribute in his article 'The Position of Freud in the History of Modern Thought'. Aschenbach is a classic Freudian case-study of the repressed man, the man who tries to disguise the reality of his feelings and the eruption of whose subconscious desires undermines his whole hold on life. From the point when he acknowledges what his feelings for the boy actually are — feelings which he regards as shameful — the diseased city mirrors the disease in his heart and his exploration of the narrow streets parallels the exploration of his own soul. By the end, in Lionel Trilling's words, 'the artist knows a reality he had until now refused to admit to consciousness'.[17]

On another level, the story can be interpreted as a prophetic tale about the death of Europe. The story begins on 'a spring afternoon in that year of grace 19—, when Europe sat upon the anxious seat beneath a menace that hung over its head for months'.[18] In emphasising the background of an oppressed, anxious Europe underneath an unspecified menace, Mann might not be indulging in specific prophecy, but he does seem to be responding to something in the atmosphere and finding the air (like Aschenbach in Venice) stifling, menacing and inimical to health. In three years time, in fact, Europe is to tear itself apart in a genocidal world war ('the thunderclap', as Mann described the First World War at the end of *The Magic Mountain*), and *Death in Venice* seems to suggest that, almost unknowingly, this is what Europe was treacherously and unerringly heading for. Aschenbach's psychological disintegration stands for the disease and incipient collapse of a whole cultured society — in some ways, a whole civilisation. An edifice (Aschenbach/Europe/Venice) which is superficially strong and secure is revealed at root to be rotten and decaying, with a deadly secret inwardly recognised but desperately concealed from view. The story in these terms is not only about the death of Venice (for the city is in peril as well as Aschenbach: it has the plague). It is by implication a prophecy of the death of the 'European soul' which the city of Venice represents (the hotel in which Aschenbach stays is represented as a microcosm of Europe — 'subdued voices were speaking most of the principal European tongues').[19] This 'European soul'[20] has been identified with Aschenbach at a very early stage in the story and it is a soul which at heart is revealed to be corrupt.

In writing *Death in Venice*, Mann was drawing on a number of sources for inspiration: events in his own life; his fascination with the last years of Goethe, in particular the poet's forlorn love for a girl many years younger than himself; the death in Venice of one of Mann's great and enduring cultural heroes, the composer Richard Wagner. The prime inspiration for the story, however, was the life and death of Gustav Mahler. After the première of Mahler's Eighth Symphony in 1910, Mann had written to the composer describing him as the man who 'represents the art of our time in its profoundest and most sacred form'.[21] It is in those terms in which Aschenbach's own artistic reputation is presented in the story. Although the specific incident which forms the basis of *Death in Venice* has no authenticated equivalent in Mahler's own life and although Aschenbach in the novella is a writer rather than a composer, Mann does use some biographical details of Mahler for his description of Aschenbach (his age and appearance; the tragic death of one of his children; some of his artistic ideals). In a letter of 1921 to Wolfgang Born, Mann revealed how the conception of the story was influenced by the news of Mahler's death, so that 'when I conceived my hero who succumbs to lascivious dissolution, I not only gave him the great musician's Christian name but also in describing his appearance conferred Mahler's mask upon him.'[22]

In Mann's conception, the chief thing shared by Aschenbach and

Mahler is that both are the last of their line, upholding a tradition which is collapsing and the collapse of which breaks them. Both are men who stand between two worlds. Aschenbach stands between the world of the conscious and that of the subconscious, between order and chaos, between classical control and romantic excess, between the mythological and the real, between life and death. Mahler too stands between two worlds — the 'dual one', as Leonard Bernstein called him, torn apart by inner psychological tensions (also acutely analysed by Freud) and this duality finding its way into his music as the highest expression of late-nineteenth-century musical romanticism and early-twentieth-century musical expressionism. Although it is always difficult to attach a precise meaning to a musical composition, there seems to be no dispute among expert observers (for example, Alban Berg, Bruno Walter, Leonard Bernstein) that Mahler's last completed work, the Ninth Symphony, is essentially a sonic presentation of death — and, like *Death in Venice*, not simply about the death of one particular artist, but about the death of a whole culture and society. 'Ours is the century of death,' said Bernstein, 'and Mahler is its musical prophet'.[23] The work is torn between an exceptional fondness for the earth and the certainty of death. Just as Aschenbach is to be riven by the chaos raging within, Mahler's symphony similarly crackles with discord, the tension between its yearning romanticism and its bitter mocking irony exploding the work from within into the dissonance and chaos of our own time.

Rather like Mahler, the final works of Luchino Visconti, who died in 1976, are all richly ambiguous farewells to life. The heroes of *Death in Venice*, *Ludwig* (1972), *Conversation Piece* (1974) and *The Innocent* (1976) are essentially divided men, unable to reconcile their public role and their private desires; striving to come to terms with a modern age that is foreign to them; failing to transcend the ideology of a society they fundamentally despise; and, in their search for freedom from the ties of family, society and religion, ironically becoming gripped by a much more imprisoning obsession. This obsession often takes the form of the pursuit of an ideal. In *Death in Venice*, one could take the boy, Tadzio, as representing an ideal of beauty and perfection which Aschenbach the artist pursues. Like most ideals, however, it is elusive, checking that it is being followed, moving on, beckoning — but always just out of reach. *Death in Venice* can also be taken as a disquisition on culture and the isolation of the artist, and here Visconti can draw on his rich cultural experience, on work accomplished not only behind the film camera but in the theatre and the opera house. This background is often felt in his films in their unabashed melodrama and the use of classical music over the soundtracks (Bruckner in *Senso*, Mozart in *Conversation Piece*, Gluck and Liszt in *The Innocent*) as important cultural reference-points. In *Death in Venice*, the disintegrating fabric of Aschenbach's ordered world is wittily signalled by Visconti in musical terms — Mahler first having to contend for attention over the soundtrack with the waltzes of Lehar and then with crude popular song.

Although Visconti's identification of the hero of Mann's novella with Mahler is fully justifiable, the specific music of Mahler predominantly chosen to accompany the action is distinctly controversial. For the reasons indicated earlier, the music of Mahler which has exactly the resonances Visconti needs is the Ninth Symphony: Visconti chooses the adegietto from the Fifth. It is much shorter than the adagio from the Ninth and therefore can be moulded much more easily to fit the film's imagery without too much violence to the musical structure. However, not only does this piece lose much from being wrenched out of its context, seeming more senti-mental and care-worn than it actually is when heard in the full symphonic argument, the Fifth Symphony itself charts a movement from tragedy to triumph, from darkness to light, which one could argue is exactly the reverse of what happens in *Death in Venice*. I suppose one could say that Aschenbach moves from the darkness of self-ignorance to the illumination of self-knowledge, but it is not clear Visconti sees him like that and, if he does not, then the associations of the music run contrary to the drift of the film. Its inappropriateness is crippling to a film that prides itself on its cultural refinement.

In fact, Visconti has difficulty in actually getting inside Aschenbach, particularly as book and film are almost entirely devoid of direct dialogue. Aschenbach never speaks to people casually, a factor which points up his artistic alienation and self-consciousness, but Mann can compensate for this with an elaborate and analytical internal discourse. Visconti has to suggest Aschenbach's artistic personality by recourse to some rather uneasily interjected flashbacks, in which the hero is intellectually terrorised by a hysterically obstreperous fellow-composer who is clearly (and crudely) meant to represent Schoenberg.

If Mann's tale, then, is slippery filmic material, there are nevertheless two crucial themes to which Visconti responds incomparably. The first is the theme of forbidden love. Visconti's films invariably document the progress of illicit relationships, either adulterous or, increasingly in his later films, homosexual. These relationships often involve two people of widely differing ages, which intensifies a sense of humiliation for the older man or woman. In *Death in Venice*, Aschenbach's forbidden passion for Tadzio is highlighted uncomfortably by his occasional confrontations with old men with made-up faces, men who, in a horrid mockery of his own situation, try to look younger than they are in order to be attractive enough for love and also perhaps to postpone their date with death. Aschenbach is similarly artificially transformed ('Now the signore can fall in love as soon as he likes,' says the cosmetician) but the façade evaporates in the merciless light of day. Visconti's deepest sympathies are roused by the anguish attendant upon the tension between surging passion and ravaging old age.

Visconti also renders brilliantly another theme strongly apparent in the story: what Mann referred to as 'the voluptuousness of doom'.[24] Visconti is an unrivalled observer of superficially cultured ways of life in their death-throes, and *Death in Venice* has all the decadent inevitability of *The Leopard*

(1963), *The Damned* (1969), *Ludwig* and *The Innocent* as a culture gives way to the pressure of social change and submits to a final orgiastic indulgence before the apocalypse. *Death in Venice* is another of Visconti's lavish reconstructions of the past, momuments to a grand style which is going out of movies as well as life. Diffuse but sumptuous, it succeeds in fixing its characters with a stare so penetrating that the society which has formed them also comes sharply into focus. It is finally perhaps the combination of unique talents which makes the experience of the film so overwhelming, for all its internal sense of three giant artistic egos from a different epoch all narcissistically indulging in cultural one-upmanship. The trinity of Mann, Mahler and Visconti makes for the kind of artistic interchange that was, in fact, one of the most glorious aspects of the pre-First World War arts, which, in Visconti's words, saw a 'whole complex of cultural change and revolution and which one must understand to follow our own history'.[25]

Barry Lyndon

Thackeray's novel *The Luck of Barry Lyndon*, as it was first called (the title was then changed to *The Memoirs of Barry Lyndon, Esq. by Himself*), was first published in 1844. It was planned by Thackeray as a riposte to the novels of Ainsworth and Bulwer Lytton, which romanticised villainy and made dubious heroes out of the criminal classes. Thackeray's hero, Redmond Barry, who becomes Barry Lyndon by virtue of a prosperous marriage, tells his story of deceit, bragging and bullying in a tone of unwitting self-disclosure. It is intended by the narrator to be the tale of the triumphs and misfortunes of a sympathetic and resourceful eighteenth-century gentleman. As intended by Thackeray, it comes across as the diary of a wicked and self-deceiving brute.

It was Thackeray's first novel and undoubtedly planned as a best-seller, although it proved to be a difficult book to sustain and Thackeray finished it in low spirits in hospital. Although it does not have the range and variety of *Vanity Fair* (1848) nor the polish of *Henry Esmond* (1852), the work does have a number of unusual features. It is, first of all, a demystification of the romantic hero, something that Thackeray felt had not been done adequately since Fielding. In his preface to *Pendennis* (1850), Thackeray laments that:

> Since the author of *Tom Jones* was buried, no writer of fiction among us has been permitted to depict to his utmost power a man. We must drape him, and give him a certain conventional simper ... You will not hear — it is best to know it — what moves in the real world, what passes in society, in the clubs, colleges, mess-rooms — what is the life and talk of your sons ... If truth is not always pleasant; at any rate truth is best.

Barry Lyndon as a character is heavily influenced by Fielding's Jonathan Wild, and Thackeray is a continuation of the Fielding spirit, in terms of his picaresque structures, his satirical tone, and his love of the eighteenth century.

Another point of interest in the novel is its pretence at autobiography. Thackeray's perception is that autobiography is a kind of fiction, anyway, both in terms of the subjectivity and selection of the point of view and in terms of the narrator's quite possibly being self-deceived (something that James and Conrad are particularly to elaborate). The hero attempts to reinforce historical verisimilitude by arrogant name-dropping, claiming friendship with John Wilkes, the animosity of Dr Johnson and the acquaintance of Boswell, Goldsmith and Sheridan: even Nora Brady has been christened by Dean Swift. However, the effect of this bragging is merely to augment the impression of an upstart's unconvincing self-justification. With a phrase like 'For the first three years, I never struck my wife but when I was in liquor,'[26] Barry Lyndon gives himself away.

Although Stanley Kubrick's 1975 film is substantially different from Thackeray's novel, it might be worth speculating on the points in common between Thackeray and Kubrick that might have drawn the latter to the novel. Thackeray's earliest ambition was to be a painter; he wrote much criticism of art; and his own work tends to break down into vivid pictures more than psychological scenes (for example, his description of the deaths of George Osborne and Pitt Crawley in Vanity Fair) — something that would be highly suggestive to someone of Kubrick's visual imagination. Thackeray's domination by his mother and his unfortunate marriage led to an uneasy and rather misogynistic attitude to women (there is an element of Thackeray's own life in Barry Lyndon here); misogyny is something equally noticeable in Kubrick's films. Above all, Thackeray and Kubrick have a tendency to take a superior attitude to the spectacle they have contrived. They do not identify or involve themselves with their characters, but observe them from a lofty remove, Kubrick's zoom lens and omniscient narrator in Barry Lyndon serving an equivalent ironic function to the harsh editorial comments about the hero in Thackeray's novel. However, this distancing has different implications for the artist. Thackeray's stance of superiority is that of the social satirist; Kubrick's that of the social scientist. Thackeray's novel is ultimately a satire on snobbery. Kubrick's Barry Lyndon is more a portrait of thwarted social mobility and a clinical study of fate.

The main difference between the two works is point of view. Thackeray's novel is narrated in the first person and Barry's crass conceit ('it is wonderful how the possession of wealth brings out the virtues of a man ...')[27] and his defensive defiance ('I spent my personal fortune as well as the lady's income in the keeping up of our rank, and was always too much a man of honour and spirit to save a penny of Lady Lyndon's income')[28] ironically furnish the evidence with which the reader can condemn him. Kubrick's film is more objective. An unidentified narrator (Michael

Hordern) provides explanatory links between scenes, and adds both irony and a sense of ominousness to the film's narrative. The first-person narration in Thackeray's novel reflects an arrogant insistence on self. But one of the consistent visual motifs of the film is the diminution of the individual. The camera will begin with a close shot, often of the hero, and then slowly move back to a middle distance. The effect is to see the individual first and then, pulling back, see him in relation to the tangled society of which he is a part and which in turn will entangle him — a major theme of the film. Also it gives us a perspective which is denied to the character himself, wrapped up as he is in his own pursuits. The camera's retreat has the effect of diminishing the hero, making him look smaller in the tide of events and foreshadowing the man's receding fortunes. There is a shot of Barry towards the end of the film as he talks to his son in his home and in which the two are almost completely dwarfed by a huge painting behind them on the wall. The film was criticised for highlighting the houses and decor at the expense of the characters, but this is one of the film's major points: houses and décor dominate because the characters become prisoners of their obsession for possession, prestige and position. Also, if the stately style seems to keep the film's world tantalisingly at arm's length for the spectator — we admire but do not enter — this is precisely the effect this world is to have on Barry himself.

The film proceeds in a series of stately events, sometimes reflected in a single majestic shot: the duel (which kills Barry's father); first love (Nora's seduction of Barry, which precipitates his whole fate); the challenge, whereby Barry (Ryan O'Neal) forces a duel with Captain Quin (Leonard Rossiter), whose outcome compels him to flee. Thereafter his journey through life is constantly being diverted through fateful encounters on the road — with the highwayman, the German peasant girl, Captain Potzdorf — which prevent Barry from reaching his intended destination and even then suggest that Barry's ultimate ambitions for himself in society will be thwarted.

The rise/fall structure of the film is unobtrusively underlined by careful pairings of detail. Redmond Barry becomes Barry Lyndon. Situations start happening in pairs, in which the second darkens the atmosphere of the first. When Barry sees Lady Lyndon for the first time, his sight of her and immediate courtship is accompanied over the soundtrack by Schubert's decorous piano trio, which puts the romance into a refined, elegant context. But the next time we hear that music, it follows the events where a crippled Barry limps out of the inn and into a carriage, and the following scene where the family hover around Lady Lyndon as, with a stroke of her pen, she writes Barry out of her life — at this juncture, the repetition of the music seems to mock Barry's early aspiration. He tells his son, Brian, of the occasion when he and his fellow-soldiers stormed a fort and chopped the heads off the enemy; but his second attempt to tell the story later in the film is uncompleted, for he breaks down by the bedside of his dying son. (There is an echo here of the father figures whom Barry has lost on his way through the film — his own father, Captain Grogan, Captain Potzdorf, the Chevalier.) He wants to step into my shoes!' cries Lord Lyndon immediately before his consumption conspires that Barry can do just that; but when Lord Bullingdon disrupts a musical recital by leading in Barry's son Brian in the young lord's shoes ('Don't you think he fits my shoes very well, your Ladyship?'), he triggers off a violent reaction in Barry that will for ever bar his entrance into high society. A duel in the first part of the film (Captain Quin against Barry) is echoed by a duel in the second part of the film (Bullingdon versus Barry). But whereas the first has an element of farce and fakery under the ritual, the second has an element of chaos and mess. The critic Michael Klein has pointed out that whereas in the first example, Barry fires from left to right, in the second he has to fire from right to left, motifs that throughout the film apply to Barry's rise and fall, respectively.[29]

Kubrick has cleverly tightened the whole structure of the novel, giving a hypnotic and fatal linearity to a narrative that in Thackeray's hands was a diffuse picaresque. He has given an oppressive beauty to a society whose sumptuous exterior conceals a mocking cruelty and severity. He has also given a sense of balance to the motivations of every character which Thackeray's first-person narration, by very definition, cannot do. One feels that every character in the film has a credible point of view — Lord Lyndon, Lord Bullingdon, Captain Quin, the Bradys, and even Reverend Runt and Mrs Barry (the scene where Mrs Barry dismisses Runt from the Lyndon household is electrifying in the way the severity of tone and harshness of argument are intensified shot by shot). The main difference of shading is in the character of Barry himself: an active, violent rogue in the novel; a resourceful but vulnerable character in the film (Ryan O'Neal is wonderfully well used here). Kubrick does not sentimentalise him. Barry's treatment of his wife is occasionally despicable and shown to be so (when Barry is caught out in his infidelity, Kubrick zooms forward with a camera movement that has the effect of impaling the adulterer like an insect). At the same time, Barry is seen to be as much victim as villain. Deprived of his father in the first shot of the film, seduced and then abandoned by his cousin, tricked in a duel, robbed, caught up in a war, it is small wonder he looks for a more comfortable position. His tactical marriage is understandable, given that a fortunate position in that society seems the only way of surviving its hellish cruelty.

Two additions by Kubrick to the novel seem in particular to emphasise the greater vulnerability and sympathy in his shading of the title character. His night of love with the German peasant woman is significant in two respects: Barry's romantic vision of it contrasts with the narrator's dry description of the girl as a whore, and relates back to his fateful fascination for the faithless Nora Brady that has set him on this road; and his gentleness to the woman's child anticipates Barry's adoration of his own son, whose death will break his heart. An even more significant addition by Kubrick to Thackeray is the duel scene between Barry and Lord Bullingdon. Bullingdon has the first shot, but his gun misfires. Barry now has him at his mercy, but he does what he conceives to be the 'gentlemanly' thing — he fires into the ground. He has always wanted to be a gentleman, and it proves to be the undoing of him. Bullingdon has no such scruples — unlike Barry, he does not need to *prove* he is a gentleman — and his next shot is to inflict a wound on his despised stepfather, which leads to the amputation of a leg.

The film closes with Lady Lyndon signing the document of her former husband's pitiful annuity, and, as has been frequently noticed, the document is dated 1789. There are two associations which particularly spring to my mind here, and take Kubrick's film into a different world from that of Thackeray. The first association is with Abel Gance's *Napoleon* (1926): the date of the French Revolution on Lady Lyndon's document provides one of the keys, and the scene is rather similar to a scene in the Gance film in which Robespierre is similarly sealing people's fate with the stroke of a pen. Kubrick's film is epic movie-making on a par with Gance.

The second parallel with another Napoleonic work is even more fundamental: the parallel with Stendhal's *Scarlet and Black* (1830). Ultimately, Kubrick's film is much closer to Stendhal than to Thackeray. Both works are historical panoramas about the difficulty of a man from humble origins in finding a niche in the higher classes and who has the prospect of glory snatched away from him at the last minute. Stendhal's ironic commentator in his novel is much closer to the narrator in Kubrick's film than to Thackeray's; and Stendhal's style approximates more to that of Kubrick's film than Thackeray's novel, Stendhal emphasising the importance of form and suggesting that the emotions of a work of art must come through its rhythm. A sentence like this in *Scarlet and Black* — 'That day Julien's happiness was near to becoming a lasting one, but our hero fell short of daring to be sincere'[30] — could be applied in several contexts to Kubrick's *Barry Lyndon*, a film which, like Stendhal, and unlike Thackeray, could actually be interpreted as a sustained search for sincerity.

Stendhal subtitled *Scarlet and Black* as 'a chronicle of the nineteenth century', in effect dealing with the Napoleonic legacy. Kubrick's *Barry Lyndon*, more than Thackeray's novel, is a chronicle of the eighteenth century, leading to the Napoleonic revolution, with the look and manners of the period being conveyed by every aspect of the film's style. It does for the cinema what Stendhal did for the novel — that is, convey at one and the same time a huge sweep of history, an extraordinary evocation of a period and a tide of events, and against this the struggle of an individual to carve an identity for himself in a society that is materially sumptuous and morally decadent. Thackeray's novel relates the downfall of an upstart. Contrastingly, Kubrick's film deepens the portraiture of the hero and broadens the social perspective. For a statement of the film's major theme, one could not do better than quote Julien Sorel's cry at his trial in *Scarlet and Black*:

Even were I less guilty, I see before me men who, without pausing to consider what pity my youth may deserve, will wish to punish in my person and forever discourage that body of young men who, born in an inferior station, have ... the audacity to mingle with what the pride of rich men calls society. That is my crime, Gentlemen.[31]

The French Lieutenant's Woman

John Fowles once said that, for a novelist in the position of having his work adapted for the screen, the director to fear is the one who swears absolute fidelity to every word. He was speaking from bitter experience. It was Woody Allen who said that, if he could live his life over again, he would do everything the same — except see the film of *The Magus*.

Fortunately, the adaptation of *The French Lieutenant's Woman* by writer Harold Pinter and director Karel Reisz is a magnificent metaphor for the novel rather than a slavish imitation of it. It obeys the cardinal rule of screen adaptation: fidelity not to the letter of the source but to the spirit. This is also sound film sense. After all, only a comparative minority of people who go to the film will be seeing it to find out how closely it approximates to the novel. Many will be seeing it to discover if the book is worth reading.

The French Lieutenant's Woman is a Victorian love story told from an avowedly twentieth-century perspective. The author makes his presence felt through confidential asides, historical footnotes, flash forwards to the ideas of Marx, Marcuse and Freud, and, most strikingly, through the construction of two alternative endings to the fiction. On the one hand, the authorial presence is an imitation of the omniscient narrator typical of the Victorian novel and most perfectly exemplified in the novels of George Eliot; on the other, it is a modernist, almost Brechtian alienation device designed insistently to draw attention to the novel as a contrived fiction rather than a mirror of life. The insistent presence of this modern point of view around the main action, as it were, is so important to the novel's sense of irony and complexity that any adaptation would have to integrate it in some way: just telling the Victorian story would not do. Richard Lester and Charles Wood, Fred Zinnemann and Dennis Potter, were only two of the director–writer combinations who were approached to solve this problem but who had finally to admit defeat. At one time, it was felt that the presence of an invisible or even visible narrator (Peter Ustinov, perhaps) could be used to approximate Fowle's interventions in his novel and narrate the author's modern reflections on the historical events he invents and describes. But this would probably have seemed irritating and artificial. The Reisz–Pinter solution to the problem is simple but ingenious. They choose a film-within-a-film structure. The love of Sarah Woodruff and Charles Smithson in the Victorian story is recounted alongside the developing affair between the American actress, Anna (Meryl Streep), and her co-star, Mike (Jeremy Irons), who are playing the parts of Sarah and Charles in their film version of *The French Lieutenant's Woman*.

This brilliant conceit seems to me to have a number of implications of absolute relevance to the novel. It is a structure which, by its very nature, highlights the *fictional* aspect of the Victorian story — something on which Fowles also insists. Just as Fowles continually reminds us in the novel that the characters are puppets of his own devising whom he can operate at will, the film persistently reminds us that Sarah and Charles are not 'real people' or even 'credible characters', but fictional roles inhabited by actors. The motif of role playing is the single binding image of the film. It is a splendidly effective metaphor for two of Fowles's most fundamental ideas about the Victorian age: namely, its hypocrisy ('an age where woman was sacred and where you buy a thirteen year old girl for a few pounds ... where more churches were built than in the whole previous history of the country, and where one in sixty houses in London was a brothel');[32] and its schizophrenia ('the endless tug of war between Liberty and Restraint, Excess and Moderation ... between the principled man's cry for Universal Education and his terror of Universal Suffrage').[33] Hypocrisy is a form of role playing: pretending to be what you are not, the appearance belying the reality. Schizophrenia sometimes takes the form of being unable to decide which of two worlds is real and which is fantasy: whether one is acting or being. These concepts are at the heart of the film.

Fowles's preferred director for the film all along was Karel Reisz, and it is not hard to see why. What Reisz brings to the material is, first of all, a fascination with the rebel. In films such as *Saturday Night and Sunday Morning* (1960) and *Isadora* (1968), he has explored the freedoms and frustrations of remarkable people at odds with the predominant norms and values of their society. In Reisz's version of *The French Lieutenant's Woman*, the outsider is ostensibly the character of Sarah as the embryonic 'new woman' in a rigid Victorian society whose certainties are beginning to crumble under the impact of materialism and Darwin. But, as the film develops, the outsider is also the character of Anna in the modern story as the American star viewed somewhat quizzically by the predominantly British cast and crew. Reisz has taken care to cast people whose faces we particularly associate with period adaptations of British classics. When we see a character like the dairyman or the private detective, we are less likely to exclaim, 'How right for the period!' than, 'Wasn't he in *Far from the Madding Crowd* or *Tess* — or both?' Reisz's play between period accuracy and transparent performance is very skilful and absolutely relevant to his theme.

What he also brings to the project is an impeccable technique. Watching it, you are reminded that this is the work of a man who once wrote one of the standard books on film editing.[34] Small details are impressive, first of all. Charles's first appearance in the film is intercut with that of his servant Sam, and this already hints at the way, later in the story, Sam is to interrupt and despoil Charles's affairs. There is a moment when Reisz cuts from a card bearing the message 'To my beloved' (a message from Charles to his fiancée, Ernestina) to a shot of Charles as he approaches Sarah, a skilful, almost subliminal visual anticipation of Charles's transference of affection from one woman to the other.

The solution Reisz and Pinter found to the problem of adapting Fowles — that is, tell a modern love story alongside the Victorian one — might actually have come to them through Reisz's editing experience. The solution is found essentially in the capacity of film montage to tell two (or more) stories simultaneously and, through visual pointing, to emphasise the relation between them. Reisz has done this before on a smaller scale when he exploited comic analogies between King Kong and his hero Morgan in *Morgan — A Suitable Case for Treatment* (1966) or implied a Dostoevskian parallel to the trials of his hero in *The Gambler* (1974).

Fowles's novel, after all, is basically a Victorian novel in modern dress. Why not take the idea more literally and compare and contrast the Victorian characters with the modern characters who are playing them? The film's first sizable frisson in its handling of the twin narratives is the moment when Reisz cuts from Anna and Mike rehearsing the scene in which Sarah falls into Charles's arms to the scene itself. When it happens in the film, it suddenly gives the moment an extra twist of ambiguity. Is the fall deliberate? Is the Victorian heroine, Sarah Woodruff, as much an actress as the modern star playing her? From this point, an audience is encouraged to watch Sarah much more closely.

Much of the credit for the working out of this adaptation is, of course, also due to Harold Pinter, who wrote the brilliant screenplay. As with Reisz, Pinter's identification with the material is clearly intense. He too is interested in outsiders, but specifically in their disruptive influence on a situation or relationship which is already fraught with undisclosed tension. He is fascinated by small gestures which, if sufficiently charged (like Sarah's surreptitious passing of a note at a stiff tea-party), can seem momentous enough to topple a whole society. He is intrigued by the different layers of society and how the callous disregard for the lower orders by the ruling class can be implied in a gesture — as in Charles's instinctive manner of handing his cane and hat to a maid without even looking at her. Several moments in *The French Lieutenant's Woman* recall Pinter's association with Joseph Losey and the themes and situations they jointly explored — infidelity, hypocrisy, suppressed passion, the tensions of class. As in *The Servant, Accident* and *The Go-Between,* the guilty lovers in this film are interrupted in the middle of a passionate embrace by the blundering intrusions of the outside world. As in *The Go-Between,* the strains of the modern story in *The French Lieutenant's Woman* begin to seep into the past, altering and complicating its mood.

No current screenwriter can match Pinter for the ability to bring a literary classic to filmic life not only with no loss of complexity, but often with additional original shafts of interpretation. He goes straight for the essential heart of the work. In *The French Lieutenant's Woman,* he has cut out

Charles's uncle who is structurally irrelevant. He has considerably rewritten and restructured Charles's encounter with the prostitute, also called Sarah, which seems crudely coincidental in the novel but in the film, by being placed later in the action, *after* Sarah's disappearance, becomes an expressive extension of Charles's descent into the depths and his embittered and twisted image of his beloved. The revelation about Sarah's virginity is handled so cleanly and quickly in the film that it makes the novel's comparable relevation look rather shrill and melodramatic.

It is an adaptation also which can assimilate Fowles's literary references without having to insist on them. Sarah's appearance in the film looks so instantly Pre-Raphaelite that all the evocations of that movement (its adherents' artistic temperament, their frank sexuality, their fascination with foreign cultures, their tendency to live every moment as if it were a crisis), inform your attitude to her character without her actually having to go to the lengths of living in the same house as the Rossettis, as is hamfistedly contrived in the novel. Indeed, the structure of the film might even have been influenced by a D.G. Rossetti poem such as 'The Burden of Nineveh' which contains a parallel treatment of time. The other major literary inspiration behind the novel is Tennyson. Fowles underlines that with a welter of literary epigraphs and by spelling out that Charles's favourite reading in his hours of sadness is Tennyson's poem *Maud*. Pinter conveys all this Tennysonian sense of inconsolable melancholia, this reservoir of regret and incipient madness, in one line that is compressed from the novel. During her monologue, Sarah comments: 'My loneliness was so deep, I felt I would drown in it.' Suddenly a whole new dimension of terror is given to the shots of her gazing out to sea.

To begin with, the modern insertions are a bit of a shock, but, as Reisz said, so initially were Fowles's references to McLuhan and Henry Moore in a novel about the Victorian period. Gradually we become accustomed to them and soon it becomes difficult to watch one of the stories without reference to the other. Some critics found that the modern story distracted from the Victorian one and robbed the Victorian characters of sympathy and audience identification. I found quite the contrary and that some scenes actually gain additional force and fascination from the parallel. For example, perhaps the greatest scene in the film, wonderfully acted by Meryl Streep, is the one in which Sarah Woodruff tells Charles about her encounter with the French Lieutenant. On the surface, it is a straightforward monologue from the heroine who finally entrusts the hero (and the audience) with previously undisclosed information. Later, however, we are to learn that, in various crucial details, this story is a lie. The meaning and motive behind the monologue are thus changed. Its purpose is clearly not simply to inform Charles but to seduce him. By posing as an enigmatic 'fallen' woman (and she falls a lot in the film, in order to bring Charles literally down to her level), Sarah wishes to attract the passions of a previously impeccable Victorian gentleman. The sense of ensnarement is delicately reinforced by a quietly prowling camera as she spins her tale —

and her web around the hero. The monologue thus becomes not a confession but a performance, its self-consciousness underlined by Sarah's very deliberate gesture of pulling herself to her feet by catching on to a branch and spinning slowly round to face the hero. It is a gesture she is to repeat when she clings swooningly to the bedpost after her love scene with him — the conclusion of her seduction.

The idea of performance not only now makes a more direct link between the character of Sarah and that of the actress Anna. The link is reinforced by Mike's having learnt in a scene shortly before that Anna has a French lover, David. The monologue, then, about the Frenchman in Sarah's life also relates to Anna and the Frenchman in *her* life. The reaction of Charles to Sarah's story — part horrified, part fascinated, part perplexed — is also that of Mike as he spies a connection with his relationship with Anna.

Thereafter the two stories begin to duplicate, complicate, make a mockery of each other. Charles's failure to find Sarah in her Exeter hotel is complemented by Mike's initial failure to get through to Anna in her London hotel. Charles's frustrated search for Sarah in Victorian London is echoed by Mike's frustrated attempt to talk to Anna about their future at a ghastly luncheon he has thrown for the cast. Charles's unexpected violence and hysteria in the last meeting with Sarah is in a way a projection of Mike's dawning suspicions that he might lose Anna. The film's frequent mirror shots are thus not only a reference to the illusions of the Victorian age, or the way that the Victorian fiction is mirrored by the events in the modern story. They also relate to Sarah Woodruff as conscious performer, a woman of imagination with a flair for lurid self-dramatisation (her sketches are further evidence of this).

The film, then, not only contrasts Victorian suppressed passion with the liberated sexual attitudes of the twentieth century. It becomes an elaborate allegory about performance, about the roles people play in their lives. Sarah Woodruff calculatedly constructs a role for herself as the notorious French Lieutenant's woman and plays on its mystery to enchant Charles, and to set herself apart from the narrow, suffocatingly respectable values of her society. The Victorian age acts out a charade of duty and respectability that not only belies the inner emotions of its people, but is contradicted by what we see of decadent London. Yet even the permissive modern age has its inhibitions, and that horrendous little luncheon party at Mike's house (as tense and as funny as Pinter's similar scenes for *The Pumpkin Eater* and *Accident*) is an extraordinary miniature of evasion, artifice and acting. The hypocrisy in the Victorian story suddenly strikes a spark in the modern. Anna professes to envy the docile domesticity of Mike's wife, Sonia, and the remark is so insincere as to be embarrassing: Anna caught out playing a role, perhaps even planting the suspicion that there is really something (someone) else of Sonia's that she envies.

The novel's famous 'dual ending' is superbly negotiated by the film. The Victorian story has concluded happily. There is now a party for the cast.

Shooting has finished but it is noticeable that both Mike and Anna are wearing vestiges of the costumes they wore for their final scenes as Charles and Sarah. Anna goes back to her dressing-room and stares at herself in the mirror, as Sarah has done before being cast out by Mrs Poulteney. Mike comes up, preparing to take her away, and pats that red Pre-Raphaelite wig that has been so much a part of Anna's performance as the Victorian lady of shame. Has he really fallen in love with Anna, or with a mirror image of her as the French Lieutenant's woman? Can he really distinguish, any more than Charles Smithson could, between the performance and the reality? He hears a car door slam and realises Anna is leaving without him. Rushing to the window, he leans out and shouts after her the last line of the film. 'Sarah!' he cries.

Notes

1. Quoted in Paul Mayersberg's *Hollywood: The Haunted House* (Penguin, 1969), p. 113.
2. Quoted in a conversation between the author and Fred Zinnemann.
3. David Lean interviewed by Melvyn Bragg on the *South Bank Show*, transmitted by London Weekend Television on 17 February 1985.
4. Charles Dickens, *Great Expectations* (Penguin edition, edited by Angus Calder, 1967), p. 411.
5. *Novelists on the Novel*, edited by Miriam Allott (Routledge & Kegan Paul, 1959), p. 250.
6. Dickens, *Great Expectations*, p. 354.
7. Jan Halliday, *Sirk on Sirk* (Secker & Warburg, 1971), p. 132.
8. Pauline Kael, *Kiss, Kiss, Bang, Bang* (Bantam, 1969), p. 344.
9. Dickens, *Great Expectations*, p. 46.
10. Richard Winnington, *Film Criticism and Caricatures* (Elek, 1975), p. 171.
11. *Agee on Film*, vol. 1 (Peter Owen, 1963), p. 267.
12. Dickens, *Great Expectations*, p. 113.
13. Ibid., p. 87.
14. Mario Praz, *The Hero in Eclipse in Victorian Fiction* (Oxford University Press, 1956), p. 187.
15. D.H. Lawrence, 'Thomas Mann', *Blue Review* (July 1913). Published in *Selected Literary Criticism* (Heinemann Educational Books, 1967), p. 265.
16. *The Letters of Thomas Mann*, selected and translated by Richard and Clara Winston (Penguin, 1975), p. xvi.
17. Lionel Trilling, 'On the Teaching of Modern Literature', in *Beyond Culture* (Peregrine, 1967), p. 34.
18. Thomas Mann, *Death in Venice*, translated by H.T. Lowe-Porter (Penguin, 1968), p. 7.
19. Ibid., p. 30.
20. Ibid., p. 10.
21. Letter to Gustav Mahler, September 1910. See *Gustav Mahler: Memories and Letters*, edited by Donald Mitchell (John Murray, 1968), p. 342.
22. *Letters of Thomas Mann*, p. 101.
23. Leonard Bernstein, *The Unanswered Question* (Harvard University Press, 1976), p. 313.
24. *Letters of Thomas Mann*, p. 72.
25. Monica Stirling, *A Screen of Time: A Biography of Luchino Visconti* (Secker & Warburg, 1979), p. 211.

26. William Makepeace Thackeray, *Barry Lyndon* (Penguin, 1975), p. 267.

27. Ibid., p. 258.

28. Ibid., p. 271.

29. Michael Klein, 'Narrative and Discourse in Kubrick's Modern Tragedy', in *The English Novel and the Movies*, edited by Michael Klein and Gillian Parker (Frederick Ungar Publishing, 1981), p. 101.

30. Stendhal, *Scarlet and Black*, translated by Margaret Shaw (Penguin, 1953), p. 111.

31. Ibid., p. 484.

32. John Fowles, *The French Lieutenant's Woman* (1969) (Triad Granada edition, 1977), p. 231.

33. Ibid., p. 319.

34. Karel Reisz, *The Technique of Film Editing* (Focal Press, 1953).

Chapter Nine

Bio-Pics:
The Literary Life on Film

The appeal that movies and biography have in common can be explained in one word: voyeurism. The subjects of biographies are life's stars, and the biography as a form is a way of satisfying the curiosity of ordinary people about an exceptional personality. In a way, it is a means of getting to know that person, a substitute for personal acquaintance. A celebratory biography functions as an affirmation of individualism, showing what one person can do in an increasingly impersonal society. On the other hand, if the subject is Oscar Wilde or Frances Farmer, for example, the biography often takes on the form of a cautionary tale. In this case, the relationship between subject and audience can be defined as sado-mascochistic, what Pam Cook has defined as 'the pleasure of looking at, and perhaps identifying with, the pain and suffering of an exceptional or particularly successful individual'.[1]

What are the possibilities for genuine complexity in this kind of portrait? How can the story be told? Traditionally, biography has taken the form of a linear realist narrative, the subject's life told in chronological order from the cradle to the grave. (American biographies, like Jay Martin's book on Nathanael West, or Douglas Day's on Malcolm Lowry, have sometimes begun, *Citizen Kane*-like, with the subject's death, but orthodox chronology has been resumed). There are two particular problems with this structure. The first is the danger of conveying an inner life through a series of external events: it offers an over-simple version of reality as 'something out there', and merely aggregates the sum of social and/or artistic achievement without defining the complex individuality of character. Connected with that is the danger of over-stressing the individual achievement at the expense of the social and political framework in which the character operates. A proper balance between individual and social, private and public, is the essence of successful biography in book and film, and as difficult to achieve in both.

The other alternative is not to go for the life of the subject so much as the *spirit*. The objection to the traditional biography here would be rather similar to Virginia Woolf's criticism of the materialist realism of H.G.

Wells, Arnold Bennett and John Galsworthy: 'that they spend immense skill and immense industry making the trivial and the transitory appear the true and the enduring'.[2] The alternative approach starts from the proposition that biography is as much a fiction as a novel, in that it involves selections, omissions, emphases and interpretations that might in the end reflect the biographer's values more than those of his subject. So Ken Russell's artistic biographies, for example, reject any simulation of a spurious realism and, by implication, the notion of biography as authentic truth, and openly espouse a style of surrealist imagination in an attempt to probe the *inner* truth of the personality and convey what he felt and thought rather than simply what he *did.* The other approach follows the example of *Citizen Kane*: that the truth of a personality is not an aggregate of what he has done in chronological order, but the sum of what different people at various stages of his life have said about him. Bob Fosse's cine-biographies — *Lenny* (1974), *Star 80* (1983) — have adopted this approach.

These are just some of the problems and issues that arise when dealing with biography on film. The bio-pic is an awkward hybrid form that falls somewhere between fiction and documentary, and it is hard to avoid a predictability of structure which sees the subject's life as a connecting string of major or minor failures and successes. The difficulties are intensified when the cinema attempts to treat the literary life, for three main reasons. The first is the problem of casting: can one believe in Fredric March as both Robert Browning and Mark Twain (in *The Barretts of Wimpole Street* and *The Adventures of Mark Twain*), or Dean Stockwell as both D.H. Lawrence and Eugene O'Neill (in *Sons and Lovers* and *Long Day's Journey into Night*)? Does the screen persona of Jane Fonda obstruct our perception of the real-life person of Lillian Hellman when she plays Ms Hellman in *Julia* (1977)? The second problem is the nature of literary creation itself. Unlike, say, musical performance or sporting prowess — the most popular subject of bio-pics — writing a book is not a very visual activity. It is static, private, and it takes a long time. Apart from Mozart's dictation of his Requiem to Salieri in Milos Forman's *Amadeus* (1984), Anna Karina's painstaking writing of a letter in Godard's *Vivre sa Vie* (1962), or the manic sheafs of papers (all containing the same phrase) that represent Jack Nicholson's writer's block in Kubrick's *The Shining* (1980), the actual visual rendering of the imagination in action has not been well handled in the cinema. This takes us to the final major difficulty of the bio-pic in relation to literary activity: that is, its tendency to expose the limitations of the cinema's capacity for filming thought. It can visualise the product of that thought; it is harder to visualise the germination of an idea. The bio-pic can only imply the nature of what writers write through its dramatisation of what they *are*. Yet it was T.S. Eliot who said that 'the more perfect the artist, the more completely separate in him will be the man who suffers and the mind which creates'.[3]

What, then, are the reasons for trying to bring literary lives to the screen? These are many and various, and the question can best be answered by looking in a little more detail at some specific examples. It seems fair to say that the famous Warner Brothers film *The Life of Emile Zola* (1937) has not a lot to offer to the lover of literature. Like many bio-pics, its evocation of the artistic environment rapidly degenerates into an exercise in name-dropping. Zola shares a garret with a 'talented' artist called Cézanne; a writer by the name of 'Anatole France' briefly flits past. (This is one of the most parodied aspects of the bio-pic, reaching some kind of extreme in the delirious film of Franz Liszt's life, *Song Without End*. In Curtis Bernhardt's Brontë picture, *Devotion*, there really is an exchange that goes: 'Good morning, Thackeray,' 'Good morning, Dickens.') Zola meets the inspiration for his Nana as if all a writer needs for inspiration and success is to meet the right person and transfer the essence of that person automatically to the page. Anyway, as the more literary-minded of the press of the time pointed out, in real life Zola had been a successful novelist for twenty years before he wrote *Nana*. The film does hint at one of the central contradictions of Zola's career: namely, that the success of his studies of poverty has made him increasingly bourgeois. This, in turn, hints at one of the major criticisms of Zola that has been levelled at him by Marxist critics like George Lukács: that his ostensibly compassionate writings about the working classes merely confirm bourgeois prejudices against them, and that a novel like *Germinal* (1885) is not so much an indictment of injustice as a bourgeois nightmare of proletarian revolution. This would be quite an interesting line on Zola to develop, but it is not that about him — nor indeed anything about him as a writer — that interests Hollywood.

What is it, then, that prompted Warner Brothers to make a film about Zola at that particular time? (One might add that it was very successful and won the Best Film Oscar of 1937.) There are two reasons. The first was Hollywood's mid-1930s quest for respectability. After the subversive incursions of dynamic gangster movies that criticised society and Mae West comedies that satirised and celebrated sexuality, various moral groups had put pressure on Hollywood to clean up its act. Warner Brothers had shifted its slogan from the early part of the decade — 'Torn from Today's Head-lines' — to a mid-1930s axiom that proclaimed: 'Good Films — Good Citizenship'. The Warners bio-pics became an important symbol of that citizenship, for they extolled the virtues of famous 'good citizens' and the films themselves were a celebration of enlightenment, progress, rational-ism, invention. In that sense, Emile Zola was not very different from Louis Pasteur, whom Paul Muni had portrayed to Oscar-winning effect the preceding year. He personified not great writing for Warners' purpose, but a more generalised liberal inventiveness and civic responsibility.

But the major interest in Zola for Warners was his involvement in the Dreyfus case. *The Life of Emile Zola* is not simply a bio-pic but a social problem picture: it should be grouped not only with *The Story of Louis Pasteur*, but also with, for example, Mervyn LeRoy's savage indictment of lynch law, *They Won't Forget* (1937). The film is basically a condemnation of anti-Semitism from a director, William Dieterle, who had emigrated to Hollywood from Germany in 1930. It was to be some time before Hollywood would take an explicit stand against Nazism in its films (Anatole Litvak's *Confessions of a Nazi Spy* in 1939 is an important breakthrough), but it can imply an attitude through a subject like *The Life of Emile Zola* which, although set in the past, has a message for the times. The memorable thing about the film — and the reason for the film's existence — is not Zola's literary reputation, but his advocacy on behalf of Dreyfus: 'By all that I have done for France, by my works, by all that I have written, I swear to you that Dreyfus is innocent. May all that melt away — may my name be forgotten, if Dreyfus be not innocent. He is innocent ...'

Hollywood's two most notable stabs at literary biography in the following decade were *The Adventures of Mark Twain* (1944) and *Devotion* (1944). The former is much the more coventional. Indeed, its structure could almost serve as a diagram of bio-pic orthodoxy: a chronological movement from birth to death; the inclusion of the moment of destiny (when Twain almost destroys his first manuscript, but then sends it off); the dark moments which almost but not quite bring the subject to his knees (the writing block after the death of his son, lifted when his wife gives him a good talking to; his bankruptcy); and the final triumph which redeems all his trials and tribulations (an honorary degree from Oxford University, following Rudyard Kipling on to the stage). It suggests a more or less direct correlation between his life and his writing, as if, as Henry Fielding said of Colley Cibber, he lived such a life simply in order to be able to write about it. Set-pieces such as steering the riverboat through fog and the frog-jumping contest are therefore first vividly dramatised and then provide the material for Twain's first successes, as if successful writing has little to do with technique or literary contacts or public demand, but is simply a matter of sitting down and writing about recent experience.

The picture of Twain it presents is more revealing about Hollywood in 1944 than it is of Sam Clemens. The most immediately striking thing is the stress on Twain as humorist and as a children's writer. Nowadays, it is more common to draw attention to the darker side of Twain, even in a work like *The Adventures of Huckleberry Finn.* The film has none of that. The savagely ironic *Pudd'nhead Wilson* is not even mentioned. Twain is simply presented as the Hans Christian Andersen of American literature. 'You've given eternal youth to every mortal who ever lived,' his wife tells him. In fact, it implies that his more serious work, like his biography of Ulysses S. Grant, is a betrayal of his natural talent. The thesis here has intriguing similarities with Preston Sturges's satire, *Sullivan's Travels* (1942), about a comedy director who wants to make a relevant social statement about capital and labour. In both films, the artist who wishes to do 'serious' work learns the value of making people laugh. The film is not only a vindication, through Twain, of traditional American folksy wisdom during a time of national unease. In showing Twain's uneasiness with the literary giants of the East, like Longfellow and William Dean Howells,

Hollywood is claiming Twain as one of its own: an instinctive entertainer not an egg-head New York intellectual, and all the better for it.

Curtis Bernhardt's film of the Brontës, *Devotion*, is an altogether peculiar affair. It does not have much of a sense of a small Yorkshire community; Erich Wolfgang Korngold's music is truly awful, for once justifying the crack about more corn than gold; and even the title is puzzling (as Richard Winnington said: 'I would like to know who was devoted to whom and why').[4] Its inspiration, if it can be so called, stems from the success of previous Hollywood forays into the Brontë world, notably Wyler's version of *Wuthering Heights* and, more obliquely, Val Lewton's fascinating variation on *Jane Eyre, I Walked With a Zombie*. (It also invites comparison with the 1944 film of *Jane Eyre*, with Orson Welles as Rochester, and scored by Bernard Herrman who, two years later, will write an opera based on *Wuthering Heights*.) From the standpoint of literary criticism, it has two propositions, neither of which is terribly original though some would still argue fiercely about them: that Emily is a better writer than Charlotte (Anne's literary gifts are scarcely referred to); and that the creator of Heathcliff and the creator of Rochester were probably in love with the same man. However, beneath all this is an odd, eccentric movie that might have more in it than meets the eye.

The film has one of those helpful Hollywood captions that introduces us to the Brontë family, mentioning that the family contains 'two with talent, two with genius'. As the film develops, this becomes highly ambiguous. Emily is one genius certainly, but is the other Charlotte or their brother Branwell? Significantly, in the film itself, the word is used of Branwell but not of Charlotte. Branwell (Arthur Kennedy) is presented as the 'genius' painter destroyed by drink. Charlotte is never talked of except in terms of weary respect, and, in Olivia de Havilland's matronly performance, scarcely suggests the authentic Hollywoodian demon of genius.

Ida Lupino's intensely committed performance as Emily is another matter, however. Emily's genius is particularly proclaimed by the fact that she dreams: a fantasised recurrent dream in which she wanders across a cloud-swept moor and is menaced by a black-clad rider on a rearing horse. 'I saw his face,' she says, 'there's so little time.' Ostensibly, this refers to her premonition of her own premature death. But it could also refer to her repressed passion for her brother, Branwell (her ostensible desire for Paul Henreid's Reverend Nichols being merely a cloak to disguise her real desire). After all, it is Branwell who is twice in the film associated with rearing horses — when he throws a jug out of a pub window, and causes the horses to rear and when he jumps on to the horses of a carriage — and in both cases it is Nichols who has to restrain them. In dreams and death, there is no restraint. 'Dreams that come true are no longer dreams,' says Emily, which might be the reason that her passion must remain suppressed. 'There's so little time,' could be her premonition of Branwell's death, rather than her own, and indeed when Branwell does die in her arms, it precipitates a rapid decline in her own health. In her final dream on her death-bed, the masked rider is greeted as lover, not fiend. Is the rider Death, or Branwell? It is difficult to know whether the incestuous sub-theme of *Devotion* is real or accidental, but then again, this is equally true of the incestuous implications in Emily Brontë's *Wuthering Heights*. (There are numerous hints in the early part of the novel that Heathcliff is, in fact, Earnshaw's illegitimate son, which would give Heathcliff and Cathy's frustrated passion a rational explanation; but the hints are never made explicit.) In Arthur Kennedy's performance, Branwell emerges as a cross between Heathcliff (the wild, fiery temperament) and Hareton (the drunken dissolute).

In *Devotion*, Charlotte has her own journey into darkness, but this is only a frivolous ride on a fairground into the 'tunnel of Mystery' with her teacher in Brussels (a surrogate of Charlotte Brontë's hero, Paul Emanuel, in *Villette*, who was based on Charlotte's own teacher, Monsieur Heger, for whom she had an unrequited passion). Throughout the film, in terms of emotional intensity, Charlotte plays Melanie to Emily's Scarlett O'Hara. She is a more superficial character all round, always showing her work, unlike Emily, who is always hiding hers — like her emotions. The film has a lot of fun with this contrast. During a Don Siegel montage of the sales of *Jane Eyre* (Siegel, incidentally, was employed on similar montages on the Twain film), we have the following conversation: 'It's a better book than *Wuthering Heights*, look at how it's selling.' 'Yes, but look at who's buying!' Is Hollywood reversing the message of *Mark Twain* and daring to criticise the tendencies of popular taste? It is more probable that the film is playing an amusing game with another popular Warners film of the period, *Old Acquaintance* (1942) — the *New Grub Street* of Hollywood cinema — where the lesser, cruder talent achieves a popular success over the more serious novelist. One should not forget Sydney Greenstreet's performance as a pompous Thackeray, pointing out Dickens to Charlotte and warning her not to be 'mixed up with that riff-raff'. *Devotion* is not a subtle film, in other words, and in the last resort, does not have much to do with the Brontës, for all Bernhardt's claim that he had 'always been interested in them'.[5] But its occasional eccentricity makes it a more interesting flight of imagination than *Mark Twain*.

Two British bio-pics, *The Trials of Oscar Wilde* (1960) and *Sons and Lovers* (1960), do not have much to say about their respective subjects — either Oscar Wilde or D.H. Lawrence — but they do have something to say about contemporary English society and cinema. Both are somewhat bewhiskered but sincere contributions to the British New Wave. The Wilde film is a good example of a facet of the bio-pic genre mentioned earlier: its facility for engaging with the present backwards, as it were. It recreates a historical period in all its nostalgia, but the current than runs through it is very much of the specific time at which it is being made. Oscar Wilde is a sympathetic portrayal of a homosexual at a time in England when attitudes are becoming slowly more liberal — Basil Dearden's *Victim* will continue the trend the following year — and it is also a scathing attack on the moral righteousness and hypocrisy of the Establishment, which Joseph Losey's *The Servant* will bring searingly up to date in three years' time. Wilde's epigrammatic genius, neatly encapsulated in Ken Hughes's fine screenplay and splendidly unfurled in Peter Finch's poignant performance, serves to heighten an audience's sympathy and liking for him, and hence to emphasise the calamity of a gifted man's fall at the hands of a degenerate Marquis of Queensbury (a performance of frightening ferocity from Lionel Jeffries). Wilde's literary gifts are placed second in dramatic importance to the social implications of his notoriety. The film audience, like the general public of the day, is encouraged to be both horrified and entranced by the spectacle of the upper classes' exposed dirty linen, a kind of rehearsal for the Profumo affair of 1963 which both scandalised and enthralled the nation. A rival version, *Oscar Wilde*, which followed the Hughes film three days later into the West End, is much inferior and almost forgotten. Robert Morley, as Wilde, is physically more appropriate casting than Finch, but has none of the latter's pathos. Ralph Richardson's performance as the QC Edward Carson, whose cross-examination of Wilde brought about Wilde's downfall, is slyer and more devious than James Mason's rather melodramatic rendering of the role in Ken Hughes's film. Although Britain felt Wilde was important enough to inspire two films simultaneously, even the superior *Trials of Oscar Wilde* seems to have had relatively little success in America, where it boasted the title of *The Man with the Green Carnation*.

By contrast, *Sons and Lovers* was an enormous success in the United States, and not simply because the Lawrence industry there was obviously more active than the Wilde, or even because of the notoriety of the *Lady Chatterley* trial in 1960, which had cleared Lawrence's novel of charges of obscenity. Basically, *Sons and Lovers* was received as a variation of *Room at the Top* (1958). The D.H. Lawrence self-portrait, Paul Morel, is perceived as a Joe Lampton of an earlier age, a working-class hero who wishes to escape from his background, this time for artistic more than mercenary reasons. As a film text, *Sons and Lovers* became appropriated under the banner of the 'British New Wave', with D.H. Lawrence represented as an early manifestation of the Angry Young Man. If it looks like *Room at the Top*, this is partly because it has the same cameraman (Freddie Francis), but also because of a certain similarity of dramatic incident. Paradoxically, it emphasises how much the British New Wave in general, and John Braine's *Room at the Top* in particular, owed to Lawrence's example. Braine's novel is a crudely modernised copy not only in its portrayal of the hero, but also in its pseudo-Lawrentian depiction of the two women in the hero's life, one sensuous, the other virginal (the latter being played in both films by Heather Sears). Both *Sons and Lovers* and *Room at the Top* have a scene where the hero is beaten up for his promiscuous behaviour (something that will occur in *Saturday Night and Sunday Morning* as well). Paul is a painter rather than a writer in *Sons and Lovers*. However, as is generally the case in bio-pics, his artistic skill is manifested not by the evidence of the art itself, but by the portrayal of his temperament: intensity, sensitivity and a passionate nature that all add up to the cinema's conception of how to portray the artist as a young man.

One of the problems of the literary bio-pic has already been mentioned: whereas writers think, screen heroes *act.* Therefore, how can you make a writer a hero? The problem might well be increased if the writer is a woman, for now the writer's sedentary posture is augmented by the screen's stereotype of female passivity. Two bio-pics which raise some of the representational problems of the writer–heroine are Fred Zinnemann's *Julia* (1977), which has Jane Fonda as Lillian Hellman, and Martin Ritt's *Cross Creek* (1983), which features Mary Steenburgen as Marjorie Kinnan Rawlings. The contexts into which these two portrayals fit is quite complex.

Julia is not a biography of Lillian Hellman. It concentrates on her friendship with the title character (Vanessa Redgrave) and particularly Julia's involvement of Lillian in a dangerous mission against the Nazis (smuggling money to help refugees to escape) in pre-war Berlin. In the context of film history, *Julia* came as a riposte to a flurry of 'buddy movies' in 1970s Hollywood cinema, like *Midnight Cowboy* (1969), *Papillon* (1972) and *The Sting* (1973), which romanticised male friendships and either marginalised, brutalised or excluded the female. *Julia* demonstrates that, in her particular way, the female is every bit as capable of courage as the male.

In a literary context, the film raised other issues. Is it enough for some-one of Lillian Hellman's impeccably liberal credentials simply to publish her views in a context of gathering social barbarity? Should not the writer be able to *do* something, and what form should this commitment take? It was a question that plagued many writers in the 1930s of Ms Hellman's political persuasion: literary intellectual despair was not sufficient. Orwell was, of course, a hero: he practised what he preached. So too was T.E. Lawrence. According to W.H. Auden, Lawrence's life is 'an allegory of the transformation of the Truly Weak Man into the Truly Strong Man, an answer to the question: "How shall the self-conscious man be saved?"'[6] T.E. Lawrence showed that it was possible for the intellectual to transform himself into a man of action and even of historical destiny through sheer effort of will.

According to *Julia,* Lillian Hellman puts her ideals into practice by risking her life. However, the portrait of her in the film is somewhat ambiv-alent. It admires her courage, but at the same time it honestly shows her love of fame and sable coats that sits oddly with her socialist ideas. She is brave enough to involve herself in Julia's plan, but she does not operate it very efficiently and needs help every step of the way on the train. This refusal to make her into an instant superspy makes her that much more interesting and credible, of course. (It is also part of the allegorical implica-tion of the film: Lillian stands for America's bungling and tentative attempt to understand and influence the European situation prior to the Second World War, without getting too deeply involved itself in the struggle.) There is some dispute as to whether Julia existed in real life, or not. The film conveys this by an intense atmosphere of dream and a suggestion that Julia could stand metaphorically as a projection of Lillian's guilty subconscious, with Julia having the political commitment and courage which Lillian admires and desires but does not possess. Julia acts; Lillian merely writes.

The three most controversial areas of *Julia*, as a biography of Lillian Hellman and particularly as a progressive portrayal of a politically aware woman, concern the film's representation of her writing, her relationship with Dashiell Hammett and the theme of lesbianism — all closely inter-woven. The early part of the film concentrates on Lillian's attempt to write a play that will later become *The Children's Hour* (1936). The physical grind of writing is represented fairly conventionally by mounds of waste paper and an over-flowing ash-tray; and the frustration with creative effort is memorably projected in the moment when she throws her typewriter out of the window. The intellectual process, however, remains obscure. We do not know what it is that Hammett (Jason Robards) finds unsatisfactory about the first version, nor what causes him to say about the final version that 'it's the best play anybody has written for a long time'. Perhaps it is unreasonable to expect the film to go into details on a relatively minor and esoteric point. But a number of feminists were dismayed by a portrait of an intelligent and politically aware woman being so dependent on masculine approval.

The other element in *Julia* that dismayed them was the film's evasive attitude towards lesbianism. By analysing Lillian's relationship with Julia at the same time as Lillian is writing her drama about two teachers accused of a lesbian relationship, the film suggests that it might have something to say on the theme. But, in fact, it is ambivalent in rather the same way as the play is ambivalent. The play *The Children's Hour* does not caricature its two heroines and its major scorn is reserved for the puritanical morality of the community. Nevertheless, lesbianism is still seen as a tragic affliction more than an expression of sexuality, and a kind of *deus ex machina* in a plot that is more fundamentally designed to show the corrosiveness of a lie and the persecution of individuals (almost a forerunner of Ms Hellman's experience under McCarthyism). The film similarly skirts around the issue. Lillian cracks someone across the face for snickeringly implying that her relationship with Julia is a lesbian one. The slap is emotionally satisfying but dramatically ambiguous: is it a justifiable rebuke for an outrageous suggestion, or for the implication that such a relationship would be sleazy and shameful anyway? The whole of *Julia* is a kind of wrestling match between conflicting emotions in the middle-class intellectual at a time of social turmoil, torn between thought and action, cowardice and courage, conformity and daring, dream and reality. Perhaps the achievement of the film is precisely the honesty with which is lays bare the hesitations of well-meaning intellectuals when faced — in personal and political terms — with the choice of sacrificing the sable coats and risking their own skin.

Martin Ritt's *Cross Creek* (1983) is on a more minor level because it is dealing with a lesser talent, the authoress of *The Yearling*. The film deals with the period in Mrs Rawlings's life when she leaves her husband in New York and moves to an orange grove in the Cross Creek backwoods of Florida, determined to fulfil her ambition to become a writer. After trying and failing to publish a Gothic novel, she is encouraged to write about her life at Cross Creek, and *The Yearling* is born.

One can imagine what Martin Ritt might have seen in this material. A woman who risks all for self-fulfilment is a theme that had run through his Oscar-winning *Norma Rae* (1978). He might well also have been influenced by the success of Gillian Armstrong's film of Miles Franklin's semi-autobiographical novel, *My Brilliant Career* (1979): *Cross Creek* also has a contemporary feminist theme decked out in soppy period charm. But, after seeing it, would the uninitiated spectator reach for the nearest copy of *The Yearling*? I doubt it. For one thing, the film is short of incident. For a long time the most exciting event is a yearling's knocking over a chocolate cake. For another, there is no evidence in either the writing or the performance to suggest the exceptional talent ascribed to her by publisher Maxwell Perkins (a cameo from Malcolm McDowell). The pompous pantheism of the narration and the cliché expressions of individuality and rustic communion ('I was desperate to express myself', 'I wondered if I'd find peace in my new world') would be quite enough in themselves to dissuade someone from a dip into her work, but when the words are also enunciated in Mary Steenburgen's buzzing monotone, they become quite unendurable. To cap it all, literary inspiration is provided with its most banal visual corollary: a thunderstorm breaks into our distraught heroine's sleepless night, and suddenly the floodgates of inspiration are opened.

In contrast to the realism of *Julia* and *Cross Creek*, both Michael Apted's *Agatha* (1979) and Wim Wender's *Hammett* (1982) try something a little more audacious;: that is, they contrive to situate their real-life authors in the kind of fictional plot only that particular writer could have concocted. Both explore the thin line that separates fantasy and reality in a writer's life; both have a suggestion that fiction-writing is a form of autobiography, and vice versa; and both use the form of the thriller to suggest that biography itself is most closely akin to the detective story, a piecing together of clues that will finally come up with the solution to the mystery of personality.

The subject of *Agatha* is Agatha Christie's actual mysterious disappearance for ten days after a literary lunch to celebrate the publication of *The Murder of Roger Ackroyd*. Screenwriters Kathleen Tynan and Arthur Hopcraft have offered what they call an 'imaginary solution to an authentic mystery' by devising a plot that is agreeably Christie-like in its slightly lunatic ingenuity. Basically, the idea of the heroine is to stage her own death in such a manner that it will implicate her faithless husband and his mistress in murder. The film's self-conscious Englishness and heavy wit are an attractive pastiche of the Christie manner; the obligatory American

(Dustin Hoffman) is a jarring note. None the less, the brooding quality of Vanessa Redgrave's performance and Vittorio Storaro's photography suggest a darker side to the usual Christie personality that beams complacently from adaptations of her slick criminal crossword puzzles. *Agatha* explicitly invites the question: what was it in this person that made her so obsessed with murder? (Vanessa Redgrave's performance suggests all kinds of undercurrents of neurosis, self-hatred, bourgeois repression.) Of other Christie adaptations, only the recent *Ordeal by Innocence* (1985) has had a similar darkness.

Hammett parallels Dashiell Hammett's writing of stories for *Black Mask* magazine and of *The Maltese Falcon* with his involvement in a case strikingly similar to the fiction he is writing. Which is generating which? The film's games with art and life, reality and imagination, are fairly rudimentary, but done with any amount of style. The link is made between private-eyes and writers — 'You try to put 'em in jail, I try to put 'em in a magazine' — to suggest the writer as a superior kind of snooper. The scenes of imagination are especially well done: dissolves which transform the characters we have seen in the main story into different figures in Hammett's mind; images being scrambled in his mind as the story fails to take shape; and a splendid section when Hammett's attempt to rethink a manuscript he has misplaced is visually rendered in terms of a fragmented flashback. End of film, solution of plot, completion of Hammett's fiction, all ingeniously converge in a final flourish that has something of the satisfaction of the ending of Virginia Woolf's *To The Lighthouse* (1927), where Lily Briscoe at long last finishes her painting at the precise moment when Mrs Woolf finishes her narrative — 'Yes, she thought, laying down her brush in extreme fatigue, I have had my vision.'[7] Considering the anguished production history of *Hammett,* Wim Wenders's feelings on being able, as it were, to type 'THE END' on the experience must have been a similar blend of exhaustion and exhilaration. Frederic Forrest's title performance is extremely fine. Almost unprecedentedly in a film about a writer, he really does look as if he has spent hours behind a typewriter.

Over the years, popular cinema has attempted to project many images of the writer. There has been the writer as alcoholic failure, with Scott Fitzgerald as the prototype (quite disastrously played by Gregory Peck in Henry King's 1957 film of the Sheilah Graham memoir, *Beloved Infidel*). The cinema's major presentation of this type is Ray Milland's Don Birnam in Billy Wilder's *The Lost Weekend.* Malcolm Lowry always thought that the success of this film delayed recognition of his novel *Under the Volcano* (1947), a kind of self-portrait of the artist as an alcoholic hero. In his book *Billy Wilder in Hollywood* (1977), Maurice Zolotow suggested that Birnam was actually a Wilder portrait of Raymond Chandler, with whom Wilder had just worked traumatically on *Double Indemnity*.[8] Whoever he is, thought the critic Eric Rhode,[9] why should an unpleasant alcoholic be forgiven so much just because he aspired to be a serious writer? Generally speaking, writers have not been portrayed as very pleasant personalities in movies. In *film noir*, artistic sensibility very often means violence and sexual aberration (see Clifton Webb in the 1944 *Laura* and Humphrey Bogart in the 1950 *In a Lonely Place*). In *Sunset Boulevard* and *Breakfast at Tiffany's* (1961), being a writer is synonymous with being a kept man: your time is paid for, but your soul is not your own. James Mason's Flaubert in Minnelli's *Madame Bovary* (1949) and Richard Chamberlain's Byron in Robert Bolt's *Lady Caroline Lamb* (1971) both present an image of the writer as a bohemian immoralist; whilst Malcolm McDowell's H.G. Wells, thrown into the modern age by his time machine in *Time after Time* (1980), delightedly finds his ideas about free love in wide currency. (His utopian socialism is negated, however, by David Warner's Jack the Ripper as symbol of bestial modern man. As Conrad said to Wells: 'You don't care for humanity but think they are to be improved. I love humanity but know they are not'.)[10] Rod Taylor's Sean O'Casey in *Young Cassidy* (1963) and Omar Sharif's poet Zhivago in *Doctor Zhivago* are sympathetic portraits of the writer as romantic but, in both cases, one remembers less the product of his dramatic imagination than its source: Julie Christie.

Two recent films perhaps embody the enormous pitfalls and yet the possible profundities of the literary bio-pic. The perils are all to be found in Christopher Miles's film about D.H. Lawrence, *The Priest of Love* (1981). Purporting to attack the Establishment view of Lawrence as a purveyor of obscene material, it tends only to reinforce the image of him as a man best remembered for erotic novels and rude paintings. *Lady Chatterley's Lover* is discussed in the film entirely in terms of its sexual frankness and not its equally important observations on industrialisation and England. The characters are artists, we are meant to infer, because they declaim and do not simply speak, and because they are serious and self-absorbed. So Lawrence's wit and charm are underplayed, and what we are given instead is a bearded bore, glumly played by Ian McKellen. The love scenes are photographed with a coy discretion that would have horrified an author passionately desirous of freeing the act of love from this kind of prurience. When strings and harps burst forth over the soundtrack to accompany Lawrence as he begins a new novel, it epitomises what he so loathed about what he saw as the spurious lusciousness of the cinema of his day. Lawrence's work is rendered as sensual massage, his life as turgid soap opera.

By contrast, Percy Adlon's film about the last months in the life of Marcel Proust, *Céleste* (1981), is an exemplary cinematic biography. The limited time-span of the action ensures a crucial concentration (the chief failing of most bio-pics is diffuseness); and this intensity is enhanced by the film's emphasis on a single point of view, that of Proust's housekeeper, Céleste Albaret, beautifully played by Eva Mattes. It is a two-way portrait of character: on the one side, of an ascetic artist dispassionately scavenging life for material; on the other, of a devoted housekeeper whose life is illuminated and romanticised by the prestige of her charge. The film's watchful camera, with its reverence for detail, catches the essence of the

Proustian style. If there is a scene that encapsulates this better than another, it is the scene where Proust and Céleste listen to a performance from musicians invited to their home of one of César Franck's final works, his String Quartet. Thematically, it is an important scene in the way it eases Proust into a contemplation of his own mortality. Technically, in the way it edits looks and collaboration and understanding shared between artists, it is one of the best-filmed concerts ever. Tonally, it is in perfect synchronisation with a film which, in itself, is a delicate and death-ridden chamber piece. A scene like this — and the way Proust (Jurgen Arndt) is shown attending to every nuance of interpretation — distils the essence and aura of artistic refinement. It is a film which gives one both a sense of the greatness of Proust's art and the kind of art it is. That must surely be the ideal of every literary bio-pic, but very few have attained it.

Notes

1. *Monthly Film Bulletin* (February 1985), p. 39.
2. Virginia Woolf, 'Modern Fiction', in *Collected Essays*, vol. 2 (Chatto & Windus, 1966), p. 105.
3. Quoted in *The Craft of Literary Biography*, edited by Jeffrey Mayers (Macmillan, 1985).
4. Quoted in *Halliwell's Film Guide* (Granada, 1980), p. 235.
5. *The Celluloid Muse*, edited by Charles Higham and Joel Greenberg (Angus & Robertson, 1969), p. 47.
6. W.H. Auden, 'T.E. Lawrence', *Now and Then*, no. 47 (spring 1934), p. 30.
7. Virginia Woolf, *To the Lighthouse* (Penguin, 1964), p. 237.
8. Maurice Zolotow, *Billy Wilder in Hollywood* (Putnam, 1977), p. 126.
9. Eric Rhode, *A History of the Cinema* (Allen Lane, 1976), p. 407.
10. Quoted in Jocelyn Baines's *Joseph Conrad: A Critical Biography* (Weidenfeld & Nicolson, 1960), p. 232.

Chapter Ten

Film and Theatre

Alfred Hitchcock had a contemptuous phrase for film adaptations of stage plays: he called them 'photographs of people talking'. He always insisted that his film of the play *Dial M for Murder* (1953) was simply undertaken by him as an exercise in running for cover and recharging his batteries. 'I didn't really need to go to the studio,' he used to say, 'I could have phoned that one in.'

Relations between film and theatre have often been seen as basically antagonistic. It is well known that actors in the early days of the silent cinema wished to remain anonymous for fear of undermining their theatrical reputation. Conversely, the Russian film-maker and theorist Dziga Vertov condemned theatricality in the cinema: 'every film which is built on a script and acting,' he said, 'is a theatrical performance'.[1] In some ways, the two forms are antithetical: theatre is artificial lighting and illusion, and cinema is open-air and realism; theatre is verbal, cinema visual; theatre is stasis, cinema is movement; theatre is live, cinema is canned; theatre is performance, cinema is photography. The two forms accommodate different acting and narrative styles, and, in particular, have a different ambience through an appeal to a different kind of audience. Theatre is still an elitist form, for which people dress up and book, and converse during intervals; cinema is still a more democratic, yet more private form, that is continuous and often solitary. David Thomson has even suggested that people sit differently in a theatre from the lounging posture that one sees in a cinema, the theatre requiring attentiveness whereas, in the cinema, one prepares to be overwhelmed.[2] The status of the text is different in both. In theatre, it can be infinitely reinterpreted. When filmed, that is absolutely its final form.

Nevertheless, the interaction between theatre and film over the history of the cinema is a long and interesting story, only parts of which can be surveyed in this essay. Cinema was in its early days predominantly a continuation of nineteenth-century popular theatre, and D.W. Griffith's early pioneering work in film was very much influenced by his work in the theatre, both in his use of melodrama and his assembly of a repertory company. There was an influx of talent from the theatre in the Hollywood of the early 1930s, because of the coming of talkies and the need to employ actors and actresses skilled in the interpretation of dialogue. The more radical Hollywood films of the late 1940s and early 1950s — films like Kazan's *Boomerang* (1947) and *Gentleman's Agreement* (1947), Rossen's *Body and Soul* (1947) and *All the King's Men* (1949), Losey's *The Boy with Green Hair* (1947) and *The Dividing Line* (1949), Polonsky's *Force of Evil* (1948) — were directly stimulated by the involvement of all those directors in left-wing American theatre in the 1930s, and stimulated particularly in that period by the plays of Clifford Odets (*Waiting for Lefty, Golden Boy*). Actually, one could trace the influence even further back and suggest that all of those films were affected by the impact on the directors of the European 'naturalism' of Chekhov, Ibsen and Strindberg, with their sceptical analysis of society and behaviour and their desire to disclose the poetry in the lives of ordinary people. Kazan expresses his indebtedness to Chekhov;[3] Losey to Brecht.[4] The contribution of modern dramatists to the cinema has been significant: Brecht, Coward, Shaw, Odets, Beckett, Miller, Williams and Pinter have all contributed important screenplays. The cinema can be said to have had its own theatre of cruelty (from Bruñuel to Peckinpah and Polanski), its own forms of Brechtian alienation (from the comedy of Groucho Marx, Bob Hope, Jerry Lewis to, pre-eminently, the politicised cinema of Jean-Luc Godard), its own theatre of the absurd (with Alain Jessua's 1964 film, *Life Upside Down*, a charming example).

The translation of a play into film has its own particular difficulties. Film has clearly more possibilities for variety of time, space, point of view than the theatre: ought it to utilise these when bringing a play on to the screen? One of the main problems is what is often called 'ventilating' the play — that is, opening it out from its static interior setting and letting in a bit more air. The theory is that an audience watching a film will get restless and claustrophobic if compelled to stare at the same setting for too long. Unfortunately, the intensity of the play might depend precisely on that kind of spatial unity, and concentration will be lost if too much of the play is taken outdoors. Shots of cars arriving in the street outside, or prefatory lines like 'Let's take a walk in the garden,' far from contributing to visual variety, are very often so obvious and contrived that one's attention immediately droops. The idea of opening Joseph Mankiewicz's film version of Anthony Shaffer's *Sleuth* (1972) in a maze is actually very effective, for it serves as a visual correlative to the twists, turns and wrong moves to be made by an ageing crime novelist who has invited his wife's lover to his mansion for a deadly purpose. Richard Lester's opening out of Ann Jellicoe's play *The Knack* (1965) in his film version is also highly effective, for it suddenly gives the material a very specific time and place, which in turn gives it a very evocative and precise social and sexual context. But the decision to open out Act II of *Who's Afraid of Virginia Woolf?* (1966) is nearly disastrous, for there seems little good reason for it and the characters are improbably compelled to drive to a deserted dance hall at three in the morning simply, it seems, to give an audience something fresh to look at.

There is also the difference in performance for the screen and the theatre. Theatrical performance is acting; screen performance is *reacting*. Theatrical performance is movement and exposition; screen performance is the kind of mastery David Lean so admired about Jack Nicholson's performance in *Chinatown* (1974) — the nerve to keep still.[5] Theatrical performance is directed at an audience; film performance is directed at a camera. The failure to observe that is precisely where Richard Burton's monologues in *Equus* (1977) go wrong, unlike Olivier's monologues in *Richard III*, which succeed because he treats the camera not as an audience but as a confidant. Theatrical performance is in the voice; screen perform- ance is in the eyes. Certain exceptional stage actors, like Paul Scofield and Ian McKellen, have rarely made a big impact on the screen, for their vocal range is so much more developed than their visual expressiveness. Conversely, screen performers of limited acting ability in a conventional sense can sometimes communicate their presence with little effort and yet extraordinary effectiveness. Montgomery Clift might have nearly all the lines when he takes the herd away from John Wayne in *Red River* (1948), but it is Wayne who commands the attention: not by acting, but by being. When asked why that splendid actor Robert Ryan had not had a more successful career as a leading man in films, director Anthony Mann replied: 'This might make you laugh, but I think the answer lies in a purely physical detail ... he has no *look*. Have you noticed that all the famous, much admired screen stars have bright eyes — Gary Cooper, Charlton Heston, Henry Fonda, James Stewart, Clark Gable, Burt Lancaster, Robert Taylor, Kirk Douglas and Peter O'Toole. The look does everything: it is a permanent reflection of the inner flame that animates those heroes. An actor who does not have this "look" can never get beyond background roles.'[6]

Another difference which can create problems is the difference of point of view between theatre and cinema. A theatrical performance is one that is viewed from a fixed vantage-point in the theatre: it can have filmic equivalents of dissolves and masking, but essentially it is a long shot or medium shot of a continuous dramatic event. A film version can fragment this experience into close-up detail, alternating angles and increasing variety of viewpoint, but at the same time it might disrupt the rhythm and the unity of the original. Filming dialogue in such a way that one attends religiously to every sentence is a delicate art that only a few directors — Hitchcock, Wyler, Losey, Cukor spring to mind — have truly mastered. It certainly involves more than a mixture of over-the-shoulder and reaction shots. With *A Funny Thing Happened on the Way to the Forum* (1966), Richard Lester has admitted that he discovered the difficulty of filming farce: however well you film the dialogue, an audience will be disorientated without the consistent viewpoint that shows the spatial relationship between the constantly opening and closing doors. Film has somehow to sharpen the rhythm of a play's narrative and scenes, and to mask the more obvious exits and entrances of the character. I am not sure that Trevor Nunn's strategy in *Hedda* (1972) of cutting shots of a character's imminent arrival into the play's *preceding* conversation is an altogether successful solution.

The precise level of realism that is appropriate to each medium has also to be calculated afresh. The stylised violence of *Equus* on stage, when the boy blinds the horses, is probably much more acceptable than the rather distasteful treatment of the same incident on film: on stage it seems symbolic, the imitation of an action; on screen it seems real, the action itself. Conversely, David Thomson has argued that the violence in Arthur Penn's film version of *The Miracle Worker* (1962), particularly in the scene where Annie Sullivan and Helen Keller have a pitched battle over the dinner table ('The room's a wreck — but her napkin is folded'), is probably more acceptable on screen than on stage, precisely because it is so realistically enacted. On stage it might seem offensive or degenerate into slapstick; the screen 'is able at the same time to present an overwhelmingly faithful picture of the physical struggle and by reducing it to a flat, intangible image, allow the audience objectivity'.[7]

There is finally the matter of audience expectation. Because a film has to reach a wider audience than a play, the play is sometimes in danger of either being simplified or diluted in order to make it more acceptable and accessible to the mass public. In some cases, these decisions come from hardened and experienced film sense and are not unacceptable. Defending his softening of Tennessee Williams's ending in his screen version of *Sweet Bird of Youth* (1962), writer–director Richard Brooks argues reasonably: 'No man says — Feel sorry for me because I have this little bit of evil; there's a little bit of evil in every one of you. No man waits to be castrated. He might think intellectually that he is going to be, but he doesn't stand and wait for it.'[8] In other cases, the elimination of material adjudged to be too adult or steamy for the filmgoing public can be disastrous. The deletion of the reference which implies her husband's homosexuality in Elia Kazan's film version of *A Streetcar Named Desire* (1951) makes Blanche's great soliloquy at the end of Scene vi well-nigh incomprehensible.

Nevertheless, the film of *Streetcar* is one of the two most significant popular films to be made out of classics of the modern American theatre, the other being Mike Nichols's film of Edward Albee's *Who's Afraid of Virginia Woolf?*. Both are cinematic landmarks. For all their hesitances and evasions, they brought a new realism to the popular cinema — in terms of characterisation in *Streetcar*, in terms of language in *Virginia Woolf*. It is true that Kazan's film of Tennessee Williams softens the ending by making everyone turn against Stanley. One also rather laments the monochrome melancholy of the photography when Williams's play is written in the kind of lurid colour that recalls Van Gogh (his preface to Scene iii — 'The Poker Night' — explicitly refers to Van Gogh and the coloured shirts of the men who are 'at the peak of their physical manhood, as coarse and direct and powerful as the primary colours'). However, the performances are well-nigh definitive. Marlon Brando's Stanley Kowalski has all of the brutish-ness that Blanche defines and despises, but also all of the vitality and insolent charm that Stella (Kim Hunter) so clearly loves: it makes the balance of sympathies so much more acute when Stanley is not seen simply as a bully and a thug. Vivien Leigh, a sort of wrecked Scarlett O'Hara from the American South whose collapsing Belle Rêve is a distant cousin of Tara, takes a while to get her bearings. According to Kazan, she had recently played *Streetcar* on the London stage under Olivier's direction and her performance was not what Kazan required ('Vivien's conception of the role was a bit of a stereotype, just as my direction of a British character might be ... in the last half of the picture, she's a hell of a lot better than in the first half').[9] After her great soliloquy, however, she becomes a walking shroud of pain. Her final scene with Mitch (Karl Malden), who has flashed a blindingly cruel light of reality on her fragile illusions, is heart-breaking.

For Kazan, Blanche was a character very like Williams, 'an ambivalent figure who is attracted to the harshness and vulgarity around him at the same time that he fears it, because it threatens his life.'[10] This ambivalence is felt right the way through the play. Blanche represents culture and poetry and a kind of feminine sensitivity that are desirable qualities in the encircling barbarity; but all these qualities are associated with the past and Blanche seems tragically ill-equipped to survive in the realities of the modern world. In Blanche, Williams invests with exquisite effectiveness all the poignancy of that fundamental feeling he has that 'to desire a thing or to love a thing intensely is to place yourself in a vulnerable position, to be a possible, if not a probable, loser of what you most want'.[11] Yet there is also a sense of spiritual masochism about this, as if some characters seek out this suffering, set themselves up for it — in Blanche's case, behaving throughout like a moth who seemingly cannot resist the light even though it burns her. Shades and blinds, as she knows, cannot protect her illusions for ever, and her movements are those of a trapped bird in the room of a stealthy cat that is closing in for the kill (the sinister bass notes of Alex North's score are very suggestive here). The ambivalence towards Stanley is of a similar kind: a recognition of his coarse materialism but also of his attractive animality and drive, and an acknowledgement that the world and the future seem to be going his way. The baby of Stanley and Stella in this context has considerable symbolic significance.

The parallels between the Williams play and *Who's Afraid of Virginia Woolf?* are not hard to see. Edward Albee also voices a fear of a future in which there will be no art, no poetry, culture, no beauty of mind, no rich-ness of spirit. Amongst other things, the play pits an emasculated Professor of History, George (Richard Burton), against an up-and-coming teacher of biology, Nick (George Segal), in a struggle between the relative claims of art and science, between humanism and Darwinism. The fears of George are precisely those that Williams expressed as one of the themes of *Street-car*: 'Watch out — or the apes will take over the world.' Also like *Streetcar*, it is a play about truth and illusion in which all the characters' major deceptions (Nick's virility, Honey's illness, Martha and George's son) will be violently torn away like labels off a bottle. The play is also a study of marriage as battlefield, in which a reticent husband has to be roused to masculinity by a vulgarly dynamic wife; and also a study of the illusions of the American Dream in which George and Martha (Washington?) fantasise a son and a future in order to compensate for the desperate frustrations they have encountered in their own lives. George and Martha, like Blanche in *Streetcar*, represent the past, cultured, warring but caring, but ultimately intellectually impotent; Nick and Honey, like Stanley and Stella in *Streetcar*, represent the future, though much more tentatively — scientific, calculating, detached, but with a disturbing sterility.

The changes made in transferring the play to the film are relatively small, though quite suggestive. For example, the dance music indicated in Act II of the play is Beethoven and Stravinsky; the film uses music from a juke-box. (Partially a recognition of different audiences, the film might also be reacting against the cultural one-upmanship of the play, also implied in the essentially meaningless title.) Some of the more explicit sexual language at the end of Act II has been deleted, and, as mentioned before, that Act has been opened up in terms of setting — into George and Martha's garden, then a deserted dance hall, and finally a dimly lit car park. The effectiveness of all this varies. George's 'bergin' monologue, so beautifully delivered by Richard Burton, seems to work better outdoors in the twilight under a tree: there is a real sense of unencumbered rumination that one does not get when the speech is done in the cluttered living-room. The dance hall setting is rather awkward and loses some of the text's concentration — one can practically hear the break in continuity and the decision to 'open out' the play. Yet it is not all loss. There is a welcome feeling of a more normal, mundane world, and the apathy of the owners to the violent emotions is a relevant confirmation of George's fears that feelings of sensitivity and human kinship are fading out of the world. The blazing argument between George and Martha in the car park is one of the most effective scenes in the film, their feelings about each other having festered to such a point that the exposure of them in public is both inevitable and a kind of relief: they no longer care whether people can hear them or not. The scene is curiously heightened by a dim light in the distance which Martha, in her angry pacings, keeps obscuring. One remembers this detail at the very end when, with all passion spent, all illusions exploded and a growing kinship of sad recognition, George and Martha come together and daylight breaks gently into the room.

Certain compositions in the film give additional emphasis to points in the play: in Act I, a triangular grouping of Honey, Nick and Martha on the couch, which pointedly excludes George and which he tries to fragment; in Act III, George and Martha coming together in the same frame to present a united front and turn on Nick. When Martha begins her monologue about her boxing match with George, the camera chooses not to stay with Martha's story but to follow George out of the living-room to that small room where he collects the toy rifle. Whatever the motives for the decision (it is a way of getting around any difficulties the film might have had with Martha's rather scandalous speech), it works triumphantly: the swaying light in that claustrophobic space suddenly conveys the atmosphere of an asylum, usefully suggesting certain things about George's past which will later come out. The emphasis on George's reaction to Martha's tale, rather than on the details of the tale itself is surely correct, for it gives an added weight to the tragedy in George's past and to Martha's genuine fear when he points the toy gun at her. Finally, it should be stressed that the film's central gimmick — the casting of Elizabeth Taylor and Richard Burton in the roles of a warring married couple — works sensationally. Elizabeth Taylor has just the right vulgar vibrancy for Martha. She courageously refuses to sentimentalise the role; does a hilarious impression of Bette Davis in her *Beyond the Forest* performance (a film which, incidentally, has a similar relationship between a dull and ineffectual husband being driven on by a dynamic and unfulfilled wife); and rises effortlessly to the moments of poignant poetry, notably in her touching rendering of the 'Sad, sad, sad' soliloquy. Richard Burton might seem miscast, but no other screen actor could have handled the intellect of the script with such firm spontaneity and nonchalant wit, as if the lines are coming newly minted into his head. The 'bergin' speech is the most prominent example of sustained greatness, but equally fine is the pulsating rhythm he finds in a seemingly ordinary line ('It's an allegory really — probably') and the exquisite depth he finds in a cliché ('Sunday tomorrow — all day,' where the last word is drawn out slightly into a heart-breaking dying fall). At the end there is a quiet intimacy in Burton's playing that, apart from this film and *The Spy Who Came in from the Cold* (1966), he rarely achieved on screen. When he did, it was pure cinema, and pure gold.

The screen's way with other American theatrical classics has resulted in some unevenness of achievement. Arthur Miller's work has dutifully reached the screen, but on film, Miller has never looked much more than either Stanley Kramer with brains or Paddy Chayevsky without the bile. Laszlo Benedek's film of *Death of a Salesman* (1952) is respectable enough, with a fine Willy Loman from Frederic March. However, outside of the opening sequence in the car, no attempt is made to convey visually what Willy's life on the road is actually like and give it a concrete reality rather than a nebulous identity as a metaphor for restless failure. The flashbacks also do not catch the crucial sense in the play that they are not memories as such but poised on a knife-edge of reality and fantastic imaginings: the solidity of the screen rather squashes that distinction. The best example of Miller on the screen is still his original screenplay for John Huston's *The Misfits* (1961) — a homage to Monroe, a requiem for the 'Westering' spirit in the American psyche, and a brilliant vehicle for Huston's fascination with the bond and struggle between human and animal life.

The bounce and colour of Tennessee Williams has led to more

memorable translations into cinema. It provides more opportunity for directorial flourishes, like the superb crosscutting in Richard Brooks's film of *Cat on a Hot Tin Roof* (1958) between the attempt of Brick (Paul Newman) and Big Daddy (Burl Ives) to make contact in the haunted cellar, and the picking over of Big Daddy's dying bones upstairs in the luxurious house by his predatory relations. Brooks's gleeful direction of the monstrous children also seems like a revenge on two decades of MGM mawkishness: it is a surprise that the studio let it through. Another masterful piece of cinema is Joseph Mankiewicz's characteristically secure handling of the long flashback monologue in *Suddenly Last Summer* (1959), splendidly delivered by Elizabeth Taylor, who has always looked an especially fine actress in her Tennessee Williams roles. One might add to this her excellent characterisation in Joseph Losey's *Boom* (1969), based on a thin Williams play but whose visual richness matches the luxuriance of Williams's language better than any other film. For all the sensitivity of Arthur Kennedy as Tom and Kirk Douglas as the gentleman caller, Irving Rapper's film of *The Glass Menagerie* (1950) is fatally flawed by a sentimental ending and the ludicrously literal visualisation of the mother's seventeen gentleman callers. Peter Glenville's film of *Summer and Smoke* (1962) intermittently smoulders but cannot defeat the schematism of the original play (a reprobate reforms at the same rate as a repressed spinster begins to degenerate). Considering that Laurence Harvey has to say that he has slid into degradation like 'a greased pig' and Geraldine Page has to compare her feelings at one stage to 'a waterlily on a Chinese lagoon', the two do rather well by their roles. Richard Brooks's film of *Sweet Bird of Youth* spoils the plausibility of Brooks's upbeat ending with a dreadful last line, but is generally first-rate, notable particularly for Geraldine Page's *tour de force* on the phone as an initially sliding but now resurrected actress, Alexandra del Largo. With its perceptions on the fear of failure in American life and on the sinister underbelly of folksy American politics, where talk of 'democracy' so often conceals a desire for demagoguery, the film makes as much of the play's social critique as it can. It wisely cuts the pretentious religious symbolism, and the romantic flashbacks eloquently mirror the bruised sentimentality of Chance Wayne's ruthless but still curiously innocent personality. Paul Newman's skilful performance makes Chance a hustler with a strange idealism.

Apart from rough-hewn adaptations like Ford's soporific *The Long Voyage Home* (1940) and Anthony Mann's melodramatic *Desire Under the Elms* (1957), Eugene O'Neill has been handled with the respect due to an elder statesman of American drama. You cannot cut O'Neill any more than you can cut the music of Bruckner: the loquaciousness is an inseparable part of the symphonic sweep and grandeur of the whole, and the trick is to find the right tempo and the correct relationship between the parts. On this count, easily the two best films of O'Neill's work are Sidney Lumet's film of *Long Day's Journey into Night* (1962) and John Frankenheimer's American Film Theater presentation of *The Iceman Cometh* (1973). Both directors know how to film dialogue in a way to compel attention, and have unexpected acting coups on their side. By the time of *Long Day's Journey*, Katharine Hepburn had aged just enough and matured sufficiently into a tragic actress to be ready for the role of the drug-addicted mother. Her performance is even finer than in *Suddenly Last Summer* and reduces her more recent award-winning roles (*Guess Who's Coming to Dinner, The Lion in Winter, On Golden Pond*) to grotesque charades. Her final descent into drugs is accompanied by Lumet with a discreet tracking shot into darkness, and, through the gloom, the words glow with a strange radiance that stops in mid-reverie: 'Then in the spring something happened to me. Yes, I remember. I fell in love with James Tyrone and was so happy for a time.' As Tyrone, Ralph Richardson has his finest screen opportunity since his definitive Dr Sloper in *The Heiress*. He seizes it with both hands, a great actor in the role of an actor who has missed greatness, Lumet making tactful use of lights and theatrical distance to underline Tyrone's former profession and his recurrent tendency to self-dramatisation. Dean Stockwell as the consumptive younger son is moving in a relatively lightweight role (O'Neill is writing about himself here, and it is the play's weakest part) but Jason Robards is supreme as the disillusioned elder son, Jamie, and does the best drunken scene in the cinema since *The Misfits*.

By all accounts, Robards was a wonderful Hickey on stage in O'Neill's *The Iceman Cometh*, and the casting of Lee Marvin in this role is the most contentious aspect of John Frankenheimer's film. As a white-haired Angel of Death, stripping people of their false hopes, Marvin seems to have stepped out of *The Killers* (1964), having an inappropriately hard heart for a character of intended inner luminosity. Marvin's skill ensures that Hickey's astonishing final soliloquy about his murder of his wife certainly grips, but it does not move and terrify as it should. The rest of the cast are first rate. Robert Ryan's Larry (another O'Neill self-portrait) turned out to be one of his last screen performances, and stands as his testament as a great actor. Larry is a man 'born condemned to see both sides of the question' and Ryan plays him with an aching self-pity and a soaring rage. Fredric March, Bradford Dillman, and Jeff Bridges all have their individual cadenzas of humour and pathos. It was Conrad who said: 'A man who believes he has no illusions has at least that one.'[12] In *Iceman*, pipe-dreamers in a house of illusion, for good or ill, confront the truth, and are compelled to scrutinise the depths of their own souls. It is a long journey towards illumination, but Frankenheimer ensures that it is an absorbingly dramatic one.

Perhaps the only other American stage classic that is particularly interesting from a cinematic point of view is Ben Hecht and Charles MacArthur's *The Front Page* (1928). There have been three interesting variations on this. Lewis Milestone's 1931 version relishes the contemporary period setting, the exploitation of good dialogue in an early era of sound, the opportunity for break-neck narrative and crisp performances, of which Lee Tracy's Walter Burns is outstanding. Howard Hawks's 1940 version, retitled *His Girl Friday*, exploits his relish for fast dialogue, but is most interesting for changing the sex of its main character, Hildy Johnson, from male to female (Rosalind Russell). 'It's better with a girl playing the reporter than one of the men,' explained Hawks.[13] However, one suspects that what prompted the change was Hawks's instinctive uneasiness about the relationship in the play between Hildy Johnson, the star reporter who wants to leave the paper to get married, and Walter Burns, the ruthless editor who wants him to stay. By changing Hildy's sex and making Burns's motives for persuading Hildy to stay as much romantic as professional, Hawks neatly side-steps the darker implications of Burns's behaviour and the heartless treatment of Earl Williams's imminent execution as a mere appendage to the Johnson/Burns struggle.

Billy Wilder's 1974 version of *The Front Page*, however — an interpretation unquestionably influenced both by the contemporary vogue of 'buddy movies' and by Watergate — brings the disquieting elements of the Johnson/Burns relationship right out into the open. Quite simply, Johnson's relationship with the demonic Burns (the name is significant) is seen as a Faustian struggle for a man's soul. Johnson must choose between the conciliating tenderness of his fiancée, or the malign promptings of his editor, which will lead to a dehumanising ruthlessness. (Whereas in the play, Hecht and MacArthur seem to love newspapermen in spite of everything, Wilder's portrait of them is as harsh as his classic denunciation of the yellow press in the 1951 *Ace in the Hole*.) Hildy and his girl do finally escape, but Burn's continuing hold over Hildy ('The son of a bitch stole my watch!') is, in this reading, really chilling. The opening out of the play is relatively discreet and well judged, but the real strength of Wilder's interpretation is its critique of the original's dazzling superficiality: here the moral issues are *felt*. Equally refreshing in the film is its use of the material to attack the reactionary tendencies of the Hollywood buddy movie (the women in this film are pushed to one side with a brutality intended to make an audience flinch, and the misogyny of the genre is laid bare). The parallels with Watergate are handled with Wilder's usual satirical touch, with Johnson and Burns as a Bernstein and Woodward inadvertently uncovering corruption at City Hall and wondering what is in it for them.

Thanks to Billy Wilder, the jump from *The Front Page* to *Dr Faustus* is not a large one, and serves as a convenient way to take us from classical American drama on film to that of the British. Outside of Olivier's magnificent Shakespeare interpretations, the only interesting film made of an Elizabethan classic is Richard Burton and Nevill Coghill's version of *Dr Faustus* (1968). It is strange that it should have been Burton's only film as a director. When he died in 1984, many critics were tempted to take a distinctly Faustian view of his career. Blessed and yet somehow dissatisfied with his inordinate gifts, Burton was the great actor who had sold his soul to that hell of artistic integrity, Hollywood. In the film of *Dr Faustus*, the chief temptation is played by Elizabeth Taylor, cast as Helen of Troy — though, to all intents and purposes, Cleopatra. The final Descent into Hell looks like a descent into second-rate special effects, a tragic fall not into damnation but into frivolity.

Yet it is not an ignoble interpretation. Burton speaks the poetry beautifully. The final soliloquy as Faustus waits for the stroke of midnight is thrillingly done. There is an especially good Mephistopheles, and the text has been embellished with some of the choicest bits of *The Jew of Malta* ('infinite riches in a little room') and *Tamburlaine* (during Faustus's conception of himself as a mighty warrior). The images of self-aggrandisement and the cheap conjuring tricks are an unsubtle but appropriate rendering of the tricky mid-section of Marlowe's play, where the frivolousness of Faustus's use of his great powers must be shown without the play itself becoming frivolous. The slapstick with the Catholic priests is not especially imaginative, or compelling, but the creepy witchcraft and the images of decay frequently are.

In terms of filmic adaptation, apart from Peter Brook's eccentric version of John Gay's *The Beggar's Opera* (1955) with a vocalising Laurence Olivier as Macheath, English drama seems to have had relatively little to offer between 1600 and 1900. (One could argue that the greatest plays in the English language from the Restoration to Suez were written by Irishmen, anyway.) Nevertheless, faithful adaptations were made during the time of popular modern plays, adaptations into which one could sink like an old armchair, with scrupulously observed performances and minimal cinematic interest. Shaw on film is most memorable not for any intrinsic film merit but for the occasional exceptional performance — Wendy Hiller in both *Pygmalion* (1938) and *Major Barbara* (1940), Laurence Olivier as General Burgoyne in *The Devil's Disciple* (1959) — and the spasmodic eccentricity: Peter Sellers's reprise of his Indian doctor routines in *The Millionairess* (1960), Dirk Bogarde in *The Doctor's Dilemma* (1958) unavailingly trying to shake off the image of Simon Sparrow from his *Doctor* films. The last two films were both directed by Anthony Asquith, who specialised in bringing the traditional English theatre to the screen. His film of Oscar Wilde's *The Importance of being Earnest* (1951) makes no pretence at being anything other than a filmed play, the credits being unrolled like a theatre programme and the curtain going up to signal the start of the action. The polish of the performances is pleasurable, though the whole exercise seems little more than an excuse to preserve Edith Evans's 'A handbag!' on celluloid. More significant was Asquith's partnership with Terence Rattigan. The film versions of *The Winslow Boy* (1948) and *The Browning Version* (1951) both suffer from implausible happy endings tacked on to the original — the suggestion of a forthcoming romance between Donat's crack barrister and Margaret Leighton's suffragette in *The Winslow Boy*, and the transformation of Crocker-Harris into Mr Chips at the end of *The Browning Version*. The opening out of *The Winslow Boy* also is not only perfunctory but at times embarrassing, as in that ludicrous montage when the spread of public interest in the case is visually realised by Asquith through shots of everyone whispering 'Winslow!' in the ear of everyone else. But there are performances in both films to savour. Cedric Hardwicke's Mr Winslow is extremely persuasive and finally moving: in the crucial scene with his son when he asks him if he stole the money order, Hardwicke is rightly so imposing and fearsome that the possibility of a lie is completely out of the question. Even finer is Michael Redgrave's old schoolmaster in *The Browning Version*, at his best when his hurt is barely concealed under a welter of self-defensive words. Asquith also contrives a superb silent moment where the master and his wife sit silently at the tea table, with the clock ticking audibly in the background: suddenly, a frightening image of time's having gradually left two people with absolutely nothing to say to each other.

Other candidates for this category of the indifferently made British film of the well-made British play must be mentioned. After his successful collaboration on *In Which We Serve* (1942), director David Lean took some time to escape from under the wing of Noël Coward, and it is not until *Brief Encounter*, his fourth Coward adaptation, that Lean's full and complex filmic personality breaks through. His films of Coward's *This Happy Breed* (1944) and *Blithe Spirit* (1945) are fairly subdued and dutiful renderings of rather fragile pieces with a dated and decaying charm. As Alain Silver and James Ursini rightly remark about *This Happy Breed*: 'The opening shots of the city and the travelling into the house establish one reality: then the "play" begins and asserts another.'[14] There is no point in establishing an 'authentic' street if, as soon as the people open their mouths, they sound like theatrical characters. The only visual interest is provided by the pictures on the walls as emblematic of character: a romantic landscape for the daughter who dreams of escape; a picture of Chaplin to indicate that the son has socialist tendencies. Guy Hamilton's film of J.B. Priestley's *An Inspector Calls* might seem to be in the same bourgeois vein, but the force of Priestley's finest play takes it in a somewhat different direction (and Alastair Sim is splendid as the Inspector). Prior to David Hare's recent *Wetherby* (1985), it is the nearest the British cinema has come to Buñuel's *The Discreet Charm of the Bourgeoisie* (1973), beginning on an interrupted meal and making free play with ghosts, with a cyclical structure of a nightmare from which there is no escape, and with a satirical attack on the complacency and irresponsibility of the upper middle classes. It is a timely attack in Hamilton's film. By the mid-1950s, the Establishment was coming under scrutiny, particularly from a new English drama whose most public and successful early manifestation was John Osborne's *Look Back in Anger*.

With hindsight, one can see that the cinema did not do particularly well by the New English Drama. One of the reasons for this can be summarised in two words: Tony Richardson. He was given the film version of *Look Back in Anger* (1959), *The Entertainer* (1960) and *A Taste of Honey* (1961) and, in all cases, they were visually cliché and insufferably condescending. *The Entertainer* gave Olivier his big break in modern drama and is quite a good 'Condition of England' piece, with the music-hall background suggesting a 'Merrie England' in decay. However, the ranting *Look Back in Anger* now looks self-pitying and sentimental in precisely the same way as John Braine's wildly overrated and appallingly written novel, *Room at the Top*. There was much more wit, irony, social observation and a feeling for urban alienation in most episodes of *Hancock's Half Hour*, and if you compare Hancock's 'Sunday' (written by Alan Simpson and Ray Galton) with Jimmy Porter's in Act I of *Look Back in Anger*, there is no question which is the sharper piece of writing. Osborne does not adapt well for the cinema, simply because he writes old-fashioned actor–manager plays, in which the company's star spends the entire drama ranting at his supporting cast. Even on stage, this can give you a headache. On screen there is no way you can make this look interesting — it is a complete denial of what the screen is for.

Clive Donner's film of *The Caretaker* (1963) was the first screen adaptation of a Harold Pinter play and is still the best. The opening out is limited, but very intelligent. It precisely plots the moves of Mick as he spies on his brother and his tramp tenant; and there is a lovely moment when Mick offers to give the tramp a lift to Sidcup, drives him round in a circle, and then deposits him exactly at the spot where they left (a visual parallel to what Mick is doing to the tramp verbally, running him round in circles and leaving him no better off). Donner stages the violence impressively (Nicholas Roeg's splendid black-and-white photography is helpful here), but the commendable thing about the film is its sense of stillness and concentration at moments it might be tempted to fragment: the still camera for the cyclical exchange of dialogue between Davies and Mick about Mick's 'funny' brother; the courageous decision to stay with Aston, without extraneous visual illustration or reaction shots, during his long monologue about his experience in the asylum.

Many interpretations have been offered of the play. Kenneth Tynan suggested that the three characters represented the Id, Ego and Superego: 'Good luck to him,' was Pinter's response. It is a commonplace to see it as Pinter's *Huis Clos* and insist that the characters are stranded in Hell: Donner refutes this by showing a world outside and showing that Aston's shed is an actual shed and not a figment of his imagination. 'It's about two brothers and a caretaker,' said Pinter: precisely. Donner's film plays it for humour and psychological realism, and goes to that crucial tragi-comic point in a Pinter play where suddenly things are no longer funny; and makes the situation of all three lost and desperate characters intense and involving. It would have been criminal if Donald Pleasence's supreme performance as Davies had not been preserved on celluloid. Whether jabbering in his sleep, or lifting the tails of his filthy coat like a concert pianist before sitting down, this is one of the great theatrical performances of our age, admirably adapted to the screen. Alan Bates memorably repeats his stage triumph as Mick. Robert Shaw is the only one who is not from the original London production, but he is both pitiable and frightening as Aston.

Finely cast in *The Caretaker*, Shaw is unfortunately miscast as Stanley in William Friedkin's fidgety film of Pinter's *The Birthday Party* (1968), seeming much too robust and powerful as the victimised Stanley. Sidney Tafler is an intelligent, intellectually menacing Goldberg, and there is more spine-tingling drama in the way Patrick Magee tears his newspaper into strips than there is in any of John Osborne's monologues. But it is not as idiomatic or as funny as it should be. I have never seen an American production of Pinter that seemed to understand either the language or the timing of his humour (I exclude Joseph Losey from this criticism since I regard him as a naturalised Englishman). Peter Hall's American Film Theater production of *The Homecoming* (1973) is a modest affair, with the original National Theatre cast repeating their stage roles, with the exception of Michael Jayston substituting for Michael Bryant as the returning brother. There are some compelling images: Ted's face at the window before going back into the home he has been away from for nine years; the soundless entrances of the sinister Lenny (Ian Holm); the four men smoking cigars together after Sunday lunch in an image of suffocating maleness (one mentally compares it with the smoking-room scene in *The Go-Between*). There is not much wit in this production, largely because the film is dominated by the grim, unbearable anguish of Vivien Merchant's performance as the rejected wife, Ruth, almost as if she is reading the part as a warped reflection of her own disintegrating marriage to Pinter and her feeling of being ditched by a now successful man who has grown out of her world.

Adultery and betrayal have always been key Pinter themes. Since 1970, he has added time, memory and jealousy to the range. Memory and jealousy figure largely in his play *Old Times*, as they do also in *Betrayal* (1983), scrupulously filmed by David Jones with careful fidelity to the text. The trick of *Betrayal* is to tell the story of an affair in reverse chronological order, from end to beginning. The procedure gives a retrospective frisson of irony to the lines and to the looks, and the performances of Ben Kingsley, Patricia Hodge and Jeremy Irons are finely judged, particularly Kingsley's. His unaccountable outburst in the restaurant is electrifying, pure Pinter in the anger of the *words* concealing rather than expressing the emotional pain of betrayal that is really nagging at the character like an aching tooth. Ultimately, though, *Betrayal* takes Pinter perilously close to J.B. Priestley: time and the Pinters, as if a conventional play has been desperately modernised simply by shifting the order of the Acts. *Betrayal* is inconsistent in its time-structures and seems oddly passionless in comparison with *The Caretaker* and *The Homecoming*. However, this is partly because of the world with which the film deals: the bourgeoisie, who courteously conduct their shoddy emotional betrayals with civility and a hypocrisy that is finely tuned to the nth degree of fragile self-restraint. At moments like this, Pinter is closest to Renoir, his characters precariously surviving by the rules of the game.

Two old-fashioned modern British theatrical classics which have been transferred with unexpected success to the screen are Fred Zinnemann's film of Robert Bolt's *A Man For All Seasons* (1966) and Peter Yates's film of Ronald Harwood's *The Dresser* (1983). Several things are interesting about the Zinnemann–Bolt adaptation. One thing worth remarking about a film of a successful play is that, unlike most theatrical repertory companies, the film can be strongly and expensively cast in depth, which in turn means that the film might not be so reliant on a star presence in the leading role. Zinnemann's insistence on Paul Scofield to repeat his stage triumph as Thomas More was undoubtedly helped by his having names in the supporting cast: Robert Shaw (as Henry VIII), Susannah York, Wendy Hiller (as More's daughter and wife, respectively) and Orson Welles (as Cardinal Wolsey). Welles seems to have been cast for his bulk as much as his talent. In Wolsey's scene with More, in a claustrophobic room dominated by shades of red (the robes of Wolsey's office that seem to threaten the prospect of blood-letting to come), the sheer scale of Welles's presence seems to make Wolsey seem a solid mass of brooding intimidation.

After much discussion, Zinnemann and Bolt had agreed to discard the character of the Common Man who on stage had linked the events and inhabited a variety of roles (steward, boatman, jailer) as he followed More's inexorable route towards execution and martyrdom. Bolt thought the character a 'bastardised Brechtian device'.[15] Zinnemann thought him an interesting self-serving survivor in a slippery world. Both finally agreed that he was too theatrical a device to work in the more naturalistic world of the screen. The parts are now played by individual actors.

It is clear why the character of More — a Tudor prisoner of conscience — would appeal to Fred Zinnemann, whose most famous films — *High Noon* (1952), *From Here to Eternity* (1953), *The Nun's Story* (1959) — are about the conflict between community and individual conscience. But what would equally attract him about the play is the political atmosphere, which seems very modern. Thematically, the play is less about Catholicism than about McCarthyism. The film has a striking atmosphere of spying and paranoia, of interrogation and informers, of scrupulous silence and the calculated taking of oaths. In his defence against the charge of treason to the King, More is effectively pleading the Fifth Amendment. Zinnemann's first-hand observation of McCarthyism in Hollywood — *High Noon* being Hollywood's most famous, coded anti-McCarthy message — clearly provided a valuable frame of reference for the film.

The trial scene is particularly well done. It is prefaced by a superb forward-tracking shot as More walks into the courtroom alone, faced by his accusers and by interested spectators: the helpless bull stepping into the political arena in anticipation of his sacrifice, entering through a passage whose narrowness not only signifies the inhibitions of More's freedom consequent upon his moral decision, but the straight narrow path which has been his route through the film — the only one he can follow. His moral ascendancy has been visually matched to his physical decline, a process exactly reversed in the characterisation of Rich (John Hurt), whose increasing corruption is signalled by his ever more extravagant finery. These two images confront each other in the courtroom — More stooped but spiritually exultant, Rich lavishly attired but, in terms of the drama, irredeemably damned. Indeed, simply by the posture he adopts, Scofield is able to convey the impression in the trial that More is judging the accusers rather than the other way round (another connection with the American political trials of the 1940s and 1950s and John Howard Lawson's famous rebuke to the House of UnAmerican Activities Committee that it is they who are on trial and not the accused).[16] Zinnemann's direction is very scrupulous during this scene, a skilful blend of film and theatre. By not moving in too close but keeping the camera at a distance, often at moments of great passion, Zinnemann can give proper weight to More's rhetoric; give the sense of him in the final moments as an actor in the theatre playing commandingly to the gallery; and give the cinema audience the equivalent viewpoint of the trial spectator, watching from the wings.

Like the Zinnemann film, Peter Yates's film of *The Dresser* seems to appeal more to lovers of the theatre than of the cinema. Film buffs feel that, as backstage dramas go, it lacks the imagination of Cukor's *A Double Life* and that Mankiewicz's *All About Eve* is a much wittier and more corrosive study of the relationship between star and dresser. But *The Dresser* is a hymn to theatrical illusion, relishing the magic even as it demystifies it.

Perhaps Ronald Harwood's play has been so successful because it offers the equivalent of Shakespeare for tourists. It has an aura of culture without being difficult or intimidating. Its star is a great actor–manager (a character partly based on Sir Donald Wolfit) who is taking his theatrical company around Britain during the Second World War. Given his mental instability, will the production of *King Lear* be all right on the night? Between snatches of the play, star and dresser enact a relationship which is something like a more accessible *Lear*, with Sir as the King (towering but ageing, with rebellion stirring in his kingdom) and the dresser, Norman, in all senses, playing the Fool.

There are entertaining lines and affectionate set-pieces, notably the backstage storm. There are also some over-familiar routines, as Sir mixes up his plays and misses his entrance (played here, mistakenly perhaps, mainly for laughs without subtle shadings of pathos). The war background could have been used more imaginatively as a correlative to Sir's psycho-logical breakdown: the period detail is decorative more than expressive. Apart from a funny scene when Sir manages to stop a moving train simply by the sound of his stentorian voice, the opening out of the play is fairly perfunctory. Nevertheless, Yate's direction is characteristically competent, making particularly judicious use of mirror shots at key moments to emphasise Sir's narcissism and Norman as a mere reflection of him.

Unlike *A Man For All Seasons*, the distinguished supporting cast (which includes Eileen Atkins, Michael Gough and Zena Walker) is as much hindrance as help because they are not given much to do and thus inadvertently underline the weakness of the play away from the central relationship between Sir and Norman. Nevertheless, Edward Fox broods impressively as an actor and aspiring playwright with a disdain for Sir's special effects and feeling that the theatre of the grand gesture is on the decline. He is intended as a harbinger perhaps of the New English Drama: possibly a witty surrogate of Harold Pinter, who once played a retainer to Wolfit's Lear and was admonished by Wolfit for getting in the way of his sweeping gestures. Pinter has on many occasions expressed his opposition to Wolfit's brand of theatrical bombast. Ironically, the parts of Sir and the Dresser are played by Albert Finney and Tom Courtenay, who were amongst the leading lights of that English drama breakthrough. Here they are upholding that opposite tradition. They put on quite a show, if you like that sort of thing.

Three more recent attempts to deal cinematically with more modern themes in recent British drama have had a varying degree of success. Lewis Gilbert's film of Willy Russell's play *Educating Rita* (1983) soundly reproduces the basic feeling of the material, which is attractively written but not very convincing. Willy Russell sets himself up as the Neil Simon of the Open University and has rewritten *Pygmalion* for the 1980s. The problem with this is that, despite a smattering of the jargon, Russell clearly does not know how the OU system works, so what purports to say something about education is really a sentimental romance between two people from different sides of the tracks. Russell is shrewd enough to see that the movement from working-class ghetto to the groves of Academe might simply be an exchange of one set of trade names for another (Chekhov displacing Frank Sinatra), and the film's emphasis on the male chauvinism in Rita's home background makes an obvious but still useful point about attitudes to education amongst the working classes and for women. But the tentative visualisation of the heroine's triumph at the Summer School is rather literal and the literary jokes are ingratiating more than inspired. Simon Gray writes more authoritatively about universities and Alan Bleasdale writes with more passion about the working class. *Educating Rita* is slick but superficial, striking a chord perhaps because, as David Puttnam suggested, it is simply a British 'rites of passage' picture which avoids the vulgarity of its American counterparts like *Porky's* (1982) and *Bachelor Party* (1984).[17]

Marek Kanievska has talked with commendable passion about his film of Julian Mitchell's play *Another Country* (1984), particularly his desire to attack a public school system that channels the emotions of its boys into a sterile and sometimes sadistic exercise of power. 'Hopefully people get the feeling that the games people play when they are at school are insane,' Kanievska says. 'When you think that for hundreds of years, the people who have governed this country have come from a public school background, where they are obsessed with the fact that they are going to be part of the hierarchy, and with ruthlessly manipulating themselves into positions of power, it seems absurd.'[18] Unfortunately, the film never defeats the absurdity of the basic situation. An ageing English spy in Moscow in the present day (and in appalling make-up) explains his betrayal of his country through a languorous and lachrymose tale about his failure to become a public school prefect. The attack on public schools is very confused and even contradictory: it cannot decide whether to be more angry at them for the injustices of privilege or for being breeding-grounds for communists. I prefer its confusions to the insufferable smugness of the Alan Bennett–John Schlesinger foray into the same area, *An Englishman Abroad* (1983), but, in both of them, any criticism of English institutions is deflected into sentimental sorrow for a promising fellow who has let the side down by flirting with homosexuality and, its political bedfellow, Marxism.

Joseph Losey's film of Nell Dunn's *Steaming* (1985) transforms the anger of the play into something which conforms to a mellow testament from a great director, whose last film it turned out to be. *Steaming* had a rough ride from the British critics but I found it very moving. It is Losey's feminine version of Richard Lester's *The Ritz* (1976): single-set bathhouse, single-sex characters, lots of humour, and a feeling of retreat and refuge from the outside world where a hazy hallucinatory surface seems to dissolve reality into dream and the prison of their lives into the freedom of their fantasies. It would be easy to relate it to Losey's other work: the basic theatricality of the piece; the class antagonism between the characters; the setting as refuge or fortress that must not be penetrated by intrusion from outside; the baths as a modern metaphor for a run-down England, uneasily trying to pull towards cohesion, and with different individuals trying to resist becoming random victims of the depersonalised argument of 'economic necessity'. What is different from usual is the indulgence by Losey of romantic licence (lovely shimmering dissolves that are an unusual technical device for him but are right for the piece) and an overall optimistic sense of human endurance and the achievement possible through solidarity of purpose. Losey avoids any ping-pong cutting for dialogue exchanges. Instead he composes a beautiful medium shot of the three main characters lined along the pool as if three dimensions of a single character; and judiciously uses mirror shots to provide visual variety, avoid cutting, and suggest that the women are ultimately confronting themselves as much as relating to each other. I have rarely seen reaction shots edited so subtly and unexpectedly. The interplay of the performances (Vanessa Redgrave, Sarah Miles, Diana Dors, Patti Love, Brenda Bruce, all superb) is a joy and the whole thing is characterised by human affection and cinematic intelligence — in fact, precisely the qualities that were so conspicuously absent from the critical response.

Of European drama as interpreted by the popular cinema, two costume warhorses are worth mentioning, Michael Gordon's film of Rostand's *Cyrano de Bergerac* (1950) and Peter Glenville's film of Jean Anouilh's *Becket* (1964). The former film suffers a little from dull black-and-white photography for a flamboyant French Fairbanks-type swashbuckler that cries out for colour; from Dimitri Tiomkin's blatantly syrupy score; and from some clumsy editing that chops messy reaction shots into key moments that destroy their poignancy, as in the moment when Cyrano declares to his friend his love for Roxane. None the less, Carl Foreman's screenplay is a racy adaptation; the scene divisions are cleanly marked by dissolves that keep the drama moving; and Jose Ferrer's Oscar-winning performance as Cyrano has a flair and dash he has never since matched on screen. The film of *Becket* suffers from a thoughtless fidelity to the text. After we have seen the suicide of the King's mistress, we most certainly do not need the King's explanatory line a minute later to Becket: 'She's dead. She's killed herself. There's blood.' Although he himself felt he hit the lines too emphatically, a legacy of his stage experience, Richard Burton brings a sombre dignity to the title role, particularly in the death scene. Peter O'Toole rants stylishly as Henry II, a character he was to play a few years on in James Goldman's sub-Anouilh text brought to the screen by Anthony Harvey, *The Lion in Winter* (1968). The visuals of *Becket* are rather routine, except for individual details (like the unemphatic shot of the two rings on Becket's fingers, one his seal as Archbishop, the other as Chancellor, which concisely expresses the duality of his loyalty to God and King) and for the final quarrel on the beach.

The commercial cinema has generally steered clear of the trinity of great European playwrights of the last century — Strindberg, Chekhov, Ibsen. Strindberg's preface to *Miss Julie* (1888) seems to encourage a cinematic reponse: 'In a modern psychological drama ... the soul's most delicate emotions should be reflected from the face rather than through gestures and noise ... if we could have the stalls raised so that the spectator's eye would be above the level of the actor's knee.'[19] Alf Sjoberg made a fine film of *Miss Julie* (1950), with a particularly sensitive use of flashback. In general, however, the cinema's attitude has been: who needs filmed Strindbeg if we have Ingmar Bergman? (There's a beautiful reference to Strindberg's *Dream Play* at the very end of Bergman's *Fanny and Alexander*, and his film masterpiece — *Persona* — owes a great deal to Strindberg's mini-drama, 'The Stronger'.) The most interesting film of a Chekhov play is probably still Sidney Lumet's honourable stab at *The Seagull* (1968), with Vanessa Redgrave a blazing Nina, James Mason a thoughtful Trigorin, but David Warner an excessively hangdog young writer and Simone Signoret struggling too much with the dialogue to suggest the grand actress demanded of her role.

Intriguingly, there were four filmed Ibsens in the space of around five years, between 1972 and 1977. Two of them were inspired by the desire to preserve an important production; two to exploit the topicality of Ibsen's themes. Trevor Nunn's film *Hedda* featured Glenda Jackson's interpretation of Hedda Gabler. In this performance, Hedda is not a hysterical egoist or middle-class prig but a tragic heroine out of her time, trapped by a pregnancy, and a bourgeois society whose narrowness she despises so much that the only outlet for her romantic spirit is in acts of perverse and petty revenge. In the film, Hedda's scene with Mrs Elvsted (Jennie Linden), who has risked her reputation, is the highlight. Hedda is both envious and contemptuous, wanting not to serve nor sacrifice like her friend, but to be and to do. (The casting of Glenda Jackson and Jennie Linden here has odd echoes of their not dissimilar roles as Gudrun and Ursula in *Women in Love*.) As a film, *Hedda* is competent more than inspired, but it faithfully treasures Miss Jackson's fine performance. Patrick Garland's film of *A Doll's House* (1973) is a similarly low-key piece of cinema, so dimly lit, indeed, that the gloom of Dr Rank (Ralph Richardson) seems as much due to inadequate lighting as mortal melancholy. Nora's dance is disappointingly staged, and the final confrontation between husband and wife a laboured and predictable exchange of close-ups. But Anthony Hopkins does Torvald's rage at Nora as well as any actor I have seen: for a sensitive woman like Nora, there would really be no going back from that kind of torrential tirade of chauvinistic contempt. Claire Bloom is rather older than is usual for the portrayal of Nora, but her sensitive playing makes this a telling point. Her desertion is not the impulse of youth, but the painful wisdom of maturity. Strangely, the strong patterning of the final act of this particular production — snow and Christmastime, the party at which the husband suddenly becomes full of desire, the disillusionment which sets in when he learns his wife does not love him as he thought, the closing close-up of the husband — reminded me of James Joyce. Is that pattern not identical to the narrative structure of Joyce's wonderful story 'The Dead', from *Dubliners*? Given the fact that Joyce's first published work was an essay on Ibsen and that Joyce treasured Ibsen's letter of thanks ('I wish to thank you for your kindness in writing to me. I am a young Irishman, eighteen years old, and the words of Ibsen I shall keep in my heart all my life'),[20] the influence of *A Doll's House* on 'The Dead' seems quite likely, but I have seen no critical reference to it and, until this production, the connection had not occurred to me.

Joseph Losey's film of *A Doll's House* (1973) appeared at about the same time as Patrick Garland's. Adapted by David Mercer, it seemed a response more to feminism than to a theatrical occasion, and starred Jane Fonda as Nora and David Warner as Torvald. In general, critics preferred Garland's principals, and certainly Warner cannot compare with Hopkins's terrifying volatility in the crucial scene where Torvald loses control and attacks his wife. Jane Fonda skilfully manages the more extrovert moments — the dance is much better done in the Losey version — but the inner tensions seem insufficiently revealed or developed. Perhaps the star's own feminist associations obscure our vision of the character's blind and painful quest towards self-awareness and undermine the shock of Nora's startling decision (startling, that is, to a nineteenth-century audience) to walk out on her husband and children.

Perhaps it should be stressed that the play's original impact was not only to do with the time at which it was first produced (1879) but also probably to its cunning structure, which must have taken its first audiences completely by surprise. It seems an absorbing but relatively conventional drama about domestic deceit until a remarkable final Act throws a time-bomb at contemporary values, as the husband's egoistic hysteria unexpectedly and irreversibly exposes the quicksand on which his marriage has been built. The shock of the structure is somewhat diluted in Mercer's and Losey's adaptation, where the elaborate crosscutting tends to fragment Ibsen's narrative drive.

Nevertheless, the film is bound together by a tight visual logic. The numerous opening and closing doors (Krogstad closes a door: cut to Nora, in a different location, opening a door) establishes a mysterious unseen interaction between characters whose separate lives are soon dramatically to intersect, and encloses them within rooms whose alternate orderliness and disarray eloquently reveal their occupant's state of mind. With that particular motif, the final moment — the most famous slammed door in theatrical history, as Nora walks out — carries a powerful charge.

At another stage, at the height of an emotional crisis, Nora straightens her hair in a mirror before, with forced gaiety, she moves to deal with her husband. Losey's camera, slowly tracking towards the mirror, establishes the moment as one where the character is most deeply divided and aware of this division — the image she has of herself, and the image she must project to her husband and friends. (This shot beautifully prepares the way for Nora's great speech in Act III when challenged by Torvald about her duty to him and her children: 'I have another duty just as sacred ... My duty to myself ...') Much later, just before the revelation which brings the relationship to a crisis, Torvald is caught in a similar way before the same mirror but does not look at his own reflection. It is a neat way of marking Torvald's own deep division but also his unawareness of his own hypocrisy.

In *A Doll's House*, the interpretative skills of Losey's camera are invariably equal to those of his excellent cast. Certainly, Ibsen's main concerns in his plays — the importance of self-realisation, his fascination with outsiders, his sense of outrage at the sterility of bourgeois society, his concept of entertainment as provocation rather than passive amusement — are sufficiently akin to Losey's own to explain the keen intelligence of his adaptation.

Steve McQueen's strange venture into Ibsen territory is another matter. If Women's Lib was the modern inspiration for Losey's version of *A Doll's House*, then the success of Spielberg's *Jaws* (1975) seems to have been in the back of the producers' minds for *An Enemy of the People* (1977). It is not a shark but pollution of the waters that threatens a spa's prosperity in Ibsen's drama. It is not a sheriff but a doctor who discovers the threat and, in both cases, it is the community's mayor who attempts a cover-up.

Amongst other things, the play is semi-autobiographical, written shortly after the furore over *Ghosts*. The doctor, like Ibsen, sees himself as a truth-teller, reviled by popular opinion for having the courage to expose some of the poisons and contaminations of modern society. Part of the play's greatness is the remorseless logic through which the individual and the society reach their implacable and irreconcilable positions (for as Arthur Miller, who adapted the play in America, said about it, 'There never was, nor will there ever be, an original society able to countenance calmly the individual who insists that he is right while the vast majority is absolutely wrong'). Its greatness also stems from its refusal to sentimentalise the hero: we never know for certain whether or not he is right; and there is an obsessive element of fanaticism and stubborn self-congratulation in his character. The weakness of the film is its blind embrace of the very things the play avoids. For all McQueen's sincere disguise of his usual screen persona behind steel-rimmed spectacles and a mountainous beard, his self-conscious presence does sentimentalise the hero and we never doubt that McQueen's doctor is right in his conclusion. Charles Durning is a fine actor but at this stage of his career, he was associated with heavies in films so, in his hands, the mayor is too quickly seen as a hypocritical villain. Neither performance is so misjudged that it could not have survived in an imaginative production, but the direction of George Schaefer (one of those prize-winning American TV directors, like Fielder Cook and Lamont Johnson, whose big-screen films are devoid of interest) is dreadfully turgid. There is little sense of context or period, with the effect that this intense drama has more the air of a debate in a lecture hall than a suspenseful dilemma that involves the morality and survival of an entire community. Leonard Rosenman's music tries to breathe some emotion into the situation, but this kiss of dramatic life comes too late.

The subject of filmed theatre would be incomplete without an acknowledgment of some great films that have been made about the theatre. Three films particularly stand out — Ernst Lubitsch's *To Be or Not to Be* (1942), Marcel Carné's *Les Enfants du Paradis* (1945) and Mankiewicz's *All About Eve*. Lubitsch's film is set in wartime Poland and is a satire on the ridiculous ideology of the Nazis (like Chaplin, Lubitsch finds Hitler, among other things, an abominably bad actor). It is also a comedy about the vanity of actors and their inability to separate illusion from reality. 'In the theatre it's important that you choose the right part,' says the collaborator, Dr Siletsky. 'In real life, it's more important to choose the right side.' Its black humour, theatrical imagery and anti-Nazi thrust were clearly great influences or another splendid backstage comedy in a much more raucous key, Mel Brooks's *The Producers* (1969), and on more sombre looks at war and theatre, like Truffaut's *The Last Metro* (1980) and Peter Yates's *The Dresser*. Lubitsch's film is also boldly Brechtian in its lightning fluctuations between the illusion of 'realism' and the acknowledgement of theatrical illusion. *Les Enfants du Paradis* is simply the most stagestruck film ever, committed to the proposition that all the world's a stage and continually blurring the line between Art and Life. Love and jealousy interact both on and off the stage, as feeling is transmuted into performance and back again. Jean-Louis Barrault's classic performance as the mime Baptiste was inspired by the real-life nineteenth-century French mime Deburau who, in protecting his wife, had accidentally killed her attacker, with the result, according to Barrault, that 'the whole Boulevard du crime had rushed to the trial not to see him acquitted but to hear the sound of his voice'.[21] Mankiewicz's *All About Eve* is an Oscar-winning study of theatrical bitch-craft, in which Mankiewicz balances his iconoclastic attitude to the acting profession against his fascination for theatre and his love for language. They are all here — the star, Margo (Bette Davis), for whom to act is to breathe; the desiccated critic, Addison de Witt (George Sanders); the touchy writer, the brilliant director, the loyal wife; and, above all, the predatory Eve herself, ruthlessly working her way to the top over the prostrate egos of her fellow-thespians. Mankiewicz has said that 'there are Eves afoot in every competitive stratum of our society where there's a top you can get to and from the bottom'.[22] Eve's ambition is unrecognised for so long because she is dealing with people who find it hard to differentiate truth from a great performance. Mankiewicz stands back and dissects the spectacle of self-dramatising people playing deadly games with a Wildean wit that could almost justify the retitling of the film as *The Importance of Being Eve*.

As a coda to this survey, I would like to make some observations about four directors whose films have often had a close association and affinity with theatre. George Cukor went to Hollywood at the onset of sound after gaining directing experience on the New York stage. His films include some of the most tasteful and dignified of Hollywood theatrical adaptations, such as *Philadelphia Story* (1940), *Gaslight* (1944), *Born Yesterday* (1950) and *My Fair Lady* (1964). *Sylvia Scarlett* (1935) and *Heller in Pink Tights* (1960) are daring and unusual comedies about theatrical people touring, respectively, Dover in the early twentieth century, and the wild West in the nineteenth, with Katharine Hepburn disguised as a boy in the former and Anthony Quinn photographed in tunic and blond curly wig in the latter. Jean Simmons plays the eponymous heroine in Cukor's film of Ruth Gordon's autobiographical play, *The Actress* (1952), a loving close-up of her entranced face at the theatre and her silent mouthing of the star actress's song speaking volumes about what it is to be stagestruck. Cukor's films are not only love letters to the theatre. In general, he adored theatrical people, whether they indulged that flair on stage, or in a courtroom (Tracy and Hepburn in the 1948 *Adam's Rib*, Olivier and Hepburn in the 1972 *Love among the Ruins*). He was a shrewd observer of the attraction of role playing in everyday life, and of the alternatively comic and tragic split between a person's public and private life. The theatre became an essential metaphor for these thematic preoccupations.

William Wyler's theatricality as a film director had slightly different connotations. Wyler's attraction to theatrical subjects like *Dodsworth* (1936), *The Little Foxes* (1941) and *Detective Story* (1951) expressed his preference for a certain kind of cinema: one that favours action in charac-ter more than character in action; that relishes words more than deeds; that finds drama in domestic claustrophobia more than the outdoors; that is fascinated by characters with a flair for the dramatic; and one that favours a style rooted in *mise-en-scène* more than montage. No director has made more expressive use of rooms or staircases to suggest the struggle for territorial advantage in a marriage or family. His films are tight dramas filmed with a minimum of photographic fuss. His approach to filming a play, he said, is 'to retain the basic construction of the original — while at the same time lending the story the illusion of movement'.[23]

Wyler's most famous association was with the playwright Lillian Hellman. He did two versions of her play *The Children's Hour*. *These Three* (1936) had to disguise the lesbian theme which makes the whole exercise rather redundant, though Bonita Granville is excellent as the evil little girl. This performance is the only element that is superior to Wyler's superb and grossly underrated 1962 remake — called *The Loudest Whisper* in the UK — which has awe-inspiring acting from Audrey Hepburn, Shirley MacLaine and Fay Bainter. 'To anyone who knows the American middle-classes of Philadelphia and Boston,' declared Jean-Pierre Melville, 'the film's a masterpiece.'[24] As Melville implied, the film is not really an examination of lesbianism but of character assassination by implication and rumour in a righteous but prurient community. Its ironies anticipate Heinrich Böll's *The Lost Honour of Katherina Blum* — though, in 1962, the specific parallel Wyler and Hellman probably had in mind was the conservative community in Hollywood that had destroyed numerous innocent lives at the behest of a collective hysteria induced by the House of UnAmerican Activities Committee and Senator McCarthy.

Wyler's film of Hellman's *The Little Foxes* is probably their most famous collaboration, and one of the best examples of filmed theatre ever. The structure of the play is fundamentally adhered to, but the struggle for superiority amongst the characters is heightened by compositions which catch people at strategically advantageous or vulnerable positions within the frame. The staircase becomes a battleground for territorial advantage that signifies a momentary economic or psychological control. Some moments would be hard to match on stage: the first entrance of Herbert Marshall, where his reaction and relationship to every member of his family are conveyed as much through fleeting looks as actual dialogue; or the wonderful scene between Oscar (Carl Benton Reid) and his whining son Leo (Dan Duryea) as they shave back to back and discuss an underhand scheme to defraud Marshall — the mirror shot conveying a complicated sense of deviousness (plots hatched back to back rather than face to face) and of nastiness infinitely duplicated. Above all, there is the famous moment when Marshall has his heart attack and Bette Davis refuses to move from her chair to help him. The camera's immobility matches hers, all the more striking in a character who has elsewhere been constantly on the move. What is going on inside the heroine's head is the principal point of interest here, even more than the husband's attempt to reach the medicine that can save him. The motionless camera on Davis's whitely determined face and her position of power within the shot would be impossible to approximate on stage and are an object lesson in how to achieve the maximum filmic intensity with the minimum cinematic means.

The relation of Alfred Hitchcock to the theatre is more complicated. On the surface, no one is more purely cinematic than Hitchcock nor more imaginative and powerful in his use of montage that is one of the cinema's most characteristic and expressive devices. He has indicated his defensive and derisive approach to *Dial M for Murder*, though it is actually a much more intriguing example of filmed theatre than he allows, the use of colour, eccentric camera angle and intensity of detail giving it a concentration hardly possible on stage.[25] Hitchcock had a great personal fondness for theatre, and used it in his films as both a dramatic and metaphoric background to suspense dramas about deception and identity. Particularly memorable is the music-hall memory man in *The Thirty-nine Steps* (1935), who is the means by which enemy agents smuggle state secrets out of the country; the use of a blood-stained dress to frighten the actress (Marlene Dietrich) in *Stage Fright*, a plot detail that has exactly the same purpose as the play within the play in *Hamlet*; or the interrupted stage performance of *Francesca da Rimini* in *Torn Curtain* (1966), when an American professor shouts 'Fire' to panic an audience and make good his escape — imagery of hellfire appropriately accompanying this peculiar Hitchcockian variation on the Faust legend. But the most interesting theatrical piece of all is Hitchcock's *Rope* (1948), his experiment with the ten-minute take, where montage is virtually eliminated and the camera becomes like an extra participant in the stage performance, following the actors, observing and emphasising key detail. *Rope* is an almost perfect match of form and content. For Hitchcock, it was primarily a technical exercise — about a murder which is itself primarily a technical exercise (two homosexuals committing the 'perfect' murder simply for the thrill of it). For them, the crime is simply the elevation of murder to an art form, filmed by a director who has made an art form from the subject of murder. The imagery of murder and art in the film are inseparably entwined. A comment about Philip's hands ('These hands will bring you great fame') ostensibly alludes to his piano-playing but actually and ironically alludes to the murder he has committed. Brandon cannot differentiate the murder from theatricality, lamenting that the crime was not committed with the curtains open, as if it were a play, and electing to close the curtains towards the end when he (mistakenly) thinks the performance is over. It might seem a conventional reproduction of a theatre performance, but Hitchcock's control of the perpetual movement of his *mise-en-scène* in *Rope* within a single set is as authoritative and authoritarian as his control of the montage of *Rear Window* within a single set. It is as good and unusual an example of filmed theatre as one can find.

In recent years, the director who has most radically explored the links between film and theatre is Robert Altman. Ed Graczyk's *Come Back to the Five and Dime, Jimmy Dean, Jimmy Dean* (1982), David Rabe's *Streamers* (1983) and Donald Freed and Arnold M. Stone's *Secret Honor* (1984) provide the basis of an extraordinary Altman trilogy, which mix favoured themes with formal experiment. All three are about modern America and particular forms of modern American experience — movie worship in the first, perennial threat of violence in the second, and political paranoia in the third. All three preserve the integrity of the theatrical experience by never letting the camera leave the single set, on the one hand preserving the claustrophobia but, on the other hand, taking advantage of the camera's ability to register the flickers and nuances on his actors' faces. Yet the quality of each depends ultimately on the technique. None of the three plays seems especially interesting in itself, but is made so by the camera innovations that Altman brings to them.

Jimmy Dean is a study of small-town oppression and illusion, of false fronts, of the dreams and yearnings of three Texas women. The interest lies in the manner in which Altman films it: flashbacks within the same filmic space as the present; mirror shots that seamlessly reflect a surface of action and reaction; and a looking-glass sense of characters dissolving in and out of each other. *Streamers*, dealing with the tense relationships of young American soldiers steeling themselves for action in Vietnam, is less radical technically than *Jimmy Dean*, but its Altmanesque themes — iconoclastic attitudes to violence, nationalism and the army — are intensified by the close camerawork which locks these young immature characters into the barracks like a womb. *Secret Honor* consists of an imagined Richard Nixon monologue, a one-man (Philip Baker Hall) show as far removed from the gigantic fresco of Altman's *Nashville* (1975) as can be imagined, yet all the more concentrated and personal. As Nixon babblingly explains how he deliberately contrived Watergate as the event in which to cut his own deep throat, Altman's camera looks at the surrounding icons of America and the technical apparatus of power, the images from the television monitors becoming endlessly expressive on the split between substance and shadow, office and private person, appearance and reality, official truth and actual truth. Alone in his presidential office, the emblems of his personal life and the symbols of Americana clank manically around in Nixon's fevered head. No film is more cynical about the Faustian nature of political office (selling your soul to the demons of wealth and power) nor more fearful of those Fausts who have no souls to sell: only an image up for grabs. If nothing else, Altman's refusal to open out the play shows a profound sensitivity to the rhythm of the writing that must really flow like a single uninterrupted, stream-of-consciousness sentence. Yet the camera permits you to get in close, to see things which would be impossible on stage, to make use of the monitors which vary the visual texture and which, as Altman says, 'emphasise the whole idea of media participation in politics'.[26]

Altman's experiment perhaps confirms that the task of adapting a play to the screen boils down to one of two alternatives: by making you forget the stage altogether; or by making you hyperaware of it. Most adaptations tinker around somewhere in between, and although there are examples of intelligent tinkering (*A Streetcar Named Desire*, *Who's Afraid of Virginia Woolf?*), they must ultimately fall short of either great theatre or great cinema. In the first category, I would group an assortment of adaptations which would include Lester's film of *The Knack*, Sjoberg's *Miss Julie*, Penn's *The Miracle Worker* and Forman's *Amadeus*, all of which retain the themes of the original but explode them in an entirely fresh and completely cinematic structure. In the second, I would include Wyler's *The Little Foxes*, Hitchcock's *Rope*, the Altman trilogy, all of which respect the basic text and spatial integrity of the original but use the unique intimacy of the camera to dig even deeper into its depths and detail. Explosion or exploration, *Amadeus* or Altman: these represent the extremes of the screen's theatrical adaptation tradition, but they have proved by far the most interesting and rewarding.

Notes

1. Dziga Vertov, *Provisional Instructions to Kino-Eye Groups* (1926). This extract is from *Realism and the Cinema*, edited by Christopher Williams (Routledge & Kegan Paul, 1980), p. 24.

2. David Thomson, *America in the Dark* (Hutchinson, 1978), p. 97.

3. Michel Ciment, *Kazan on Kazan* (Secker & Warburg, 1973), p. 136.

4. See the extract in which Losey describes Brecht's influence on his cinema in *Coming to Terms with Hollywood* (British Film Institute, 1981), pp. 36-7.

5. *Stills Magazine* (March 1985), p. 34.

6. *Framework*, Issue 15/16/17 1981, p. 19.

7. David Thomson, *Movie Man* (Secker & Warburg, 1967), p. 62.

8. *Movie* (spring 1965), p. 8.

9. *Movie* (winter 1971-2), p. 5.

10. Ciment, *Kazan on Kazan*, p. 71.

11. Tennessee Williams, foreword to *Sweet Bird of Youth*, *New York Times* (8 March, 1959).

12. Joseph Conrad, *Under Western Eyes* (Penguin, 1969), p. 175.

13. *The Men Who Made the Movies*, edited by Richard Schickel (Elm Tree Books, 1977), p. 111.

14. Alain Silver and James Ursini, *David Lean and his Films* (Leslie Frewin Publishers, 1974), p. 27.

15. Robert Bolt, preface to *A Man For All Seasons* (Heinemann, 1960), p. xvii.

16. See *Thirty Years of Treason*, edited by Eric Bentley (Thames & Hudson, 1971), p. 154.

17. See James Park's *Learning to Dream* (Faber, 1984), p. 67.

18. Ibid., p. 98.

19. Strindberg, *Miss Julie*, translated by C.D. Locock. Quoted in Lionel Godfrey's 'It Wasn't Like That in the Play', *Films and Filming* (August 1967), p. 4.

20. James Joyce's letter to Henrik Ibsen, 28 April 1900. Reproduced in Richard Ellman's *James Joyce* (Oxford University Press, 1966), p. 77.

21. Jean-Louis Barrault, *Memories for Tomorrow* (Thames & Hudson, 1974), p. 151.

22. Gary Carey and Joseph L. Mankiewicz, *More About All About Eve* (Random House, 1972), p. 29.

23. *Focus on Film*, no. 24 (spring 1976), p. 9.

24. Rui Nogueira, *Melville* (Secker & Warburg, 1971), pp. 94-5.

25. For an interesting comparison between the play and Hitchcock's film, see Peter Bordonaro's article in *Sight and Sound* (summer 1976), pp. 175-9.

26. *Monthly Film Bulletin* (January 1985), p. 5.

Acknowledgements

I would like to thank the following for advice and encouragement during the writing of this book: Dr Tony Aldgate, David Castell (of *Films Illustrated*), Melanie Crook, Dr W. Hutchings (of *The Critical Quarterly*), Brian McFarlane, and Adrian Turner. Needless to say, the faults of the text are entirely my own.

This book is dedicated with love to my wife Lesley, who was as always the greatest help of all, and to my daughter Natalie, who was born as this text was being completed.

Index